GROUND TRUTH

3 Para: Return to Afghanistan

PATRICK BISHOP

ISIS

LARGE PRINT

Oxford

First published in Great Britain 2009
by
HarperPress
An imprint of HarperCollins*Publishers*

Published in Large Print 2010 by ISIS Publishing Ltd.,
7 Centremead, Osney Mead, Oxford OX2 0ES
by arrangement with
HarperCollins*Publishers*

British Library Cataloguing in Publication Data
Bishop, Patrick (Patrick Joseph)
    Ground truth: 3 Para - return to Afghanistan.
    1. Great Britain. Army. Parachute Regiment.
    Batallion, 3rd.
    2. Afghan War, 2001– – - Campaigns.
    3. Afghan War, 2001– – - Personal narratives,
    British.
    4. Large type books.
    I. Title
    958.1'047–dc22

ISBN 978–0–7531–5237–9 (hb)
ISBN 978–0–7531–5238–6 (pb)

Printed and bound in Great Britain by
T. J. International Ltd., Padstow, Cornwall

To Douglas and Richenda

Contents

Maps xi

Introduction: A Big Ask................................xxiii
1. Going Back...1
2. Through the Looking Glass 10
3. KAF 29
4. Hearts and Minds..................................45
5. Hunting the Hobbit...............................75
6. Green Zone 91
7. IED 110
8. The Stadium 149
9. Facing the Dragon...............................168
10. Sangin Revisited...................................200
11. The White Cliffs of Helmand 241
12. Convoy...266
13. The Enemy..287
14. Close Quarters 302
15. Fields of Fire...320
16. "Something our Parents will Understand" 343
17. Homecoming...368

Abbreviations, Acronyms and
Military Terms..379
Acknowledgments 382

List of Maps

1. Regional Command South xiii
2. Upper Sangin Valley ....xiv-xv
3. Kandahar.................................xvi-xvii
4. Maywand.............................xviii-xix
5. Kajaki.....................................xx
6. Upper Gereshk Valley xxi

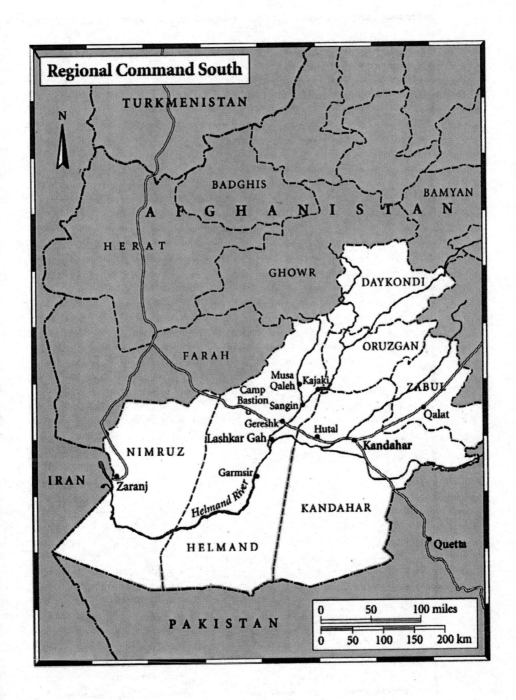

Regional Command South

TURKMENISTAN

AFGHANISTAN

BADGHIS

BAMYAN

HERAT

GHOWR

DAYKONDI

FARAH

ORUZGAN

Musa
Qaleh   Kajaki

Camp
Bastion   Sangin

ZABUL

Qalat

Gereshk   Hutal

Lashkar Gah   Kandahar

NIMRUZ

IRAN

Zaranj

Garmsir

Helmand River

KANDAHAR

HELMAND

Quetta

PAKISTAN

0   50   100 miles

0   50   100   150   200 km

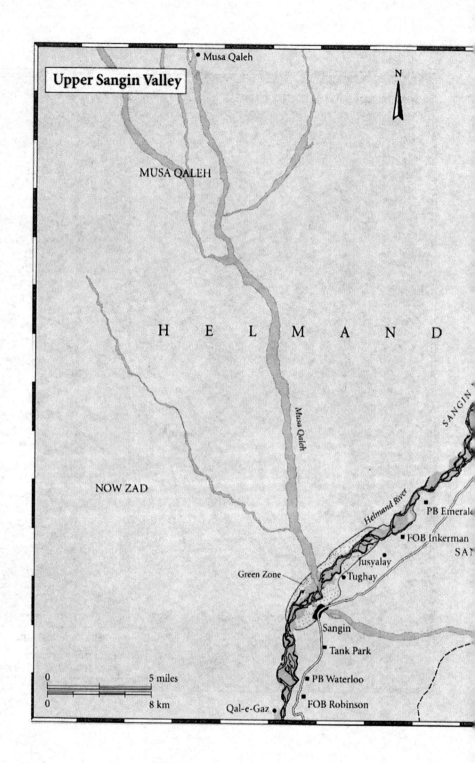

Upper Sangin Valley

N

Musa Qaleh

MUSA QALEH

H E L M A N D

Musa Qaleh

NOW ZAD

SANGIN

Helmand River

PB Emerald

FOB Inkerman

SAN

Jusyalay

Green Zone

Tughay

Sangin

Tank Park

0   5 miles

0   8 km

PB Waterloo

Qal-e-Gaz

FOB Robinson

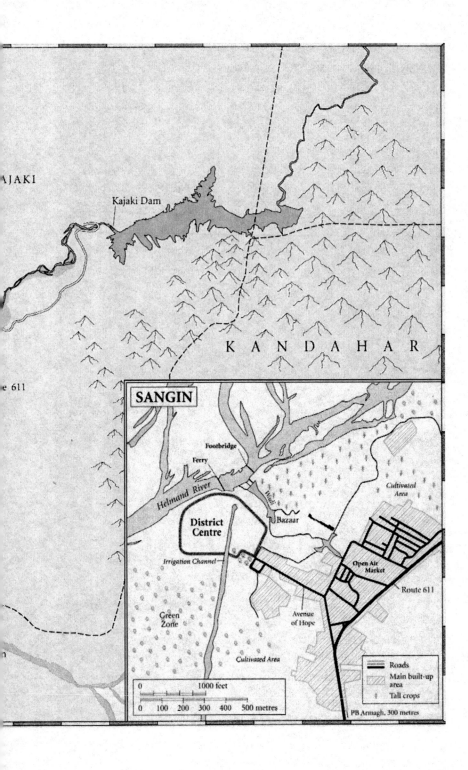

AJAKI

Kajaki Dam

K A N D A H A R

e 611

SANGIN

Footbridge

Ferry

Helmand River

District
Centre

Irrigation Channel

Wadi

Bazaar

Cultivated
Area

Open Air
Market

Route 611

Green
Zone

Avenue
of Hope

Cultivated Area

| 0 | 1000 feet |
| 0 | 100 200 300 400 500 metres |

Roads

Main built-up
area

Tall crops

PB Armagh, 300 metres

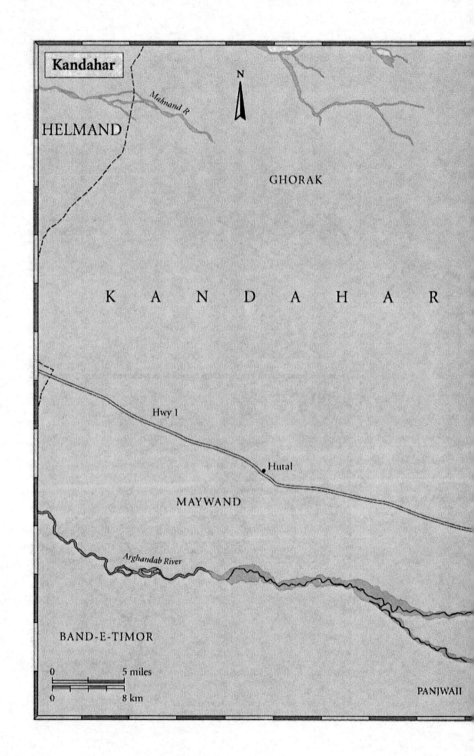

Kandahar

HELMAND

Mahnand R

N

GHORAK

K A N D A H A R

Hwy 1

• Hutal

MAYWAND

Arghandab River

BAND-E-TIMOR

0   5 miles

0   8 km

PANJWAII

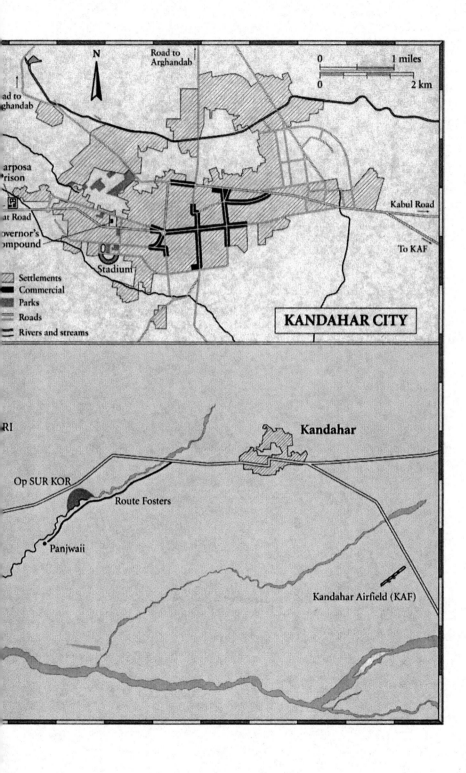

Road to
Arghandab

N

Road to
Arghandab

arposa
rison

Kabul Road

at Road

overnor's
ompound

To KAF

Stadium

Settlements
Commercial
Parks
Roads
Rivers and streams

0   1 miles
0   2 km

KANDAHAR CITY

RI

Kandahar

Op SUR KOR

Route Fosters

Panjwaii

Kandahar Airfield (KAF)

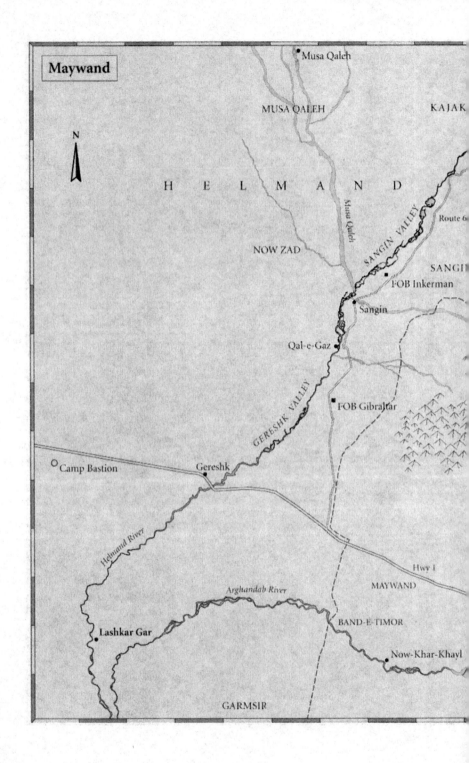

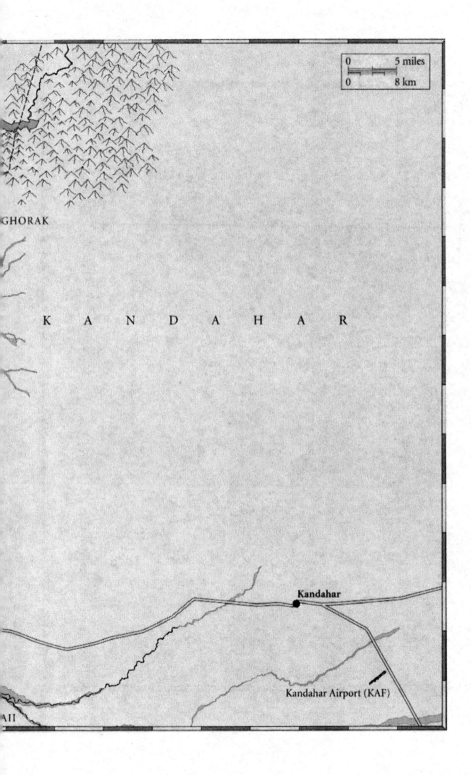

GHORAK

K A N D A H A R

Kandahar

Kandahar Airport (KAF)

AII

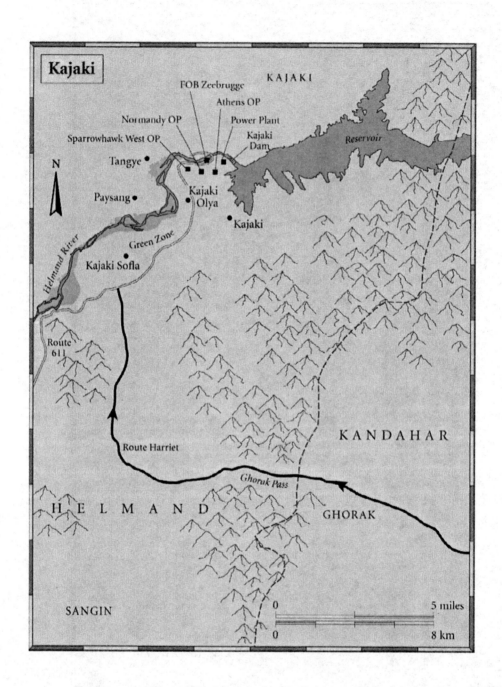

Kajaki

KAJAKI

FOB Zeebrugge
Athens OP
Normandy OP
Power Plant
Sparrowhawk West OP
Kajaki
Dam
Reservoir

Tangye

N

Paysang

Kajaki
Olya

Kajaki

Green Zone

Kajaki Sofla

Helmand River

Route
611

KANDAHAR

Route Harriet

Ghorak Pass

HELMAND

GHORAK

SANGIN

0   5 miles

0   8 km

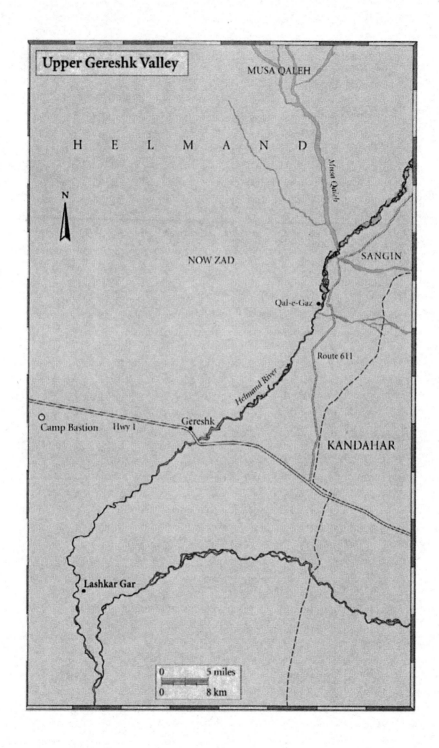

Upper Gereshk Valley

MUSA QALEH

H E L M A N D

Musa Qaleh

N

NOW ZAD

SANGIN

Qal-e-Gaz

Route 611

Helmand River

○
Camp Bastion   Hwy 1   Gereshk

KANDAHAR

Lashkar Gar

| 0 | 5 miles |
| 0 | 8 km |

Introduction: A Big Ask

When 3 Para arrived back in Colchester in the autumn of 2008 after their second tour of Afghanistan in three years, their commanding officer, Huw Williams, pointed out the difference between his generation of soldiers and the very young men he was leading.

"When I joined the army we thought we would have to go to Northern Ireland and might possibly have to go somewhere else to fight," he said. "But these guys knew when they joined that they would be expected to go off, more or less straight away, to a full-on war."

A British soldier's job today is much more difficult and dangerous than it was in the last decades of the twentieth century. Then it was easily possible to go through an entire career without hearing a shot fired in anger. Now, a new recruit to a combat unit is virtually certain to see action. Thanks to Afghanistan, before long almost everyone will have a war story to tell. Since the British Army went there in force in 2006, about 40,000 servicemen and women have come and gone. That represents more than a third of the country's ground troops. Some of them have now been twice. Force levels are rising steadily. There is no end in sight to the conflict and no obvious short cut that would allow an early but honourable exit. A spell in "Afghan", as the soldiers call it, is becoming as routine as an Ulster roulement was thirty years ago.

There are some similarities. The skills and drills honed on the terraced streets of Belfast and Londonderry and the fields of Fermanagh and Tyrone have proved surprisingly useful in the river valleys of Helmand.

The differences, though, are far bigger. Ulster was grim, but Afghanistan is harrowing. The violence is deeper, darker and more disturbing. There were no suicide bombers in Northern Ireland. Life in Afghanistan's front-line forts is harsh, squalid, exhausting and dangerous. Soldiers know that once they step through the gates they are facing six months of knackering patrols, regular fire-fights and the constant nerve-fraying fear that the next step they take may trigger a buried bomb.

They are operating in an extreme climate in wild country among people whose culture, try as the soldiers might to understand it, remains baffling and opaque. There's nothing in the recent memory of the British Army to draw on for help. You have to go back more than a hundred years to match the experience. Any soldier reading Winston Churchill's account of his time with the Malakand Field Force fighting Pathan (Pashtun) tribesmen in the North West Frontier in 1897 would feel a buzz of recognition at his tales of Tommies and their native allies battling with heat, thirst, slippery local leaders and opponents steeped in a culture of violence.

"The strong aboriginal propensity to kill, inherent in all human beings, has ... been preserved in unexampled strength and vigour," he wrote. "That

xxiv

religion, which above all others was founded and propagated by the sword — the tenets and principles of which are instinct with incentives to slaughter and which in three continents has produced fighting breeds of men — stimulates a wild and merciless fanaticism."[1]

The strain of a tour is enormous, reflected in the number of soldiers diagnosed with mental disorders.[2] But the burden also lies heavy on the folk they leave behind. For those with families, Afghan duty means being absent from hearth and home not just for the six months of the deployment but also for lengthy preoperational training exercises. By the end of 2010, some members of 3 Para will have done three Afghan stints in five years.

It is, as the soldiers say, "a big ask". It is not as if they are going to fight in a popular cause. British public opinion remains resolutely sceptical about the value of the campaign. Most people seem unwilling to accept the government's assertion that by fighting in Afghanistan we are defending the home front against a threat as great as that posed by the Nazis. The scepticism shows no sign of eroding. Progress, military and political, is deemed to be non-existent or far too slow to merit the cost in blood, money and effort.

At the same time, the public are full of admiration

---

[1] Winston S. Churchill, The Story of the Malakand Field Force: An Episode of Frontier War, Project Gutenberg, E-Book 9404.

[2] In 2007, according to the Ministry of Defence, 375 Armed Forces personnel who had previously served in Afghanistan were assessed as having a mental disorder.

for the soldiers. The standing of the services in civilian eyes is probably higher than at any time since the Second World War. It is not difficult to see why. Their culture of stoicism and comradeship are points of light in a world of blighted materialism and egocentricity. They remind us, perhaps, of the way we like to think we once were.

The soldiers are pleased to be appreciated. But they, who pay the price of Britain's policy, do not share the civilians' pessimism. From what I have seen and heard, there is no significant reluctance to serve in Afghanistan and if necessary to do so again and again. "Are we prepared to do it?" asked 3 Para's former regimental sergeant major John Hardy. "Yes we are. Every time." The soldiers are driven back by a number of impulses. One is professional satisfaction. Almost every soldier in a volunteer army welcomes the prospect of action. Another is their sense of duty, which has stood up well to the climate of self-interest prevalent in civilian life.

But there is more to it than that. Soldiers have a refreshingly clear-cut sense of right and wrong. They sympathise with the Afghan people, caught between the cruelty of the insurgents and the venality of the authorities, and want to help them. The job is tough and dangerous and brimming with frustrations and disillusionment, but the prizes of safety at home and a better Afghanistan are considered, if they can be won, to be worth it. The soldiers' enthusiasm, though, is finite. A military stalemate will eventually lower morale and degrade performance. If there are no signs that the

Afghan government is serious about governing, that process will accelerate.

The phrase "ground truth" is a military expression, meaning how things are compared with how they are imagined to be. Soldiers know the ground truth better than anyone; yet, it seems to me, their voices have not been given the attention they deserve. They have some extraordinary tales to tell. This book reveals some of their stories as well as their thoughts, fears and anxieties about a conflict that, for good or for bad, is shaping both them and us.

CHAPTER
ONE

Going Back

He had imagined this moment often during the last two years. Now, after an hour-long climb along a rocky, sun-baked ridge line, it had arrived. Corporal Stuart Hale shielded his eyes from the mid-morning glare and looked down at the corrugated hillside. The slope was the colour of khaki, bare apart from a scattering of rocks. It was just like a thousand others that undulated across Helmand. There was nothing to show that it was here that his life, and the lives of several of his comrades, had been swept so traumatically off course.

His mates left him alone to enjoy the satisfaction of having made it up unaided. It was cool up here after the baking heat of the valley, quiet too, the silence disturbed only by the occasional boom of mortars in Kajaki camp and the rustling noise the bombs made as they flew past.

Eventually he spoke. "I was up there when I spotted them," he said, pointing to a crag above. "They looked like Taliban, and they seemed to be setting up a checkpoint to stop people on the road down there." That morning, 6 September 2006, he had grabbed his rifle and bounded down the hill to get a better look.

1

When he reached a dried-up stream bed he hopped across without thinking. "Normally I jump with a two-footed landing 'cause that's how you're supposed to do it. A good paratrooper lands feet and knees together. But this time I got a bit lazy and just jumped with one foot." The lapse was a stroke of luck. It meant that only his right foot was blown off when he landed on the mine. The detonation was the start of a long ordeal for him and the men who went to his rescue. Four more soldiers were injured and two lost limbs. Corporal Mark Wright was killed.

Hale was rescued after hours of muddle and delay. Back in hospital in Britain he was plunged into a new trauma. Recovering from surgery, he suffered vivid paranoid hallucinations. He believed the doctors were plotting to kill him and that his girlfriend was so horrified by his injuries that she was frozen with fear on the other side of the ward door, unable to face him.

Eventually the nightmares passed. Hale did everything the doctors and physiotherapists asked, determined to regain as much as he could of the fitness he had been so proud of. Now, two years later, he was standing on the peaks above Kajaki, a welcome breeze drying the sweat on his face, after climbing 300 metres up a goat track on one real leg and one artificial one.

In the summer of 2006, Stuart Hale was a private soldier, serving as a sniper in Support Company of the Third Battalion of the Parachute Regiment. 3 Para had formed the core of the battle-group tasked with bringing stability to the province of Helmand, which until then had been virtually ignored by the international force occupying Afghanistan. Helmand was a peripheral province, a pitifully backward corner of a very poor country. No one knew precisely what would happen when British troops got there. Certainly no one anticipated the storm of violence that blew up after the Paras' arrival. From June onwards, all over the province, the soldiers were pitched into exhausting battles with bands of Taliban who fought with suicidal ferocity to drive them out.

The British were soon stretched to snapping point. They found themselves stranded in remote outposts, dependent almost entirely on helicopters to get food and ammunition in and to take casualties out. At times it seemed they might be overrun. But, showing a bravery and determination that have hardened into legend, they clung on. Their courage was reflected in the medals that followed, a haul that included a VC, awarded to Corporal Bryan Budd, who died winning it. Another thirteen men from the battlegroup were killed. Forty more were seriously wounded.

Now the Paras were back. Since they had bid a thankful farewell to Helmand in the autumn of 2006, three more British expeditionary forces had arrived, fought for six months, and gone home. In that time another fifty-four soldiers had been killed and scores more seriously wounded. The arrival of 16 Air Assault Brigade in the spring of 2008 put more troops than ever on the ground. They lived in fortresses planted near the main settlements and the rough roads that joined them together. They were squalid places, unsanitary, cramped and uncomfortable. But despite

3

their gimcrack construction they looked as if they were going to be there for a long time.

There was no end in sight to Britain's Afghan adventure. Even the politicians who had launched the deployment into southern Afghanistan in a cloud of optimism admitted that. In the summer of 2006 the 3 Para Battlegroup had won virtually every encounter they had fought and killed many insurgents. No one knew an exact number but a figure of up to a thousand was mentioned. These were heavy losses for a small guerrilla force, living off the land and among the people. The beatings had forced them to change their tactics of reckless, head-on attacks. But they seemed as determined as ever to keep on fighting. As long as they did so there was little chance that progress would be made with the activity that the government said was the real point of the British deployment. The soldiers were there to make Helmand a better place, by building roads and schools and hospitals, but more importantly by creating an atmosphere free of fear within which Afghans could begin to take charge of their lives.

Looking down from the ridge line towards Route 611, the potholed, rocky track that links the mud villages strung along the Sangin Valley, it seemed to Stuart Hale that morning that, if anything, things had gone backwards since he was last there.

On the day he was wounded, he had decided to descend from the OP and engage the Taliban himself with his sniper rifle, rather than calling in a mortar strike on them. "I didn't want there to be any risk of collateral damage because there were women shopping, kids playing," he said. "The place was really thriving." Now he looked down at the silent compounds, the empty road and the deserted fields. "No one wants to live here any more," he said sadly. "It's a ghost town."

The area is called Kajaki Olya. It lies a few kilometres from the Kajaki dam, a giant earthwork that holds back the Helmand river. British troops had been sent to Kajaki in June 2006 to help protect it from attacks by the Taliban. The insurgents saw it as an important prize. Its capture would be a propaganda triumph that would also give them control of the most important piece of infrastructure in the region. The chances of them succeeding were tiny. In the regular squalls of violence that swept Kajaki it was the civilians who suffered most. The number of innocents killed so far in this Afghan war is not known, but it is many more than the combined total of the combatant dead. Soon, living close to Kajaki became too dangerous, even for the farming families whose customary blithe fatalism always impresses Westerners.

But now it seemed that life was about to get better, not only for the people around Kajaki but in towns and villages all over southern Afghanistan. We were waiting for the start of a big operation, the high point of the British Army's 2008 summer deployment. If it succeeded it would give much-needed support to the claims of the foreign soldiers that they were in Afghanistan to build and not to destroy. 16 Air Assault Brigade was about to attempt to realise a project that had been under consideration for two years. It had been postponed several times on the grounds that it was too dangerous, and probably physically impossible. The plan was to deliver the components for a turbine which, when installed in the dam's powerhouse, would light up Helmand and carry electricity down to Kandahar to turn the wheels of a hundred new projects. It involved carting the parts on a huge convoy across desert and mountain and through densely planted areas of the "Green Zone" where the Taliban would be lying in wait. The Paras, together with a host of other British and Afghan soldiers, were now gathering in the last days of August, to protect the convoy as it reached Route 611 and the last and most dangerous phase of its epic journey.

Now, as we toiled along the ridgeway that switchbacked up and down the three peaks dominating Kajaki, we could hear the sounds of fighting drifting up from the Green Zone. Our destination was Sparrowhawk West, on top of the most southerly crag. Stu Hale led the way in. The OP gave an eagle's-eye view of the whole valley, from the desert to the east to the green strip of cultivation, watered by the canals that run off the Helmand river, across to the wall of mountains that rears up on the far bank. A team of watchers has sat there night and day, winter and summer, since the spring of 2006. The operation to clear the way had already begun. Down at the foot of the hill we could see sleeping bags spread out like giant chrysalises in a compound at the side of the 611, which 3 Para's "A" Company had taken over the night before.

Through the oversized binoculars mounted in the sangars we watched a patrol moving southwards along the road. They were from 2 Para, which manned the Kajaki camp, pushing down towards a line of bunkers known as "Flagstaff" and "Vantage" — the Taliban's first line of defence. A thin burst of fire drifted up from the valley. "That's coming from Vantage," said one of the observers. It was answered immediately by the bass throb of a heavy machine gun, followed by a swishing noise, like the sound of waves lapping the seashore, as .50-cal bullets flowed through the air. 2 Para's Patrols Platoon, lying up on the high ground overlooking the road to provide protection, were shooting back.

The firing died away. For a while, peace returned to the valley. On the far side of the river there were people in the fields. The bright blue burkas of the women stood out from the grey-green foliage like patches of wild flowers. Then, noiselessly, there was an eruption of white smoke at the foot of the hill, followed by a flat bang. "Mortar," said someone, and the binoculars turned to the west. We strained our eyes towards a stretch of broken ground on the far side of the river, scattered with patches of dried-up crops and dotted with abandoned-looking compounds. Somewhere in the middle appeared a spurt of flame and a puff of smoke. This time the mortar appeared to be heading in our direction. We ducked into a dugout and it exploded harmlessly a couple of hundred metres away. The Taliban had given themselves away. The trajectory was picked up on a radar scanner and the firing point pinpointed, a compound just under a kilometre off. Then we heard a noise like a giant door slamming coming from the battery of 105mm guns on the far side of the Kajaki dam and the slither of the shells spinning above our heads. There was a brief silence followed by a flash and a deep, dull bang, and a pillar of white smoke stained with pulverised earth climbed out of the fields.

The exhanges went on intermittently for the rest of the morning, settling into a sort of routine in which each hopeful prod by the Taliban rocket-propelled grenades (RPGs) and machine guns was met by a great retaliatory thump from the British mortars and artillery. The silence rolled in quickly to fill the spaces between the explosions. In the middle of the quiet, from high overhead, another sound drifted down, distant and familiar. Miles above, a faint white line was crawling eastwards across the cloudless sky. There were no high-flying bombers on station. The condensation trail came from an airliner, one of the dozens that pass to and fro every day and night, carrying tourists and business people from London and Paris and Rome to Delhi and Singapore and Sydney. It was noon now. The trolleys would be passing along the aisle while the cabin crew offered passengers the choice of beef or chicken. Perhaps, eight kilometres up, someone was looking out of the window at the pinprick flashes and scraps of smoke and wondering what was going on. Down below, in a medieval landscape of mud houses and dirt roads, the violence was petering out. For ten minutes there was no shooting from the Taliban. 3 Para's Regimental Sergeant Major Morgan "Moggy" Bridge had decided it was a good time to head back down the mountain. Stu Hale took the lead, bounding over the first boulders. The distant drone of the airliner faded away.

The only sound was our breathing. It seemed to be all over. Then, after 100 metres, we heard behind us the throb of the Sparrow Hawk .50-cal machine gun opening up and the sound of violence rolled once more over the harsh and beautiful landscape.

CHAPTER TWO

Through the Looking Glass

On the morning of Monday, 3 March 2008, a cold, blustery day on which spring seemed far away, the headquarters party of the Third Battalion of the Parachute Regiment arrived at Brize Norton airbase to await the RAF flight that would take them to Kandahar and a new Afghan adventure. The departure lounge was crowded with men and women from all branches of the British services. They sat hunched in what little pockets of privacy they could find, making a last call on their mobiles or stretched out on the carpet catching up on sleep. Brize was where they passed through the looking glass. On one side lay the muddy pastures and bare trees of Oxfordshire. On the other, the mountains, deserts and poppy fields of Helmand. The physical journey was nothing compared to the psychological distance they were about to travel. Here there was security and comfort. Beyond lay a realm of fear, danger and hardship.

Many of the Paras who flew out during the following days had taken part in the great events of the summer of 2006. In the eighteen months they had been away, though, much had changed. The 3 Para Battlegroup had written the opening chapter of Britain's latest Afghan war. But the plot had moved on and the shape of the action had altered. The battalion looked different too. The Paras had a new colonel and a changed cast of characters. Four out of ten of the veterans of the last tour had left, having quit the army or transferred to other units. They also had a new role that would require skills other than the sheer fighting ability that had sustained them last time.

The battalion was now led by Huw Williams, a lean, relaxed Welshman. He inherited a unit that was still preoccupied with its recent history. The 2006 tour had already entered military folklore, and if some of the prominent original players had departed, their ghosts still lingered on.

Williams had taken over from Stuart Tootal, a complex figure who had sublimated himself in the drama of the campaign, reacting emotionally to its triumphs, crises and setbacks and taking each death and injury as a personal tragedy. His demanding personality had made him a few enemies among his senior officers. There were many more, though, who admired and respected him.

Tootal's two-year command period ended in November 2007. Early in 2008 he announced he was leaving the army. The news came as a surprise. His bosses thought highly of him and he was assumed to be on a rising path that could take him to the upper reaches of the army. Tootal was close to several

11

influential journalists. He used his departure to publicise what he said were serious failings in the way the government equipped the men they sent to war and the shameful treatment the wounded received when they returned home. Out of uniform he continued to speak out as a part-time media commentator, which he combined with a top job at Barclays Bank.

To some, his decision to leave was easy to understand. Nothing could ever match the prestige of commanding an elite unit like 3 Para on the most intense operation it had faced since the Falklands War. Tootal told friends that if he had continued his army career, subsequent postings were unlikely to come close to matching the excitement and satisfaction he found in Helmand, no matter how far up the ladder he climbed.

Tootal was still commanding 3 Para when it was announced that the battalion would be returning to Afghanistan in the spring of 2008 for Operation Herrick 8. The Paras would be playing a multiple role. Their main function was to act as the rapid reaction force for the NATO commander of southern Afghanistan, going wherever he thought they were needed. But they were also expected to work with 16 Air Assault Brigade, their parent formation, which was deploying at the same time in Helmand.

During early planning meetings for Herrick 8, the brigade got used to the battalion harking back to the experiences in Herrick 4. "There was a feeling in 16 Brigade that . . . 3 Para were a backward-looking organisation who only wanted to talk about Herrick 4 and didn't want to look forward," said an officer.

12

"Everything [the Brigade] tried to do or talk about was greeted with 'well, on Herrick 4 it was like this' and 'of course, you don't understand what it's like'. The battalion wasn't overly popular and there was a feeling that they were pulling in a different direction."

Huw Williams knew as much as anyone about Herrick 4. He had been 3 Para's second-in-command during the tour, carrying the unglamorous responsibility of keeping the battalion machine running while the colonel got on with the exhausting but exhilarating job of command. But he felt it was time to let the experience go. He was determined that the shadows cast by the legends of 2006 would not obscure the new tasks and changed circumstances facing him and his men. After taking over in November 2007 he told his men that Herrick 4 belonged to the glorious past. Everyone was to look ahead and prepare for a different situation and different role.

The British Army had gone to Helmand in 2006 with only the sketchiest plan, which had been erased by the first contact with reality. They had been sent to a place which most soldiers regarded as being of only peripheral strategic importance. Once there, they were soon stuck with it, enmeshed in a process whose direction they were unable to control. 3 Para Battlegroup was supposed to create a climate of stability in a small area around Helmand's provincial capital, Lashkar Gah, in which development and reconstruction work could begin. Instead they found themselves riding to the rescue of the Afghan government whose thinly spread forces were under attack from the Taliban. Their area of operations expanded out of the original triangle bounded by Lashkar Gah, the town of Gereshk and the Camp Bastion logistics base to the northern settlements of Sangin, Musa Qaleh and Now Zad.

In the process they became the main targets of the Taliban and sank into an intense attritional slog that lasted throughout the summer. The conflict was later presented officially as the "break in battle", the fighting that has to be done to establish a force in-theatre. But the term was a *post facto* justification and no such exercise had been envisaged when the soldiers set out. The break in battle decided nothing. The Paras, in the judgement of one of their senior officers, were intent on "just surviving". It was exhaustion which eventually brought the fighting to a close, and the welcome onset of winter.

When spring came the Taliban re-emerged to face a new British force. The Paras had been succeeded by 3 Commando Brigade. They were relieved in turn six months later by 12 Mechanised Brigade. Then in October 2007 their place was taken by 52 Infantry Brigade.

By the spring of 2008 there was an established pattern to the annual fighting cycle. The Taliban remained relatively inactive during the winter. The conditions were against them. Life in the open was harsh and miserable. The fields in the fertile valley floors were bare and provided no cover from which to launch attacks. They used the time to stay in their home villages and rest, or travel to their hinterland across the border in Pakistan to recruit and resupply and confer with their high command sitting safely in the border town of Quetta. By late spring they were busy again, not fighting but farming. The most important task was to harvest the poppies that dance in the breeze in the opium fields covering southern Helmand. The milky sap that oozed from the bulbs was the main source of wealth in the local economy. It was the fuel that powered the insurgency. Some of the fighters grew poppies themselves. The others earned the approval of the peasants by working alongside them in the fields. Once the crop was gathered in, the Taliban took their cut of the profits, using the revenue to pay wages and buy weapons.

Then, rested and invigorated, their armouries and ranks replenished, they were ready to begin another summer of fighting. The Taliban were slow learners. It had taken them two fighting seasons to refine their tactics. They had started out in the summer of 2006 trying to drive out the British by weight of numbers, throwing themselves against the bases at Sangin, Now Zad and Musa Qaleh in frontal attacks that lost them many men but failed to dislodge the defenders. They seemed able to suffer remarkably high casualties without losing their will to keep fighting.

The weight of the losses that they suffered in 2006, though, was unsupportable. Gradually the Taliban developed new approaches which reduced their own casualties while increasing the damage they could inflict on their enemies. By the start of Herrick 8 both sides were engaged in what looked like a classic "asymmetric" conflict.

Wars with insurgents were always unbalanced. One side had modern conventional weapons. The other fought with what was cheap, portable and easily improvised. But in Afghanistan the scale of asymmetry at times seemed blackly absurd. Supported by the Americans, the British had an ever more sophisticated armoury of jets and helicopters, missiles and artillery, operated by men but controlled by computers. The Taliban's basic weapon was an AK47 rifle of Second World War design, augmented by machine guns, RPGs and latterly home-made roadside bombs. The Allies' satellites and spy planes and unmanned drones roamed the skies like hawks, sensitive to the slightest scurrying creature on the ground. The insurgents relied on their own eyes or those of their spies, the teenaged "dickers" who appeared on rooftops or loitered at roadsides as soon as the soldiers arrived. The NATO soldiers were encased like armadillos in body armour and stomped across the fields and ditches in boots, laden with half their own body weight in kit. The Taliban wore cotton shifts and sandals.

But the Allies' lavish assets were failing to alter the direction of the war. The Taliban showed no sign of losing heart. The level of attacks had been mounting steadily since 2006 and their methods were growing more skilful and effective. The main change on the battlefield when the Paras arrived in 2008 was the use of improvised explosive devices (IEDs), home-made bombs, packed with powder from old shells or chemical fertiliser and set off by simple electric triggers. They also had to deal with the increased threat from suicide bombers. Anti-American rebels had made great use of IEDs and suicide bombs in Iraq but they had been late arriving in Afghanistan. Together, they now kept the troops in a constant state of alertness and anxiety. The insurgents' new methods carried less risk to themselves than did their previous confrontational tactics. Even when they suffered losses, though, there seemed to be no shortage of replacements.

Since the first deployment there had been a progressive lowering of expectations about what the British could achieve on the military front in Helmand. One of the articles of faith of the counter-insurgency catechism was that you could not defeat an uprising by military means alone. Twentieth-century armies had shown themselves to be remarkably inefficient when it came to dealing with insurgencies. Guerrilla forces had defeated the French in Algeria, the Americans in Vietnam and, most recently, the Russians in Afghanistan.

Victories, when they were achieved, took a long time, far longer than victories in conventional wars. In the British experience, the struggle to defeat the communist rebels in Malaya lasted from 1948 to 1960. The campaign against the Mau Mau rebels who rose against British rule in Kenya in 1952 took eight years to suppress. The British Army's active involvement in Northern Ireland stretched for thirty-eight years. As became clear in the spring of 2009, the embers of rebellion still glowed.

Nonetheless, the high casualties that the Allies were inflicting on the Taliban encouraged initial hopes that, in a relatively short time, the insurgents might be worn down to the point where they were ready to give up or start negotiating. Brigadier Ed Butler, the senior British officer in Helmand during the Paras' 2006 tour, declared as they left for home in mid-October that "the Taliban [are] on the back foot and we are in the ascendancy". He claimed the insurgents were "having trouble with their resupply lines, getting resources and ammunition through" and that "the morale of the foot soldier has lowered". He was speaking after the fighting in Musa Qaleh had been halted by a deal brokered by the tribal elders of the town. They promised to raise a local militia to police the area if the Taliban and British withdrew. The ceasefire that followed lasted until early February 2007, when the Taliban took over the town following the killing of one of their leaders in an American airstrike. They murdered the elder who inspired the plan and terrorised the inhabitants. It was not until December that the Alliance retook the town.

The Alliance commanders tended to be cautious in their military assessments, avoiding talk of "winning" and "victory". Instead they emphasised the holistic nature of the operation. The fighting was unfortunate. But it was necessary to establish the climate of security that would allow southern Afghanistan to be healed, physically and morally.

Throughout the summer of 2007, 12 Mechanised Brigade maintained pressure on the Taliban, mounting vigorous sweeps through the Sangin Valley and driving them out of Sangin town. Whenever they encountered the insurgents they defeated them. But, as their commander, Brigadier John Lorimer, acknowledged, this, on its own, achieved little. "When we close with the Taliban we beat them," he said. "But the critical part is what happens after that . . . we need to make sure that we can clear the Taliban from those areas so that the government can extend its influence and authority to help the local people."

His successor, Brigadier Andrew Mackay, who led 52 Infantry Brigade into Helmand in October 2007, shared Lorimer's analysis. He said as he took over, "we are concentrating our efforts towards a balance between offensive operations we know are required to counter the Taliban . . . against those operations we know will make a difference in the medium to long term, such as the reconstruction and development, bringing on the Afghan National Army and the Afghan National Police". He concluded: "What I'd like to be able to do is a lot more of the latter than the former."

But that was not how things worked out. Measured by the volume of shooting, the level of violence in Helmand showed a steady upward curve in the eighteen months after the British arrived in 2006. In the course of the "break in battle", the 3 Para Battlegroup fired 470,000 rifle and machine-gun bullets. In Herrick 5, a roulement that covered the supposedly quiet winter months, the number more than doubled to 1.225 million. In Herrick 6 it doubled again to 2.485 million. In Herrick 7, despite Brigadier Mackay's intentions, it dipped only slightly to 2.209

million. These figures are only for bullets fired by rifles and medium and heavy machine guns on the ground. They do not include tens of thousands of 105mm and 88mm rounds fired by the artillery and mortars, and the thousands of cannon shells, rockets and bombs showered down by the British and NATO helicopters and jets.

There was little to show for all the spent ammunition. Following the ousting of the Taliban from Musa Qaleh and Sangin, some but not all refugees from the fighting returned home. The bazaars stirred back into life and farmers resumed their weekly trek to the markets to sell their crops, sheep and goats. This was progress, but only if the situation was being compared with the dark days of the summer of 2006. No one would claim that the civilians' existence was better now than it had been before the British arrived.

The high hopes at the start of the mission had encouraged visions of grand construction projects that would help pluck Helmandis from medieval squalor and ease them into the twenty-first century. By the spring of 2008 there were few improvements to report. The task of supervising the rebuilding programme lay with the Helmand Provincial Reconstruction Team, drawn from the Foreign Office, the Department for International Development (DfID) and the Ministry of Defence. The dangers of life in Helmand had severely restricted their activities. Their work was limited to funding and managing at arm's length small schemes such as refurbishing schools, cleaning the streets and improving small stretches of road.

Like the military, the civilian players in Helmand had learned to dampen optimism about what their presence could achieve. They discouraged attempts to measure progress in terms of new hospitals, schools and colleges. They downplayed their own role in the great enterprise. They were there to aid a metamorphosis called "Afghanisation", a transformation by which the government and people of the country turned away from factionalism and alienation and took charge of their own affairs.

The soldier leading 16 Air Assault Brigade to Helmand was finely attuned to the realities he was facing. Brigadier Mark Carleton-Smith impressed almost everyone who came across him. He was short and slight with blue eyes, fair hair and light skin. Despite a traditional upper-class military background he was a very modern British warrior. He was educated at Eton and Durham University and was commissioned into the Irish Guards in 1986. He spent the following years alternating sharp-end soldiering in dangerous places with high-powered staff appointments. Much of his active service had been spent in Iraq and Afghanistan. When appointed to lead 16 Air Assault Brigade he was forty-two, the youngest one-star general in the British Army, and he was being given charge of its newest and largest brigade.

Carleton-Smith was charming and intelligent. He had a winning ability to translate his thoughts into pithy, inspirational language. In the pre-deployment preparations he devoted time to going around his units, explaining what he thought they should be doing and

21

how they were going to do it. He talked to everyone, from majors down to privates fresh out of the depot.

"He made a real point of articulating what he saw as the strategic direction," said Huw Williams. "He talked to all of us, the soldiers as well. Where we were going, not just in Herrick 8 but where we were on the path and where that path ultimately led. We didn't have any of that last time. Then it was really a case of 'well, let's go out and see what happens'."

Carleton-Smith started his talks by stating that violence was not a measure of success. "He said that we actually wanted to be coming back saying we hadn't fired that many bullets or had that many contacts and we didn't kill that many people," Huw Williams remembered. "His line very much was that we were not going out to fight at every opportunity and should consider sometimes withdrawing from a battle which we could win but which would have no strategic effect. We hadn't got that sort of direction before."

Among those sitting in the planning meetings was Major Ben Howell, of 7 Parachute Regiment Royal Horse Artillery, who would be commanding the batteries providing fire support to the Paras. Howell was clever, well read and had a sceptical and enquiring mind. He thought he recognised the source of some of Carleton-Smith's ideas. "He talked in Rupert Smith terms," he said, a reference to a recently retired and famously intellectual senior officer who had produced a mammoth study of modern warfare entitled *The Utility of Force*. "The people were the prize, the battleground was not the fields of the Green Zone. It was actually the minds of the Afghans. So that's where we should be focusing our attention, and that pouring blood and treasure down the Helmand river really wasn't the way forward."

In his first statement after taking over Carleton-Smith made barely any mention of fighting. The task was, he said, "continuing to improve the sense of security for the people — not just physical security but their human security in the round. It's all about effective governance, rule of law and the provision of the basic necessities of life."

If he made no mention of war, it was because in his mind the army was not engaged in one. "What I wanted to avoid was this sense of 2006," he said later. The intensity of the fighting in Helmand, he felt, had caused people to lose sight of the nature of the campaign they were there to prosecute. There was an inevitable tendency among the soldiers to reason that "if it looked and smelt and sounded like war fighting, then for God's sake, we must be fighting a war". In his view, however, "we're not fighting a war. We're supporting a democratically elected government to prosecute a counter-insurgency campaign, the nature [of which] is much more political than it is military."

From this perspective, the "core of the matter was not the Taliban". It was "the Afghan people and what they thought was happening". The prize was "the human security of the people. The Taliban were to be marginalised and isolated, not made the absolute focus of the operation."

Carleton-Smith had more resources than any of his predecessors with which to carry out his plans. There had been about 3600 soldiers in the 3 Para Battlegroup. 16 Air Assault Brigade, with all its attachments and additions, numbered around 8,000. Nonetheless, this was still nowhere near enough to exert control over more than a fraction of Helmand. He decided to "recognise the relative limits of our resources on the locals, and [that] there was no point getting ahead of ourselves". Rather than extend their area of operations beyond what they were able to hold, the intention was to "try and deepen the government's control and influence and authority in those areas where we actually have the capacity to bloody well hold the ring, and not find ourselves stretched further".

The British were now effectively fixed in four places, Lashkar Gah, Sangin, Musa Qaleh and Kajaki, with a presence in the outposts of Now Zad in the north and Garmsir in the south. Carleton-Smith had no intention of expanding out of these places or trying to join them up. To do so would simply mean displacing the Taliban to another location and spreading their contagion to a previously benign area. The intention was to deepen the mission in Helmand, not to broaden it.

Carleton-Smith also had a civilian plan to work to which laid out in fairly concrete terms what the British presence was hoping to achieve in Helmand. The overall framework for the UK's efforts was set out in the "Helmand Roadmap", which pledged support to programmes in seven "core" fields: politics and reconciliation, governance, security, rule of law, economic development, counter-narcotics and strategic communications. The plan began with the idea that attention should focus on the few areas where there was some fragmentary infrastructure and the ghost of governance and laid down some milestones to mark progress over a two-year period. In that time, it was hoped, Lashkar Gah would develop into a centre of sound government and administration. Gereshk, 80 kilometres to the east, would be promoted as a financial centre. The focus would then switch northwards to Sangin and Musa Qaleh. If possible a fifth centre would be developed, either at Kajaki or Garmsir in the south. None of this thinking was new. The 3 Para Battlegroup had arrived in Helmand in 2006 with much the same ideas. But now these had solidified into a design for action. Coordinating the activities of the army, the Foreign Office and the DfID was to turn out to be complicated, however.

Huw Williams reinforced Carleton-Smith's message as he prepared his men psychologically for the new deployment. He found that most of them were receptive to the constructive mood abroad in the brigade. The response may have surprised some observers of the regiment. The Paras' reputation is based on their fighting prowess. It was won during the Second World War in Normandy and Arnhem, then reinforced at Suez and in the Falklands. The Paras genuinely believed themselves to be the best soldiers in the British Army, by which they meant the best in the world. Their exploits in Helmand appeared to justify that claim.

About four hundred of the six hundred men in the battalion had been in Afghanistan in 2006. The new members had arrived from other units or were raw young "Toms" straight out of training. Many of these eighteen- and nineteen-year-olds had been inspired to join up by what they had heard about the last operation and were, in their commander's words, "keen to prove they were the same as the guys last time, that they matched their stature".

But among the older men and the young veterans of 2006 the attitude was more considered. They knew the reality of combat. Many of them had relished the chance to test their skill and courage. But the thrill of fighting had faded. It was something you endured rather than enjoyed. Jamie Loden had taken over command of "A" Company during the defence of Sangin in June 2006, one of the most intense passages of fighting of the tour. Now he was taking the company back again, supported by another veteran, Sergeant Major Steve Tidmarsh. Their attitude, according to Loden, was that although they were "more than happy to deal with whatever we came across, at the same time we weren't going to go out of our way looking for trouble".

It was shared by the "corporals and lance corporals and senior private soldiers who had been there before, who were very content with doing their job. They knew what they had to do, they had the right resources and equipment to do it, but equally there was an element of be careful what you wish for." The mixture of cautious veterans and newcomers determined to get their share of action, in Loden's opinion, made for "a very balanced company group".

Those who had served in the 2006 tour were pleased that this one would be different. It was not only because they did not relish the thought of another six months spent in static positions slogging it out with the Taliban. The Paras are more thoughtful than their public image, and the picture painted of them by their army rivals, might suggest. At every level of the unit there were those who felt that the concept of excellence embraced more than just fighting prowess. It meant demonstrating the ability to carry out the non-kinetic, "influence" operations aimed at persuading local people of the soldiers' good intentions that were vital for the ultimate success of the campaign.

"I'm sure", said Huw Williams, "that there were some people who thought, 'Oh, 3 Para. They're just going out there to see how many bullets they can fire. It's all going to be kinetic.' But a lot of us wanted to prove we could do all sides of it . . . We were very keen to show we could do 'influence', we could do reconstruction, stabilisation, anything we were asked to do. We could bring security without wielding the big stick." Even so, it was clear to everyone that "at some stage during the six months we would still have to show that we carried the big stick".

The Paras were setting off to war in a domestic political climate that was much altered from the one that existed at the start of 2006. Then, Iraq was the dominant issue in British foreign policy. Few Britons knew much about events in Afghanistan. Two years of conflict had changed that. Afghanistan replaced Iraq as a staple of the news bulletins and almost all the stories emerging from there were depressing. A perception was growing that going to Afghanistan was a bigger mistake than going to Iraq.

The government's faith in the mission, though, remained, outwardly at least, unshaken. Ministers continued to claim progress was being made and was worth the cost in effort, expenditure and lives. On the death of the 100th British soldier to die in Afghanistan since 2002, they reached for old-fashioned words to justify the losses. The soldiers, claimed the then Defence Secretary, Des Browne, were engaged in "the noble cause of the twenty-first century".

As the Paras began boarding the buses at their barracks in Colchester for the drive to Brize Norton for the eight-hour flight to Kandahar their mood was very different from the excitement and anticipation that had gripped the battalion when they had set off two years previously. They were on their way to fight an unpopular war in a faraway place where progress was measured in centimetres, to face death, injury and constant discomfort. It seemed to some of them that the campaign had reached a point where real progress would have to be made or the enterprise would sink into a pointless and demoralising test of endurance. The next six months would answer the question that was echoing in many heads. Was it all worth it?

CHAPTER
THREE

KAF

Kandahar airfield was the NATO capital of southern Afghanistan, a gigantic logistical hub that seemed to radiate both might and hubris. It was built by American contractors in the late 1950s, then taken over by the Soviet Air Force in 1989 soon after Russia invaded Afghanistan to go to the rescue of the communist government in Kabul. From the 3-kilometre-long runway Russian jets took off to pound the mujahedin fighters who harried the invaders on the ground. The disembodied tailplanes of two burnt-out transport aircraft lay in an unused corner of the camp, all that remained of the Soviet air fleet after the rebels captured the base.

"KAF", as everyone called it, lay 16 kilometres south-east of Kandahar city. The town was invisible, blocked from view by a range of mountains. The only signs of the local inhabitants were the gangs of labourers who arrived each morning and the merchants who turned up on Saturdays to sell carpets, knick-knacks and fake Rolex watches at a ramshackle bazaar. Visiting the base was a risky business. The Taliban regarded any commercial dealings with the foreigners as collaboration, a charge that could bring a sentence of death. A story went round that the insurgents had presented a stallholder with the severed head of one of his children, wrapped in a sack.

The base was scattered over bare desert, the flatness broken here and there by stands of spindly, grey-green pines. The accommodation blocks, workshops, warehouses, offices and compounds had grown with the mission, spreading out along a grid of gravel roads. A stream of heavy trucks, armoured vehicles, buses and four-by-fours trundled continuously along them, churning up a fog of fine dust that never settled.

The base was under British control. There were 14,000 people at KAF, from about forty different countries. The majority were not soldiers but civilians, working for international companies that supplied many of the base services. The managerial jobs were taken mostly by Britons. The next level down was filled by workers from Poland, Romania, Lithuania and other upwardly mobile European nations. At the lower levels, washing dishes, cleaning floors and emptying the Portaloos, were small, unobtrusive men from southern India, the Philippines and Bangladesh.

Great efforts had been made to make KAF comfortable. The inhabitants ate in big food halls which served pasta, curry, steak and vegetarian specials. There was a hamburger bar, ice cream and espresso machines and plenty of fresh fruit, vegetables and salad. The social life of the base centred on a square stretch of raised decking known as the boardwalk, which was lined with cafés and shops. At one corner sat a branch of Tim Hortons, a Canadian coffee house chain founded by an ice-hockey star, where you queued for iced cappuccino, the house speciality. Near by were the Dutch and American PX stores selling electronic goods, paramilitary clothing and tobacco and confectionery. There was a chintzy Dutch café, the Green Bean, a Starbucks-style hangout which stayed open all night, and a NAAFI.

Coffee was the strongest drink available in KAF. The base, like everywhere in-theatre, was dry. Newcomers were surprised to find an establishment advertising itself as a massage parlour, staffed by ladies from former Soviet republics. But the sign over the door described accurately what went on inside. A story was told about a gullible British soldier who had been tipped off by his company sergeant major that extra services were available. He was shown into one of the cubicles by a masseuse. After stripping off and lying down he listed his requirements. The masseuse told him to wait a moment and slipped away. The next person through the cubicle door was a military policeman and the poor dupe was sent home on the next plane.

The enforced abstemiousness did not seem to dampen spirits. In the evenings, when the day's work was done, the cafés filled up with men and women, soldiers and civilians who chatted, laughed, flirted and smoked. They were there because of a war, but for much of the time there was no charge of anxiety in the air. Occasionally the Taliban fired a rocket into the base, which usually exploded harmlessly in the wide open spaces between the buildings.

The Paras had mixed feelings about KAF. The normality of the place was unsettling. It should have been a relief to go back there after a spell "on the ground". Instead, it could seem artificial and irritating, an affront to the sensitivities of those doing the fighting. Most of the inhabitants, soldier and civilian, never left the camp and had little idea of what life was like in the FOBs, the forward operating bases on the front line. The cushy existence of the KAF-dwellers could easily provoke feelings of contempt. "Have you noticed there are an awful lot of *fat* people around here?" remarked a Para company commander as, returning from the helicopter landing site after a spell in the field, our Land Rover passed two stout Canadian female soldiers trundling along, each holding a supersized milkshake. Kandahar airfield did at times seem to exemplify flabbiness and waste. Modern armies inevitably trail long logistical tails behind them, but the ratio of "enablers" to fighting soldiers in Afghanistan seemed absurdly high.

Now and again, however, the realities of the conflict intruded. During the summer came regular announcements that "Operation Minimise" was now in force. This was the communications blackout imposed whenever a soldier was killed, shutting down Internet and phone cabins to prevent news of the death reaching the outside world until the victim's next of kin had been informed. Some evenings, a "ramp ceremony" was held on the runway before the body of a soldier was flown home. Hundreds of soldiers from dozens of nationalities would troop through the dusk to the aircraft carrying the dead man or woman home, and for a while everyone was touched by the gravity of the mission.

The Paras were quartered in Camp Roberts, named after Alexis Roberts, a major in the Gurkhas and mentor of Prince William during his Sandhurst days who had been blown up by an IED in October 2007. Officers and men lived in rows of air-conditioned tents. It was noisy, right next to the runway, and a twenty-minute walk away from the boardwalk and canteens. The location had one major advantage. It seemed to be blessedly sheltered from the stench of shit that drifted from the inefficient sewage farm in the south-west corner, polluting much of the base.

The battalion is the basic social block in the army edifice. It numbers about six hundred men, which is big enough for it to have a real identity in the wider organisation but small enough for everyone inside it to know everyone else. A battalion's mood is to some extent set by its commanding officer. A change in leadership can alter the unit atmospherics. Officers and men agreed that under Huw Williams, 3 Para was more relaxed than it had been in the Tootal era. That did not mean that the essential character of 3 Para had changed. Williams had no intention of trying to alter it. Each of the three regular Para battalions liked to think they had their own clearly marked identity. 3 Para's nickname was "Gungy Third".

"I would say we are more laid back, more relaxed, slightly scruffy, not too worried about army-bullshit-type stuff," said Williams. "The blokes take a genuine pride in being a little bit off the wall. Yet no matter what happens, they perform to the highest standards and because they do that the whole hierarchy of 3 Para and certainly myself give them a lot of leeway."

Williams was breezy, good natured and straightforward. He carried his authority lightly. A stranger watching him chatting with a bunch of fellow officers in the dining hall would not automatically assume that he was the boss. But when he spoke everyone listened. There was wisdom and shrewdness beneath the easy surface manner. He was born and brought up in Cardiff and joined the army at eighteen straight from school. He had been a soldier now for twenty-two years. He first heard of the Paras through a book on his father's bookshelves on the 1942 Bruneval raid, an operation full of all the dash and daring that the regiment relished. A small airborne force had parachuted on to a clifftop near Le Havre, attacked a strongly defended German radar base, captured a top-secret new electronic detection device and escaped by boat.

During his career Williams had served in 3 Para as a platoon commander, intelligence officer, commander of "B" Company and as the battalion's second-in-command. Commanding a battalion on operations is regarded as the most challenging and stimulating job an officer can do. He is out with his men on the ground, putting his and their capabilities to the test. It is the peak of active soldiering and the promotions, if they come thereafter, will take him farther and farther away from the real action. Having served as number two was no guarantee that he would eventually take over as boss. Williams regarded his promotion as "a dream job . . . not just being made CO but the fact that I was going to get to spend another two years in the battalion".

His deputy was Major John Boyd, a tall, thoughtful Ulsterman, who uncomplainingly accepted the role of enabler. "I'm the oil that makes the machine work," he said. "I take the burden off the CO and let him go out and command." He had grown up on a reading diet of "*Commando* magazine, War Picture Library, the *Victor*. I used to wait every Friday for the comics to come in. At the age of five I just knew I was going to join the army one day."

Many in 3 Para talk about a feeling of vocation when they examine their reasons for joining up. The army seemed to offer an identity and a sense of community that the civilian world could not provide. Boyd had grown up on the Loyalist streets of East Belfast. The Troubles were at their height and many of those around him had served with the Ulster Defence Regiment and the Royal Ulster Constabulary. "My first platoon sergeant was a Catholic from Belfast and in those days we would never have socialised," he said. "But we've gone on to become very firm, good friends. I thought it was amazing that one of the few places where Irishmen could sit together without trying to stab each other or shoot each other was the British Army. I love the army and I love the regiment."

Boyd had been posted away from the battalion during Herrick 4 but there were many senior figures among the officers and NCOs to provide continuity. Two of the 2006 company commanders remained, though they were to move before the end of the tour. Major Jamie Loden, who had taken over "A" Company when it was under constant attack from the Taliban in the district centre at Sangin, was still in-post. So too was Major Adam Jowett, who commanded the hard-pressed defenders of the outpost at Musa Qaleh. Paul "Paddy" Blair, who had commanded "C" Company, had gone off to lead the Red Devils, the Parachute Regiment skydiving team, and Giles Timms, who commanded "B" Company, had moved on to another role outside the regiment.

Timms was replaced by Major Stuart McDonald, a pale, shaven-headed Scotsman, whose aggressive tactical approach was to make him stand out even within the Paras. He was to win a Military Cross for his courage and leadership. Stu McDonald had light blue eyes that sparkled with what some interpreted as a quasi-mystical light. They had inspired a visiting German journalist to compare him to Jesus Christ, which provided the battalion with many laughs.

He had become a soldier, almost on a whim, at the time of the 1991 Gulf War. "My friend and I were sat on the train one day and had this great romantic notion that we would join the Territorial Army and be sent out to the Gulf to fight," he remembered. "At the time I was incredibly ignorant. I knew nothing about the army . . ."

The idea took hold. He did some basic training with the TA. Then his parents showed him a newspaper ad seeking recruits for the Paras' territorial battalion. He had seen a documentary describing the rigours of "P" Company, the brutal physical and mental selection process through which all Parachute Regiment recruits have to pass, and decided that this was for him.

He joined the Para reserves before going to Edinburgh University to study commerce. "I had asked originally to join as an officer and was advised to spend a year as a private," he said. "At the end of that year I was offered promotion to lance corporal, which I took, and spent the next three years as a junior NCO. I absolutely loved it."

At the end of the course he decided against a business career and that it was "definitely army all the way, or rather more specifically the Parachute Regiment". He went through Sandhurst then joined 1 Para. Over the next dozen years he moved around the regiment, serving in Northern Ireland, Macedonia and Iraq. There had been moments of excitement and satisfaction but no real exposure to full-on fighting. He regarded his command of "B" Company as the high point of his career and the opportunity to get his "first experience of the sharp end".

The battalion started the tour with the same regimental sergeant major who had shepherded it through some of its darkest hours in 2006. John Hardy was everything an RSM was supposed to be. He was tough but just, and the sternness that went with the job overlaid a paternal temperament. Hardy had the unusual distinction of serving in two successive operational tours with 3 Para in the post but was commissioned halfway through the tour, which obliged him to return home. He was replaced by Morgan "Moggy" Bridge, who was good-natured, shrewd and funny.

The old and bold of 2006 were well represented throughout the battalion. Several of the senior NCOs had added a stripe to their sleeves and were now staff and colour sergeants and company sergeant majors, and the Toms of Herrick 4 had also moved up the ladder to become lance corporals and corporals.

There were many new faces among the CO's staff. Williams was lucky in having as his operations officer one of the stars of the last show, Captain Mark Swann, who had led the Patrols Platoon through many alarms and adventures with skill and good humour. Among the staff officers was a man who had been a background presence in the ops room in 2006. In this tour, though, he was to play a far more significant role, and his opinion would be sought on virtually everything the battalion was engaged in.

Captain Steve Boardman did not fit the popular image of a soldier. He wore glasses, seemed shy and spoke with a soft Northern accent. At forty-nine years of age he was, in military terms, almost a geriatric. Boardman had been involved in civil-military cooperation (CIMIC) affairs in 2006, charged with coordinating reconstruction efforts. As it had turned out, there was very little of this work for him to do. The Paras were more engaged in smashing things down than building them up, and after the first few weeks there was no call for his expertise. Instead Boardman took the drudge job of head watchkeeper, spending long hours on duty in the ops room, overseeing all the incoming and outgoing communications.

He had begun his military career in the Royal Artillery, then left the army but maintained strong links by joining 4 Para, the regiment's territorial unit. He founded a business specialising in print, design and reprographics. His work had taken him to India and the Far East and he had set up a joint venture in Sri Lanka. Visiting these places, he felt, "gave me a good insight into the process of how people operate in this part of the world, how they think, what their values are. It exposed me to massive cultural differences from what we are used to in the UK."

Boardman managed to keep his business running while spending long periods in Iraq and Afghanistan attached to 3 Para. Stuart Tootal had asked him to stay on after the previous Afghan tour. His CIMIC background and his regional knowledge made him the obvious candidate for the role of "influence officer" when the Paras went back. It was, he said with characteristic self-deprecation, "better for me to be doing the job than forcing a young captain in his mid to late twenties to do it, who would rather be out on the front line". In fact Boardman spent as much time on the front line as anyone, taking part in almost every operation of the tour and tabbing out on scores of tense, dangerous and exhausting patrols, alongside men who were less than half his age.

Steve and his assistants formed the NKET, the non-kinetic effects team, or "Team Pink" as they were known. They acted essentially as diplomats, representing the Paras to the tricky tribal leaders and mistrustful peasants of Helmand, explaining their mission and reassuring them of their good intentions. It was a task that required patience, fortitude and an underlying faith in the fundamental goodness of human beings. The last quality was hard to sustain in Afghanistan, especially when dealing with those who were supposed to represent authority. Boardman's belief, however, never seemed to corrode in the ground mist of nihilism that sometimes appeared to hang over the place.

The essential purpose of the Paras' existence, though, was fighting, and at all levels of the battalion there were men who were among the most experienced soldiers in the British Army. Their knowledge and skills would be passed on to the new boys, the young, green Toms who had been in training when the battles of 2006 were being fought. The tales that they heard from the veterans had only increased their thirst for action. Darren Little, from Lockerbie in Scotland, was only sixteen during Herrick 4. He had turned down a place in his father's building company to enlist in the Paras and was now a private soldier in 4 Platoon, "B" Company. Like all the newcomers he was going to southern Afghanistan "with big expectations because what the lads did last time was tremendous".

As they settled in to Camp Roberts in the first weeks of March, it was unclear whether those high hopes would be fulfilled. It had taken some time for 3 Para's precise role in the new deployment to be defined. Initially it appeared the battalion was going to be split in two. One half would go to Kabul for the unglamorous and boring job of guarding the airport while the other went to Kandahar to provide a rapid reaction force. By the end of 2007 their mission had been changed. They were designated the Regional Battlegroup for southern Afghanistan.

The task would give them many opportunities to demonstrate their versatility. Their duties meant they would be expected to roam all the provinces that fell under the control of Regional Command South of the International Security Assistance Force (ISAF) in Afghanistan. ISAF was the multinational military coalition that had evolved following the American invasion of Afghanistan in 2001. The "assistance" part of its name was a diplomatic nicety. ISAF troops in the spring of 2008 were doing most of the fighting, though Afghan units that had passed through training camps set up by the Allies increasingly accompanied them on operations. In the seven years since they had invaded, America and its allies had talked much about the need to create Afghan forces that were capable of guaranteeing their own nation's security. Progress had been made but it was slow, and the Afghan army was still a long way from being able to plan and conduct major operations on its own.

ISAF had been set up under a UN Security Council mandate in December 2001 following a meeting with Afghan opposition leaders under UN auspices in Bonn which began the process of reconstituting the country post-Taliban. Britain led the negotiations to create the force, which initially operated with soldiers and assets from the UK and eighteen other countries, under the command of a British lieutenant general, John McColl. The coalition of nations willing to commit assets to the mission was to expand over the years so that by 2008 there were forty-one countries contributing about 50,000 troops. In August 2003 NATO took over the command and coordination of ISAF, and two months later the UN authorised it to operate everywhere in Afghanistan. The initial task had been to provide security in and around Kabul. There was a gradual expansion outwards into the more benign and pacified regions of Afghanistan where Taliban support had been lightest. In December 2005, a few months after the country held its first parliamentary elections in thirty years, the Afghan government and its foreign supporters agreed to extend ISAF's operations to six provinces in the troublesome south.

Despite the terminology emphasising the collective nature of the international military presence in Afghanistan, it was the Americans who dominated. They contributed nearly half the ISAF troops spread around the country, leaving Britain trailing a distant second. In the spring of 2008, ISAF was under the command of one American general who a few months later handed over to another.

Apart from dominating ISAF, America was conducting its own separate war in Afghanistan under the aegis of Operation Enduring Freedom (OEF), the anti-terrorism campaign established after the 2001 attacks

42

in America to hunt down and kill or capture Taliban and al-Qaeda leaders. But the apparent separation of structures did not greatly simplify operations for ISAF and the British. America was the senior partner in NATO and insisted on following its own instincts and methods, even when these clashed with the approach that the British were trying to pursue.

The lines of command inside ISAF itself were complex, an inevitable result, apologists would say, of the number of nations involved in the alliance. There would be occasions on 3 Para's tour when they suffered as a result of the friction caused by the machine's numerous moving parts. A bigger problem was the differing degrees of commitment that the participants brought to the mission. Most countries were anxious to keep their troops out of the firing line, and all operations were subject to "national caveats", which meant that governments held a veto on the use of their troops in missions that they regarded as unsound or too risky. The fighting was essentially done by the Americans, the British and the Canadians, with gallant support from small nations including Denmark, Holland, Romania and Estonia and special-forces contributions from the likes of Australia and Poland.

In the spring of 2008, ISAF's Regional Command South (RCS) was under the command of a Canadian, Major General Marc Lessard, who arrived at his post in February. Lessard had more bureaucratic than operational experience. He had seen no combat, unless you counted a spell commanding a UN Protection Force battalion in the comparatively quiet arena of

Croatia in 1993 and 1994. He was regarded by the Paras as pleasant and capable with a managerial approach to leadership. He had responsibility for an enormous swathe of Afghanistan, made up of the four provinces stretching from Zabul in the east on the Pakistan frontier, across Oruzgan, Kandahar and Helmand to Nimruz on the Iranian border in the west. He had only 12,000 troops at his disposal. As the RCS Reserve Battlegroup, 3 Para were to provide an emergency force that could be helicoptered in anywhere to do anything. Their task was described as "full-spectrum". It involved, according to John Boyd, "addressing the threat as it matured, going wherever the enemy decides to raise its profile".

They would also be used to try to stretch the thinly spread ISAF presence more widely across the RCS domain. "If there was an area that we hadn't managed to influence because troops had not been there for some time," said Stu McDonald, "we were all clear that that's where we were likely to be sent." Given the scale of the military task in southern Afghanistan, it was clear that the battalion was going to be kept very busy.

CHAPTER
FOUR

Hearts and Minds

Towards the end of March, the Paras set off on their first mission. They were going to a place that carried dark historical associations for the British Army. Maywand, in the far west of Kandahar province, was the site of an ignominious defeat. On 27 July 1880, on a sun-baked desert plain during the second Anglo-Afghan war, a British and Indian force was smashed by an army of Afghans. Nearly a thousand of the 2500 troops were killed. The battle was still remembered locally. According to legend, among the victorious fighters was a woman called Malalai, who was killed in the battle. The Taliban, overcoming their habitual, murderous misogyny, revered her as a heroine.

Now the British were back and little had changed, physically or culturally, since their last visit. Maywand was a good place to expand ISAF's area of operations in Kandahar province. Until now, the Canadians, who made up most of Major General Lessard's combat troops, had concentrated on Panjwaii, a densely cultivated area west of Kandahar city. It had been infiltrated by the Taliban, whom successive operation had failed to dislodge. The arrival of a substantial

British force would allow Lessard to broaden his horizons. The insurgents were believed to have a presence in the Maywand area. But the operation was less concerned with fighting than "influence", persuading the local population that their best chance for a secure and prosperous future was to lend their support to the government of Afghanistan. It was a perfect opportunity for the Paras to show that, contrary to the assertions of their critics, they were comfortable with the "warm and fuzzy stuff".

Their efforts would be centred on Hutal, the administrative centre of Maywand district. Maywand lay on the border with Helmand. Afghanistan's main east-west road, Highway One, ran through it, connecting Kandahar with the important southern Helmand towns of Gereshk and Lashkar Gah. Until now ISAF troops had paid only fleeting visits. The idea was to establish a strong presence in Maywand that would act as a link in the chain of "development zones", the bubbles of relative safety that the alliance was trying to form around Kandahar, Gereshk and Lashkar Gah.

Hutal was a town by the standards of the region. It had a few run-down public buildings, a school, a number of mosques and a population of several thousand — no one knew exactly how many — living in a cluster of mud and breeze-block compounds. It was close to the Arghandab river system, which irrigated a wide swathe of cultivated land. The main crop in the springtime was opium poppies.

To the south-west of the town was the district of Band-e-Timor. This lay across an important route used by the Taliban to get men and supplies from safe areas in Pakistan to the south to the Sangin Valley in the north, where they had been fighting since 2006. They used the same route to take out opium to Pakistan. It was thought that the absence of foreign troops made Band-e-Timor a potential haven for fighters recuperating from their battles in neighbouring Helmand.

Hutal, which appeared on some maps as Maywand town, occupied a strategic location on Highway One, which ran through the middle of the town. This was a vital social and economic artery, but driving on it required strong nerves. Travellers ran a high risk of running into Taliban checkpoints where they would be forced to pay a "tax", or bandits who simply robbed them. The road was also studded with IEDs, planted by the insurgents to menace the convoys that supplied Camp Bastion, the large British base in the desert north of Lashkar Gah.

The mission was code-named Sohil Laram III. All designations were in Pashto now, to give a more "local" feel. The Paras approached the task with enthusiasm. Most of the soldiers who had been there in 2006 felt sympathy and concern for the people they were fighting among. They were moved by the harshness and poverty they saw in the villages and fields. They were contemptuous of the indifference and cynicism of those who supposedly ruled them, and the cruelty of the Taliban, who wanted to take their place. Their experience in Hutal was to teach them that anyone going to Afghanistan with good intentions should expect to be disappointed, not least by Afghans who were supposed to be on your side.

3 Para had two tasks. They were to secure Hutal so engineers could build a forward operating base (FOB) there. The base would then be taken over by the Afghan National Army (ANA), which would secure the town and the neighbouring stretches of Highway One. The Paras were also to roam the neighbouring district of Band-e-Timor, disrupting Taliban operations, fighting them wherever they found them, and preventing them from launching attacks on Hutal. Initially "A" Company were to take charge of the town while "B" Company dealt with the countryside. Later they would swap roles. If the operation succeeded it would establish a centre of stability and security and lay the foundations for growth. The long-term intention was to make the local people friends of the government and their foreign backers, and enemies of the insurgents.

Sohil Laram was, said Williams, "very much an influence operation". But influencing the people of Hutal and the surrounding countryside was going to be a delicate task. Afghans had grown to mistrust foreigners and their extravagant promises. They had been listening to propaganda prophesying good times ever since 2001. In many places little had happened. In large parts of southern Afghanistan things had got drastically worse.

The Paras began deploying on 26 March. At first light, "B" Company were dropped by helicopter in Band-e-Timor. "A" Company had set off by road shortly before. It was less than a hundred kilometres from KAF, but the journey took twelve hours. There were ninety vehicles all told, a mixture of Viking and Vector troop carriers, Canadian Light Armoured Vehicles (LAVs) from the Kandahar Task Force and low-loader lorries carrying the stores. There was also a detachment of ANA troops mounted on Ford Ranger pick-up trucks, the advance party for the force that would eventually man the FOB that was to be built in town. They travelled with a Canadian mentoring team.

The convoy moved without headlights. The Afghans had no night vision goggles, which made initial progress painfully slow. It was two o'clock in the afternoon before they arrived. They stayed a few miles to the south-east of the town, setting up a camp in the desert on the far side of the highway, a "leaguer" in army parlance, which would be the logistical base for the operation.

They spent the night there, and the following afternoon "A" Company, the ANA and their Canadian mentors moved into town, travelling along a back route and making many detours to avoid damage to the poppy crop, which was flowering nicely in the surrounding fields.

The company commander, Jamie Loden, together with the colonel in charge of the Afghan force, went straight to the town's ramshackle administration centre to meet Haji Zaifullah, the leader of Maywand district, and his chief of police. Zaifullah had a residence in the town but spent only part of his time there, preferring to return to the more civilised surroundings of Kandahar

49

city at weekends. He appeared to be in his late thirties, wore a sleek black beard and seemed friendly and hospitable. "He was very charming and he was always very welcoming," said Loden. But it was clear from the beginning that behind his smiling manner he was determined to resist any challenge to his authority from the newcomers, British, Canadian or Afghan. Governor Zaifullah was to give the Paras a masterclass in the complexities of local power politics and teach them that dealing with their supposed friends could be as demanding as tackling their enemies.

The first item to discuss was the site of the proposed ANA strongpoint. The ANA colonel overrode the translator's efforts to keep up and began talking directly to the district leader, to the bafflement of the non-Pashto speakers. "Inside the District Centre there was quite a high tower," Loden remembered. "We went up there, myself, the district leader, the chief of police, the Afghan colonel and his Canadian mentor. And we got into this sort of pissing contest about where we were going to locate this place." Zaifullah bristled at any perceived slight to his authority. "The district leader was trying to say you can go there and the Afghan army guy was saying [no] we want to go over there." The point at issue was "who was the most important". As the argument ground on Loden's anxiety mounted. Dusk was falling and his men had nowhere to stay. Eventually they agreed to suspend the debate until the following day. Everyone dossed down that night in a partially built police station located on some waste ground directly opposite the District

Centre on the northern side of the town. The police compound, after being properly reinforced, was to end up being the Paras' base for the duration of their stay.

The following day the discussion resumed. This time the party made a tour of the town while the colonel and Zaifullah "argued the toss about what could and couldn't go where". Finally agreement was reached that the FOB would be centred on a series of compounds that lay below an old fort, behind the main bazaar, 250 metres to the west of the District Centre. The colonel departed a contented man. The following day Zaifullah announced that he had changed his mind again. It was only after a further wearying round of talks that he allowed the decision to stand.

When detailed discussions got under way to award the labour contracts for the project there was more trouble. The Provincial Reconstruction Teams' standard procedure was to give work to locals wherever possible. But the district leader began by insisting that the contracts would go to his nominees. Once again there was a further bout of wrangling before the matter was settled.

The Paras began patrolling as soon as they arrived. The locals seemed friendly. There had been no trouble in the town itself for eighteen months. The Taliban's interest lay in Highway One. Mainly the reaction was one of curiosity. The inhabitants had seen ISAF soldiers from time to time but in small numbers and not for very long. Now there were several hundred troops in town and they were eager to know what they were planning.

Huw Williams was determined that the Paras would leave Maywand better than they found it. He had tasked Steve Boardman, the head of the NKET team, whose *raison d'être* was "influence", with identifying some projects that could be completed in the four weeks the battalion was scheduled to be there. Williams "said to him I want to have an immediate impact because I'm going to be standing in front of locals and they're going to say 'what can you do for us?'"

Working on information gleaned from previous ISAF visits, Team Pink decided the school would be a good place to start. "We'd been told that the structure of the building wasn't too bad," said Boardman. "But they were in dire need of desks and chairs and pupils." The story of the school would be dispiriting for anyone going to southern Afghanistan expecting quick and lasting results. The building was almost new. It had been built only four years before by a Japanese charity, which had arrived in Hutal while the Taliban was still recovering from its 2001 defeat, done its good deed and moved on. Now, when Jamie Loden saw it for the first time, "the windows were broken and the paint was peeling". There were, as reported, no chairs, no desks and few pupils. The school building could accommodate nearly a thousand children, but no more than a hundred were turning up, and then only intermittently. The teachers' attendance was equally haphazard. Their absence was partly due to Taliban intimidation, and partly because most of them lived in Kandahar which, although not far away, was still a difficult and dangerous commute. The reasons why the building had fallen into such disrepair were never explained.

Within a few days of the Paras' arrival life began to return to the school. "It didn't need very much work from us to freshen it up," said Loden. "We arranged for it to be repainted and for a whole load of new desks and tables to be brought in as well as exercise books and Afghan flags." They also distributed footballs and found, as British soldiers did everywhere they went, that the game was "a universal language. We went in and through an interpreter talked about football and had all the kids cheering."

At the end of the Paras' time in Hutal there were 450 children and adolescents going to classes, drawn from the town, the surrounding villages and nearby nomadic settlements. They were being taught Pashto, some maths and the Koran. All the pupils were male. Local custom did not allow boys and girls to be taught together, and to extend education to females would require building a separate school.

The builders and suppliers all came from round about, paid by Williams from funds put at his disposal to help the influence effort. One source of money was the Post Operational Relief Fund, which had been established to soothe local feelings if fighting had destroyed buildings or killed humans or livestock. In total, Williams had £20,000 a month to spend, which went quite a long way in Afghanistan.

"A" Company had not anticipated much trouble during its deployment in Hutal. "B" Company under Stu McDonald, along with Huw Williams and his

Tactical HQ group, landed in the countryside to the south-east of the town in the expectation of a fight. Intelligence reported that it was home to a number of low-level Taliban leaders who lived in compounds in the fertile strip along the Arghandab river. The company had been supplied with a list of likely targets. They were also expecting to encounter Taliban fighters on their way to and from the Sangin valley from Pakistan, whose border lay about 200 kilometres to the south. At the same time the Canadians were conducting another operation to push the Taliban out of Panjwaii, which lay east, along the river. The hope was that the insurgents would flee into the guns of the waiting Paras. "As it transpired," said McDonald ruefully later, "nothing happened." He led raids on several compounds that were supposed to be occupied by insurgents to find empty beds and blank faces. The Paras soon suspected that the intelligence they were working on was old, and if the Taliban had ever been in the locations they were targeting they had now moved on.

The exercise did at least have the merit of familiarising the newcomers to the battalion with the sights and sounds of rural Afghanistan. The scenes they witnessed in the fields and compounds of Maywand seemed strikingly rough and primitive. To Lieutenant Tosh Suzuki, a twenty-five-year-old who had chosen the Paras over a banking career, "it was really like going back in time. They were using the same irrigation methods almost as in the Middle Ages. The way they were channelling their water, building their mud huts, the tools they used . . . It's pretty impressive that they have such a hard life but they're still very determined to carry on with that livelihood".

The cultural gulf between soldiers and peasants was brought home to him the first time he went out on patrol. Suzuki and his platoon had been tasked with searching a compound. It had attracted attention because of its size and the apparent affluence of its owner, whose tractor and two trucks made him a man of substance in Maywand. This wealth pointed to a connection with the drugs trade, and the drugs trade was enmeshed tightly with the Taliban.

Suzuki took a six-man section through the front door, leaving another section of ANA soldiers to wait outside. It was a mistake. They were surrounded instantly by "screaming, banshee women, hysterical essentially". There was no man present to act as an intermediary as the males of the household had apparently fled at the first sight of the soldiers. Suzuki and his men beat a retreat. He then sent the ANA in to try to calm the situation. Eventually the women agreed to gather together in one room and the search went ahead. The lesson was that Afghan faces should front such operations and that, if things were to go smoothly, you needed a male in the compound who could usher the women out of sight. On subsequent searches, Suzuki was always careful to push the ANA to the fore.

Ten days into the deployment a similar search turned up an interesting discovery. The Paras stumbled on two large shipping containers lying in a corner of a compound. They broke open the doors and found five new electricity generators, which, it turned out, had been trucked in for use in UN offices in Kabul but had been hijacked somewhere along Highway One. McDonald, frustrated at the lack of action, consoled himself that the discovery was "worth something". The generators had cost £2 million new and if they had made it across the border to Pakistan could have been sold to buy weapons or hire gunmen.

The Paras now had to decide what to do with the loot. It seemed easiest to regard it as Afghan government property, and the generators were moved to Hutal for disposal. District Leader Zaifullah decided that the prizes were his to distribute and had to be persuaded to release one for use in the local clinic and another to power the new FOB. He was given one for his compound where, it was reckoned, it would at least have some valid use, providing electricity for the room set aside for shuras, meetings with representatives of the local communities. The ANA decided that they were taking the other two. "They said they were taking them off to their general to show him, because they had seized them," said McDonald. "When we pointed out to them that we had seized them and they had no part in the operation they said don't worry, we'll bring them back. We told them they couldn't [take them]. We woke up one morning, they were on the back of their truck and they were driving through camp." McDonald was told not to worry about it and to regard it as a heartening display of initiative.

There was a simple explanation for the calm in Band-e-Timor. The Paras had arrived just at the start of the poppy harvest. It was a laborious business involving every able-bodied member of every farming family from the ages of eight to eighty. They moved through the fields, making incisions in the bulb below the delicate pink and white petals with a multi-bladed knife. The plants were left for a few days for a milky sap to ooze out, which was then scraped off with a wooden spatula. The process was repeated two or three times until all the resin had been collected.

The arrival of a patrol in the fields was the signal for work to stop and suspicious and hostile eyes to turn towards the interlopers. "Their initial concern was that we were there to eradicate the poppies," said McDonald. "As soon as it became clear that we weren't, they were quite happy." The message was reinforced at the impromptu shuras the Paras held in every village they visited. "The elders would come out and want to speak to you," McDonald said. "And in order to get our message across as to why we were there and to reassure them, we sat down and had a chat with them at every opportunity and said, listen, we're not here for the poppy . . . we understand that it's your only means of support for your family and until an alternative livelihood is found you can continue this."

As long as the harvesting went on the calm was likely to continue. The insurgents were as keen as anyone to get the crop in. Some of the men toiling in the field belonged to local Taliban groups or were tied to them by blood or sympathy. The organisation as a whole depended on the profits from opium, through their own processing or marketing of it or the "taxes" they raised from farmers, to fund their operations. In the words of Mark Carleton-Smith, opium "supercharged" the insurgency. When in power, the Taliban had been fierce opponents of the opium trade. Now they relied on it to finance their comeback. The ideological difficulties this turnaround presented were easily overcome on the grounds that it was Western unbelievers who would suffer most from the flood of heroin pouring out of southern Afghanistan.

The Taliban's intimate connection with the trade was brought home to McDonald a little later, after the company moved into Hutal. He was called up on to the roof of the base to witness an alarming sight. A huge convoy of pick-up trucks was trundling down the wadi, a dried riverbed that ran through the town, heading for Highway One. "It was about two hundred vehicles," he said. "I counted about eight hundred fighting-age males coming down the road, which clearly alarmed us." A team from the National Directorate of Security, the Afghan intelligence bureau which worked closely with the soldiers, raced out to question them. The men replied innocently that they were just transient workers on their way to help with the poppy harvest. It was clear to McDonald, though, that "they were the same [men] we would be fighting in months to come". The harvesters climbed back into their pick-ups and "drove down the wadi. They waved at us and we waved at them."

"B" Company's stint in the countryside settled down into a routine of daily patrols during which they tried to make friends with the farmers, holding shuras and setting up a clinic where the medics could treat minor aches and pains. The willingness of the local people to talk was an encouraging sign. The patrols came across leaflets produced by the Taliban, warning locals that the penalty for fraternising with the occupiers was death. But it seemed to the Paras that the population felt they had more to fear from the Afghan National Police who were supposed to protect them than they did from the insurgents. The police were under the control of District Leader Zaifullah and appeared to be concerned only with their own interests and his.

The conduct of the police came up at every shura. "Every village we went into, they complained to us," said McDonald. The locals pleaded with him "to stop the ANP coming here, saying they beat us up and they steal our money". The police were not only corrupt but potentially hostile. Early on the morning of 10 April, a patrol in the vicinity of the desert leaguer came under small-arms and mortar fire from what seemed to be an ANP position. The Paras refrained from shooting back. The police chief later claimed that the shooters were not his men but Taliban masquerading in stolen uniforms.

The identification of friend and foe was a constant preoccupation, whether in town or country. Soldiers were always alert to the presence of dickers, bystanders who passed on information to the unseen Taliban about their movements. Even the most innocent-looking activity might well turn out to be a hidden signal. It was noticed that whenever a patrol set off from the base in Hutal, smoke from a nearby chimney turned from white to black, and one of the children who hung around a taxi rank in the centre of town would run away and talk into a mobile phone when a helicopter came in to land.

The combination of stretched nerves and erratic Afghan driving resulted in some tragic blunders which damaged the soldiers' attempts to portray their presence as benign. Just after 7 a.m. on 1 April, a Toyota was seen driving erratically near a Para position. Almost daily, the intelligence briefings were warning of the likelihood of suicide bombers, whether in cars, motorbikes or on foot. Often the information was quite specific, detailing the location of the likely attack and the make and year of the car involved. The soldiers all knew the drill for dealing with a suspicious approaching vehicle. First they fired a few rounds over its roof. If it kept coming they shot at the engine block. If that failed to deter the driver they aimed at the occupants. In this episode, as was by no means uncommon, the driver seemed oblivious to the rounds flying around him and continued driving towards the soldiers. They opened up, wounding him and his passenger. There was a similar incident two weeks later when two men on a motorbike were shot after they failed, after repeated warnings, to stop at a checkpoint. In both cases the casualties were evacuated by helicopter to KAF for emergency treatment in the base hospital. They recovered, apologies were issued and compensation paid. But the incidents reinforced the feeling in the fields and the bazaars that the arrival of foreign soldiers brought more harm than good.

McDonald had found on his travels around the villages of Band-e-Timor that for all their antipathy to the police and ambivalence towards foreign troops, people welcomed the presence of the Afghan army. ANA soldiers usually came from outside the immediate area and had no ties to corrupt local officials or to tribal leaders. The news that a fort was being built in Hutal which would establish a permanent army presence was welcomed. When Huw Williams arrived back from Kandahar on 4 April, however, he found that progress on the FOB's construction was being held up. Once again, the district leader was at the root of the problem. Haji Zaifullah had showed little sign of bending to the new wind blowing through his fiefdom. His response to the arrival of construction workers had been to try to divert them away from their task of building the FOB in favour of carrying out improvements to his official residence. When Williams vetoed the project he tried another ruse to wring some advantage from the situation.

It came to light that when truck drivers tried to load sand from a local wadi to fill up the Hesco Bastion containers that formed the walls of the fort, they were stopped by Zaifullah's men, who demanded a tax for trucking the ballast away. When Williams heard about the new scam he decided to adopt an emollient approach. The politics of the situation left him no other choice. The British were in Afghanistan to reinforce the authority of the government. That meant doing nothing to erode the standing of its local representatives, no matter how venal and corrupt they might be. The CO trod carefully when he called on the district leader to broach the subject: "I said that he was obviously a powerful man with much influence in the area and I needed his help." Williams explained what had happened at the wadi, without letting on that he knew who was behind the extortion attempts, and warned that if the situation was not sorted out the FOB could not be built.

There was "a lot of sucking of teeth" before Zaifullah admitted that it was he who was taxing the trucks. He claimed that the revenue raised would be used on local services and that the system was "good for the people". Williams countered deftly by saying that in that case he would pay the money himself, directly to the government in Kabul. "He said, oh no, you can't do that, it has to be paid here. I said, well, maybe we can pay it in Kandahar." After accepting finally that his bluff had been called, Zaifullah issued a letter exempting the truck drivers from the sand tax.

These encounters were wearing and frustrating but Williams understood the necessity of keeping cool and playing the game. "I couldn't go in there and say 'stop taxing me' because I would have been undermining him. I knew that I was dealing with someone who is corrupt but I was conscious of the difference between the person and the office he represented. Sooner or later he would be moved on. But the office would still stand and I couldn't be seen to be weakening it."

From the outset, Williams had also done what he could to communicate directly with the local notables, calling a shura soon after his arrival to introduce himself. The meeting took place in the open in the district leader's compound. About seventy elders turned up, men who owed their authority to their relative wealth or membership of a prominent family. Williams and his team explained their mission and asked their guests for their reactions. The response was sceptical. "We got the normal accusations," said Williams. "That you always come and offer but you never deliver." He had decided that the best hope of winning any degree of confidence was to "humanise myself so I appeared not just as a Western soldier there on a task. I said I was a family man. [I told them that] we didn't need to come to Afghanistan but the government that you elected has asked us to."

Williams had reported his difficulties with Zaifullah to his superiors in Kandahar, who passed the information up the political chain. The district leader's behaviour was annoying and frustrating. It started to become alarming when it became clear that, contrary to the assurances the Paras had given the farmers, he was determined to mount a poppy eradication programme in the area. On 3 April ANP vehicles that had been escorting a convoy of tractors on their way to destroy some crops came under fire from what were said to be Taliban gunmen in fields about eight kilometres north of Hutal. Jamie Loden received an urgent request from the district leader to help his men. Loden was determined not to embroil his troops in a shoot-out over opium and replied that he would assist in extracting casualties but there would be no question of sending reinforcements. By the end of the day no casualties had been reported. The incident, though, had opened a new and dangerous front in the Brits' dealings with the local authorities.

Zaifullah's eagerness to wipe out the poppy crop aroused immediate suspicions. For one thing, he was under no compulsion to do anything about opium cultivation in his district. The government eradication programme was selective. It was only in force in areas where there was a viable alternative cash crop available to growers. That was not the case in Maywand, where, as Huw Williams put it, "they grow poppy and get money for it or they starve". When Zaifullah was challenged he maintained that he was under specific orders from the governor of Kandahar province, Asadullah Khalid, to mount an eradication effort.

Enquiries uncovered an alternative explanation for the district leader's unusual zeal. Zaifullah, it turned out, had extensive poppy fields of his own. His intention, the Paras suspected, was to wipe out his rivals' crops in order to increase the value of his own. Rumours were later picked up on the ground that farmers could exempt their produce from the attentions of the police by paying a hefty bribe.

In the absence of any intervention from outside Afghan authorities, Williams had little choice but to appear to cooperate. On the evening of 8 April, Zaifullah visited him and told him that an eradication operation was taking place the following day. By now the distict leader had managed to obtain reinforcements from the provincial ANP to support the local police, who, it was increasingly clear, functioned when needed as his personal militia. Williams agreed to position vehicles from his Patrols Platoon near the fields scheduled for eradication but said they would intervene only if the ANP got into trouble. There would also be air support available if needed. As it was, 9 April passed without incident. The dangers of coalition forces being seen to support the nefarious activities of a notoriously corrupt official were obvious. But still nothing was done by the provincial or national authorities to restrain their man in Maywand.

On 11 April the Paras were told that the police would be carrying out a week-long eradication mission in the area of Now-Khar-Khayl, which lay on a bend of the Arghandab river about sixteen kilometres south-east of Hutal. Williams agreed that Patrols Platoon would watch over Afghan policemen involved in the operation but go to their aid only if they were in serious difficulties. Intelligence gleaned from intercepts reported that the Taliban were aware of the operation and were prepared to attack the police once the work got under way.

The operation began the following day. Around noon, Patrols Platoon heard gunfire coming from the fields. Williams ordered it to stay put and await instructions. The district leader, however, radioed his men to tell them to stand and fight, shoring their morale with the news that the British would shortly be coming to their rescue. When it became clear that no reinforcements were on the way he contacted Williams with ever more alarming reports from the battlefield. Just after 1 p.m. he claimed that fifteen to twenty of his men were dead and those remaining were running out of ammunition.

Williams was sceptical. He requested an overflight by a Predator Unmanned Aerial Vehicle (UAV) equipped with an on-board camera. The images it beamed back told a less dramatic story. There was no sign of any major clash and the Paras stayed put. The district leader's appeals had also been relayed back to Kandahar via the ANP. The Americans responded by sending two attack helicopters. They hovered over the supposed battlefield but found nothing to report and returned without engaging. The true story of what happened in the fields of Now-Khar-Khayl never emerged. It seemed probable that any shooting directed at the ANP was as likely to have come from farmers defending their livelihood as from the Taliban. In this instance, the two groups could have been one and the same thing.

Zaifullah's failure to inveigle British forces into backing him rankled and he complained to the governor of Kandahar, Asa dullah Khalid, to whom he was closely allied. The governor backed his protègè in Maywand, issuing a media statement claiming that a senior British officer in the district was encouraging local farmers to grow poppies. The row bubbled up the political chain until it reached Kabul and the British envoy, Sherard Cowper-Coles. The ambassador dismissed the accusation and declared that the Paras were obeying the government's own instructions, which stated that the eradication programme did not apply to

Maywand. The row subsided, but in the Paras' eyes the district leader had forfeited all respect.

Zaifullah's standing with the people he governed was made clear a few days after the eradication debacle. At mid-morning on 14 April, four men turned up at the base at Hutal asking to see the senior British officer. They were representing a group of forty elders from Band-e-Timor who had come with them to the town. Williams was away at a meeting in KAF and they were welcomed by Stuart McDonald, who had moved with his men to the town to change places with "A" Company. The visitors were angry and agitated, complaining about a raid that had taken place in their area the previous night. Men had been arrested, compounds had been damaged and vehicles set on fire. McDonald replied truthfully that it had nothing to do with the British. Later it transpired that it was an American operation that the British had not been informed of, a regular occurrence in southern Afghanistan. McDonald was backed up by an Afghan army mullah, who was as vociferous as the elders. "[He] spent about five minutes angrily shouting them down, saying I've been with these people for a number of weeks and they're genuinely here to help you." He also emphasised the common religious ground between them, claiming that the soldiers were "good Christians". He assured them that "whereas we believe in different gods they do have our respect for religion [and] this isn't part of some crusade". The mullah was a valuable ally in the struggle to win trust. "His presence was probably the single greatest factor in creating a very amiable atmosphere right from the outset," said McDonald. "They seemed to be quite reassured by virtue of the fact that he was there."

As they talked it became clear that anger over the raid was just the catalyst for the visit. They wanted to talk of many things, and most of all about the behaviour of the district leader.

McDonald invited them to return with the rest of the group later in the day when the CO would be back. The initial plan was to hold a shura in the schoolhouse, but an intelligence tip warned that there was a threat that the meeting would be attacked. They gathered instead, at five o'clock, out of the sun in a large room inside the Paras' compound. Williams sat with McDonald, Steve Boardman and the ANA mullah at the front, facing the visitors. The first ranks were filled with the most venerable of the elders. Behind them came the younger men, who would move forward to whisper their contributions in the ears of their seniors.

The spokesmen started off by spelling out to Williams the simple facts of their harsh life. "They said they were just farmers," he recalled. "They had families and they simply wanted security for them and their children. They didn't want to fight us and they didn't want to fight the Taliban. They just wanted to get on with farming." They were disarmingly frank about the source of their livelihood. "They told me they did grow poppy but they didn't care what they grew. It made no difference to them whether it was poppy or wheat — but no one was buying wheat. People were buying poppy. So what choice did they have?"

The men seemed to be between about thirty and eighty, though it was hard to tell precisely. The harshness of life and the scorching sun dried skin and ironed in wrinkles, ageing adults far beyond their actual years. Only a few dominant males spoke. Occasionally, when they made a forceful point, others would jump to their feet in passionate agreement. They told Williams that the Taliban had been active in their area but insisted that none of them was a Taliban supporter, though Williams was disinclined to take this at face value. They certainly seemed to have no reason to have any warm feeling towards the Taliban. "They said they take our food and don't give us any money, move into our compounds, beat us."

The local police, however, treated them just as badly. An old man got to his feet to show off a large bruise, the result of a beating at the hands of the ANP the previous week. Then the elders came to the point. They had come to ask for the Paras' help. They hated and feared the police. Only the British could provide real security. What they wanted was an army base in Band-e-Timor like the one that was being built in Hutal.

Williams was impressed by what he had heard. "I was convinced that they were genuine because it wasn't all good news. They weren't saying we don't grow poppy and we don't let the Taliban in. They were saying, yes we do, because it's the only thing we can sell. And we let the Taliban in because we're scared and how can we not? If we don't put them up for the night they'll kill us."

At the close, Williams promised to hold another shura to which every elder in the district would be invited. He promised to try to secure the attendance of a senior government official from the province as well as a general from the Canadian-led Task Force Kandahar. Local and national media would be invited to make sure that their concerns were given the widest possible airing. If all went well there would be more than a hundred people coming, so to accommodate everyone they would have to meet at the school and a security plan was drawn up to protect against suicide bombers.

The great shura never took place. The meeting would mean little without the presence of the main power broker in the area, Governor Asadullah Khalid. But when the Canadians at the head of Regional Command South approached him to request his presence he flatly refused to attend. A few days before, the Canadian Foreign Minister, Maxime Bernier, had visited Afghanistan and received briefings from NATO officers, diplomats and Canadian soldiers on the ground in southern Afghanistan. By the time he met Afghan President Hamid Karzai he had formed a low opinion of the president's representative in Kandahar. He accused Asadullah of corruption and of holding up Canadian humanitarian aid donations to the area. At a press conference after the encounter he effectively called on Karzai to sack him. Bernier's intervention was presented as a diplomatic faux pas and nothing happened. Asadullah ceased cooperating with the Canadians in protest and the elders of Hutal lost their chance to vent their feelings. It fell to Stuart McDonald to break the news. He found it "professionally embarrassing. You tell these people in good faith that you'll do your utmost to try and help them and then it didn't happen. There were a few disappointed looks coming across the table."

After the shura with the elders of Band-e-Timor, McDonald had come to the conclusion that any further operations in their area would "do more damage than good given that it [affected] the same people who had come to us and asked for our help". Williams agreed and a plan for "A" Company to raid some suspected insurgent compounds was called off. Instead they were sent on another mission, in line with the Paras' role as Regional Command South's mailed fist.

Williams passed a report of his meeting with local elders up the line. The truth was there was nothing he could do then and there to meet the elders' concerns. No matter how cautious Williams had been with his promises, the Paras' presence had raised expectations that, owing to the dearth of men and resources, they could not fulfil. "We weren't about to expand down there and I wasn't going to build a base," he said. There were many other places that demanded ISAF's attention before they reached Band-e-Timor. It would be another four months before the Paras returned to the region.

Nonetheless, as they prepared for their withdrawal on 25 April, they could feel some sense of achievement. The FOB was finished and ready for the arrival of a company of ANA soldiers, who would patrol the town and secure the neighbouring stretch of Highway One.

More than $200,000 had been spent on reconstruction. School attendance figures had gone up fourfold. The reactions of the local people suggested they could be persuaded to see the British as potential friends rather than aggressive interlopers.

The Paras could also claim that their stay in the area had hastened the end of Haji Zaifullah's colourful political career. At one of the shuras organised by McDonald, the district leader had been left in no doubt about how people felt about his rule. "They made some pretty strong accusations," said McDonald. "They were pointing at him, saying, 'You've done nothing for your people. You're here to line your own pockets.'" The police present carefully noted the names of anyone who spoke out against their boss.

Zaifullah, though, seemed unconcerned by the criticism. He told McDonald afterwards that his accusers were "all Taliban". Jamie Loden had had plenty of time to study Zaifullah. He felt that he had learned something important from their encounters about the subtleties of local power structures and the fluidity of interests and allegiances. "He wasn't noticeably anti-government and he wasn't pro-Taliban. He was just concerned with improving his own lot in life. In many ways what that operation illustrated for those who hadn't appreciated it was the complexity of the Afghan problem." Anyone involved in development had to understand that "individuals in power will be corrupt to varying degrees, and their interests will be dictated by furthering their own influence or power". There was a lesson there for everyone. "Perhaps some of the people and particularly the young soldiers thought that when you get to Afghanistan [the people you come across] are either good people or enemy. This made them appreciate that it is actually far more complex than that."

Nonetheless, the Paras' reporting of Zaifullah's activities and attitudes had emphasised his unsuitability in the brave new world of good governance and accountability that they were there to promote. The stories also added evidence to the dossier piling up against his patron, Asadullah Khalid. Although the Canadian Foreign Minister's candour concerning the Kandahar governor was interpreted in the media as a blunder, his remarks could not be ignored. Four months after the Paras left, Khalid was sacked and Zaifullah was fired with him.

The Paras got back to KAF to a warm welcome from Major General Lessard. For a while Sohil Laram III was talked of as a model influence mission. But long-term success required continuity of commitment and energy. The British were replaced in Hutal by soldiers drawn from Portugal's contribution to the ISAF force. There had been some uncertainty about the date of their arrival following discussions about the terms and conditions of their deployment. The Portuguese had requested the same standards of comfort that they were used to in KAF. They included canteen-quality food and an ice-cream machine. They also wanted air-conditioning units for their accommodation and a cash dispensing machine. The requests were all rejected.

On 24 April the Portuguese arrived in Hutal. "B" Company under Stu McDonald were there to conduct the handover. The new arrivals went to the now almost completed FOB. The Portuguese commander announced that he and his men belonged to a crack unit, a claim that was met with some surprise by the Paras. "They were overweight, sweaty and wore very tight uniforms," said one. "They did not look like serious soldiers." The commander sought confirmation from McDonald that the Paras patrolled in vehicles. McDonald replied that they patrolled on foot. The commander said that they would be operating mounted patrols as they were "only a company strong". McDonald pointed out that the Paras were only in Hutal in company strength themselves.

Later that day a convoy arrived bearing the Portuguese stores. The Paras watched them unloading the containers. "When they cracked the first one open it was full of booze," said one surprised onlooker. That night the newcomers strung up lights and held a party. In the morning the Paras waited at their base to formally hand over to their replacements. At the appointed hour no one had appeared. After twenty minutes, a platoon commander arrived who seemed the worse for wear from the previous night's revelry. McDonald left "with a twinge of sadness . . . we genuinely felt we were making a difference in the latter stages". At least some of the local people would agree with that assessment. As always in southern Afghanistan, the question was: how long would it last?

CHAPTER
FIVE

Hunting the Hobbit

A successful influence operation brought its own satisfaction, but so too did a good fight. It was a prospect that the soldiers looked forward to. No one joined the Parachute Regiment who did not relish the chance of combat. The news that they were to be sent on a risky daylight mission to grab a Taliban commander who had so far eluded the grasp of special forces snatch squads was very welcome.

The operation required exhaustive planning and crisp timing and coordination if it was going to come off. The target was Haji Sultan Agha, code name "the Hobbit". The ID mugshot issued to the troops revealed that, unlike his Tolkien namesake, he had a glossy black moustache and grey beard, thick eyebrows and warm brown eyes. His guru-like appearance belied his reputation as the number-one bomb-maker in the Zari district, a bucolic stretch of vineyards and poppy fields that lay along the Arghandab river near Highway One. His activities had placed him on Regional Command South's wanted list.

The task was given to "A" Company, who had finished their tour of duty in Hutal and were in a holding pattern following the decision to suspend search operations in Band-e-Timor. The RCS planners were hoping that their luck would change with Operation "Sur Kor" ("Red House"). Specialist teams had launched several missions to collar the Hobbit and his men, who were believed to build the IEDs that were found constantly along Route Fosters, a track that led south off Highway One into the Green Zone.

The raiders had been dropped at a distance from their targets and tabbed in on foot, hoping to surprise them. Instead, when they reached the target compounds their quarry had disappeared. Once they found a group of males of fighting age still in their beds. But there was nothing to link them to any insurgency activities and the conclusion was the men had received a tip-off in time to clean up any evidence.

The Paras' plan was based on boldness rather than stealth. According to Jamie Loden, "the idea was that we were going to go in in daylight and instead of putting down some way off to give them loads of warning time, we were going to land right on top of them and give them no chance of getting away".

The hope was that they would be able to catch the Hobbit in the act of making his bombs. Intelligence reports said his IED factory was in a compound, one of a cluster that lay by a fast-flowing irrigation canal in the middle of some vineyards not far from Route Fosters. The location was named "Gold". Three hundred and fifty metres to the west lay compound "Silver", which was also believed to be connected to the Hobbit's operation. Beyond that was "Bronze", home to the band's wives and children.

The site presented many practical difficulties. Landing on top of the target sounded like a good, if potentially dangerous, idea. The Taliban had so far managed to shoot down only one helicopter in southern Afghanistan, but it seemed only a matter of time before their luck improved. The immediate difficulty, though, was the terrain, which made landing a Chinook very difficult. The land to the south of the compound was more promising, but it was bounded by a canal. It was 6 feet deep and 5 wide and there was no question of even the most athletic soldier being able to jump across it burdened with body armour, weapon and the usual mountain of kit.

The only way across was via three footbridges which it was prudent to assume were mined. Clearing the route would take time, giving the Hobbit and his men the chance to escape. The pathways leading away from the compound were sheltered by trees which gave good cover. The problem facing Loden and his men was "how were we going to isolate these three compounds simultaneously to prevent anyone getting away and also land relatively close, given the limitations we had on landing zones?"

Finding a solution was complicated by the restrictions that the different elements taking part in the action placed on their men. Like almost every major operation in Afghanistan, Sur Kor was a multinational effort. The political benefits of having many nations engaged in the coalition to stabilise

Afghanistan were often cancelled out by the military disadvantages as each contributing country imposed its own caveats on what its troops would and would not do.

In this case it was the British who were causing difficulties. The policy of the joint force command that controlled the RAF, army and navy helicopters was different to that of the pilots, who Loden had always found to be "fantastically willing and wanted to do everything we wanted". British helicopters, though, were providing only part of the lift. Another two Chinooks were being supplied by the Dutch. Their commanders were willing to let their pilots land as close as physically possible to the compound walls.

The British imposed another condition on daylight assault operations. They insisted on especially thorough surveillance. These preparations took time, delaying the start. In the leaky atmosphere of KAF this was plenty of time for news of the operation to trickle out.

The operation was eventually slated for the morning of 16 April. Loden had 150 men in his group. As well as his own company platoons he could call on the heavy machine guns of the Fire Support Group (FSG) and a mortar team carrying three barrels. They were supported by explosives experts from the Royal Engineers, a Royal Military Police team, and an Afghan anti-drugs team. The force also included Corporal Sainaina Wailutu, a twenty-nine-year-old Fijian company clerk who had joined the British Army seven years before, to search any women they detained. Loden planned to fly one of his platoons in Sea King helicopters to the west of the compounds to cut off anyone fleeing in that direction. The others would put down in the Dutch helicopters next to objective "Gold", where, it was hoped, they would find the Hobbit at work. Loden, his headquarters team and the mortar men would land in the British Chinooks in an open field several hundred metres to the north-east of the target, to mop up any fugitives and give indirect fire if needed. A reserve platoon of Canadians would be waiting to the south of the canal, providing a blocking force. The Canadians had a special interest in the operation. Route Fosters was one of their main access roads to the fighting area and they had suffered several casualties as a result of the Hobbit and his IEDs.

They took off from KAF at 7.30 a.m. Half an hour later the Chinook carrying the headquarters group settled on what looked like a firm, dry poppy field. The Paras scrambled down the ramp, high on adrenaline and excitement, and immediately sank up to their knees in mud. Next off was a quad bike, used to carry ammunition around the battlefield and extract casualties, which stuck fast in the glutinous soil.

At the same time, the Dutch helicopters were touching down inside Gold compound only 33 metres from the main building. 8 Platoon, the company point men, bundled out of the back door, crouching and levelling their rifles as soon as they hit the ground, bracing for the first gust of AK47 rounds. But if anyone was inside the house they were holding their fire. As the Chinooks lifted off, they advanced cautiously towards the silent, mud-walled building. The platoon commander, Lieutenant Lev Wood, approached the door with an Afghan anti-drugs officer and peered into the dark and stuffy interior. "The place was completely bare," said Wood later. "It was as if it had been stripped of everything." They moved on to the outhouses. Several of them were piled to the roof with bundles of dried marijuana, which in an area awash with opium was considered hardly worth mentioning.

The Paras pushed on rapidly to Silver compound, leaving the engineers and military police team to go through the house. At the second location they found about twenty women and children but no fighting-age males. It was the same at Bronze. The adrenaline fizz subsided. The soldiers resigned themselves to a day of combing through the grape storage sheds and numerous mud-wall enclosures that dotted the fields and vineyards, searching for weapons and stores. It was a delicate task. The Canadians, who had been operating in the area since 2006, warned them of the risk of booby traps in the grape houses. They were also on the alert for IEDs laid along the pathways, covered by innocuous-looking cooking pots. The insurgents had developed a technique by which they waited for a patrol to approach then buried a small plastic anti-personnel mine just below the track surface and near the hidden bomb. The pressure of a footfall would set off the mine and detonate the bigger charge.

But just as they were about to begin the search, the Taliban announced their presence. Back at the helicopter landing site (HLS), Company Sergeant

Major Andy Schofield was supervising the effort to extract the quad bike from the mud. At 8.45 a.m. their work was abandoned as bullets began to buzz around them. The fire was coming from the fields to the north but no one could see the gunmen. The HQ group and mortar team who had set up near by began shooting back. Corporal Wailutu was caught in the open next to the quad bike when the firefight began. Normally her duties kept her behind a computer in the company administration office in Colchester. She had been sent to Afghanistan for a one-month tour; now she was flat on her stomach in the middle of a soggy poppy field with only the stranded quad for cover while rounds whipped over her head. "I'd never been in a contact before," she said. "I couldn't help feeling that one of the rounds was going to get me. I didn't want to risk putting my head up to see what was going on. I just lay there with my face down in the mud waiting for it to stop." Eventually, when the firing faded, she ran over to the treeline to join the others.

Loden had moved down to Gold compound. He was on the roof of the main building when the shooting started. Amid the flat crack of rifle fire he heard a sound he remembered only too well. The Taliban were engaging with RPGs. "It reminded me immediately of Sangin," he said. "There was the old pop and whizz and this thing went flying over the top. Everyone ducked. We heard the bang behind us and that was that."

Loden's initial thought was that the Taliban were preparing to attack. Something was hidden in their base

81

that was so valuable to them they were prepared to launch a full-on assault to recapture it. The pilot of an Apache attack helicopter that had been on station overhead since the start of the operation reported seeing men entering and leaving what appeared to be a bunker system. It was some distance away, however, 1500 metres to the north of Gold compound, and too far to pose an immediate threat.

The shooting began to fade but Loden was concerned that the HQ group and mortar team, who had not yet had time to set up their barrels, might come under attack again. He ordered Lev Wood to stop searching the compounds and to take his men over to the HLS.

More reports were coming in from the Apache. At 9.04, nearly twenty minutes after the initial contact, the pilot picked up further activity around the bunker. Eight men were moving around outside. He described seeing "a guy walking away from it, going a certain distance out, putting something in the dirt, coming back". Loden surmised that he was laying a mine and that the inhabitants of the bunker "were preparing themselves for a fight". Eight minutes later the pilot spotted six men entering the bunker through a hole in the wall. The pilot was eager to engage. Instead of requesting permission from the company commander on the ground, however, he asked for clearance from Kandahar. The killing of innocent civilians by Coalition forces had soured relations between President Karzai, America and ISAF, and the president was insisting greater care be taken, particularly in air attacks. The helicopter had to wait while the request was passed up the chain of command. Eventually the message came back that the pilot was not to engage.

As Loden absorbed this, Kandahar passed on an intelligence alert, stating that the Hobbit was still in the area and was holed up at a location 800 metres to the north. The report gave a rough location. British troops operated with maps taken from aerial photographs on which all the features were numbered. The trouble with the map in Loden's hands was that the imagery had been captured eighteen months before at the start of the Afghan winter. In the meantime foliage had grown, compounds had been built up and knocked down and the reality in front of him sometimes differed markedly from the representation. Eventually he matched the reference to the landscape and made his next move. It seemed clear that if the Apache was not going to take out the bunker they would have to do so themselves. By pushing forward they were also moving towards where the Hobbit was said to be lying up. Loden decided to order an "advance to contact".

He would need all his men. He called the Canadians and asked them to cross the canal and secure the compounds, freeing up his two platoons to come forward. They gathered for a conference at the HLS. The bunker would have to be dealt with before they could move on to the Hobbit's supposed location. To reach the bunker meant passing through a straggle of compounds connected by a long alleyway.

The lead section had gone only a few dozen metres when a gunman popped up from behind a compound wall ten metres away and sprayed AK47 fire in their direction. "How the hell he missed I have no idea," said Loden. "He was that close that he really should have hit someone." The Paras hit the ground. After a few minutes, Sergeant Shaun Sexton from 2 Platoon took one of his men, raced forward to the door of the compound and flung in a grenade. When the smoke cleared they peered in. The only thing visible was a tethered goat, which looked up calmly from its feed to check out the intruders.

The advance continued. The Paras came to an irrigation canal, part of the web of arteries and capillaries that channelled the waters of the Arghandab into the vineyards and poppy fields. It was too wide to jump. As they waded across, someone noticed a plastic disc glinting on the stream bed. It looked like an antipersonnel mine. Everybody hopped rapidly on to the opposite bank.

The landscape was empty now. The workers who had been dotted about the fields when the helicopters first arrived had all disappeared. Occasionally a head would pop up on a distant rooftop as a Taliban dicker tried to spot the Paras' movements. Each time he would be scared away by a volley of rifle fire.

The Apache had gone back to KAF to refuel, taking its devastating Hellfire missiles with it. Loden halted the company 400 metres south-west of the bunker. He told Lev Wood to take his platoon forward while the rest provided covering fire. They set off across the fields until they came to a wall and ditch. One section "went firm" behind the cover while the other, led by Corporal

Shane Coyne, set off on a crouching run straight towards the low, humped structure that merged almost invisibly with the surrounding earth and mud. They hurled grenades at the firing slits and doorways and threw themselves down to avoid the blast. When they raised their heads there was no returning fire. Coyne closed on the bunker and ducked inside. The place stank of cordite from the explosion. As the smoke and dust subsided they could see that the place was empty.

"They were obviously very good at guessing what we were going to do and bugging out," said Captain Mike Thwaite, the company second-in-command. The bunker was impressive, just like the ones they came across when training on the mock battlefields of the Brecon Beacons. It was well dug in with overhead cover, small firing slits that gave the occupiers good fields of fire and tunnels that led out the back into zigzag trenches allowing them to escape from it unseen, as they appeared to have just done.

The Paras set off again, towards the Hobbit's last known location, about 450 metres to the west. By now there was little expectation of finding him, however. When they reached the target compound it too was empty. There were a few old men near by who watched them carry out a search. Loden went over with an interpreter and started talking to them. They were dignified and courteous, as the soldiers found the Afghans usually to be, but had no information they were willing or able to pass on. It was nearly 1 p.m. The sun was high and the Paras were hot and thirsty. The silence was heavy and, Loden thought, eerie. Abruptly it was split by a deafening cry of "*Allahu Akhbar*" as the loudspeaker on the minaret of a tiny mud-walled mosque burst into life with the call to prayer. The recorded voice of the muezzin was immediately overlaid by the ripple of automatic fire coming from behind. Loden had left the Fire Support Group to his south to provide cover, and they now joined in, firing at the flashes lighting up the foliage with their General Purpose Machine Guns (GPMGs). Eventually the exchange died out and Loden took stock of the situation.

It appeared that, contrary to early indications, the Taliban were not interested in a stand-up fight and did not feel that anything they may have hidden in the area was worth the losses involved in trying to force the Paras out. The search of the initial compounds had turned up some bomb-making components, such as car batteries and circuit boards. On their journey north the Paras had recovered an RPG launcher and destroyed it with a plastic explosive bar mine. All this was easily replaceable. The real object of value in the area was the Hobbit, and it looked as if he had got away. The Taliban seemed content to harass the Paras while minimising their own exposure to danger.

It was now getting on for 2p.m. Time was running out. The helicopters were due to extract everyone at 4p.m. from a new landing site on the far side of the canal from Gold compound. That was nearly a kilometre away, a fair distance when you had to cover it on foot, carrying a ton of kit, over soggy, obstacle-cluttered ground, manoeuvring to protect yourself as you went. Any further delay now meant they would have to stay the night. They had enough rations to last them, and if they ran out of water they could drink canal water treated with purification tablets. Loden's main concern was radio batteries. They were heavy and used up power fast. If he decided to stay they would have to switch the radios off to save electricity, turning them on only when, as seemed likely, the Taliban launched a night-time attack.

As he was deliberating there was another burst of fire from behind as another gunman popped up, sprayed bullets in their general direction and disappeared. The search continued a little while longer before Loden decided they were going to try to make the rendezvous. He led the two platoons with him back to the mortar position, just by the field where they had landed six hours previously. The quad bikes were useless in the boggy ground; all hands would be needed to carry the unused mortar bombs, packed in plastic "greenies", to the new HLS.

As Loden and his HQ team reached the mortars it seemed that the end was in sight. "I think we were slightly lulled into a false sense of security," he said. "We'd had these fleeting glimpses of the enemy that hadn't really materialised into anything." The Taliban, however, were saving their best effort for last. "They had looked at where we were, seen where we'd gone, worked out where we were going to have to come back to and set up an ambush."

The insurgents opened up just as the last element of the company arrived at the mortar position. It was a fortunate mistake on the insurgents' part. If they had attacked early the company would have been split in two, with 8 Platoon bringing up the rear. The soldiers dived flat as bullets whipped in low, shredding the poppies a few inches above their heads and kicking up mud.

The fire was coming from a compound 200 metres to the north. Instead of another "shoot and scoot" this contact was a determined, sustained attack with machine guns and rifles. 8 Platoon were belly down in the mud with little scope for returning fire. Lev Wood was in the middle of the line. He raised his head to see a ruined storehouse in the middle of the field and made for it. "It was quite convenient for me but not so convenient for the rear section," he said. The rear was being brought up by the platoon sergeant, Danny Leitch. He brought his men forward in a crouching run while his comrades battered the firing point with rifle fire and underslung grenades. Among them was Private Ollie Schofield, who had volunteered for 3 Para after hearing about their previous exploits while in training. Now he was "living the dream". He found the experience "kind of scary", but at the same time he was feeling "the biggest buzz you will ever get. You can't match it anywhere."

The Paras paused for a few minutes then scrambled forward again another 33 metres, heading for a drainage ditch at the edge of the field. They tumbled in, gasping for breath, while the rounds continued to crack and buzz overhead. There was fire coming the other way now from the sniper team left to protect the mortars, who were also engaging the compound, and the fields echoed with the thump of heavy 8.6mm Lapua Magnum rounds. Loden had run forward with his mortar fire controller, Corporal Pete Preece, to get better "eyes on" the Taliban position. They took cover in a ditch, but for a while the weight of fire was too heavy for Preece to get his head up long enough to obtain a precise fix on the location. Eventually he was able to work out the coordinates and brought in smoke rounds on the compound, which covered the Paras' withdrawal.

Corporal Wailutu watched the contact from the mortar line. She had learned a lot during the day. At one point she had been ordered to fire warning shots over people approaching their position. As the latest fighting flared up, her first instinct was to join in. "It was very exciting," she said. "I couldn't wait to use my weapon." With so many friendly forces spread around there was less chance of hitting an insurgent than one of her own side, however, and she held her fire.

Loden now asked Wood whether he thought it was possible to assault the compound head on. It was, undoubtedly, "a big ask". It meant charging over more than two hundred metres of open ground through thick, slippery mud in full sight of the enemy. "As far as I was concerned, it wasn't [on]," said Wood. He told Loden it was "pretty suicidal" to go straight at the compound but suggested approaching it with a right flanking movement instead. Loden accepted his judgement, declined the offer and told 8 Platoon to stay put, "watch and shoot".

As they waited, the firing from the compound stopped. It was replaced by shooting from the south. The Canadians had come under fire and were replying with everything they had. Loden had an hour and a quarter until the rendevous with the helicopters. The aircraft would soon be taking off and if they weren't going to make it he should tell Kandahar immediately. By now there was air cover overhead to suppress any further attempt to slow their withdrawal. He decided to go for it. They picked up the "greenies" mortar round containers and began hobbling back across the fields, covered by the snipers, who were the last to "collapse".

The helicopters arrived at 4p.m., putting down in a wadi south of the canal. It had been a day of mixed results. They had missed the Hobbit and failed to uncover his cache of materiel. The Taliban had avoided the temptation to come out and fight, as they would certainly have done a few years before. To the veterans of 2006 it was becoming clear that the days of pitched battles were probably over.

On the other hand, the Paras had performed skilfully and professionally and, most importantly of all, had come through without a single casualty. It was a good feeling. "The company got back to Kandahar that night on a real high because they'd finally done something," said Loden. "The previous two weeks had been patrolling around Hutal with nothing much happening. I think for the first time everyone realised that the role we were in could offer significant variety." For his deputy it was "a good run out". Now the rest of the battalion were about to get theirs.

CHAPTER
SIX

Green Zone

3 Para were returning to Helmand. On 25 April, Williams began preparations for a British-run operation to push back the Taliban in the upper Gereshk valley. The fact that this was necessary was a reminder of how little the military mission had progressed in two years. The insurgents may have been driven from Sangin and Musa Qaleh. But clearing them from the countryside was a harder task, and successes were usually only temporary.

The Paras would be under the control of Mark Carleton-Smith, who had now arrived in-theatre with 16 Air Assault Brigade. The brigadier had been clear that he was more interested in building stability than fighting battles. The ground truth he met on arrival, though, meant that his first big operation would be a "kinetic" one.

The objective was to tighten ISAF's grip on the area north of Gereshk. When the British arrived in 2006 the town had been chosen as a good place to start deepening security. Gereshk had escaped the trouble that had engulfed Sangin and Musa Qaleh. But the process of extending the security bubble outwards to the surrounding areas had been slow and costly.

The upper Gereshk valley, which ran north of the town, was thick with Taliban. It fell under the responsibility of the Danish troops of Battlegroup Central, who worked alongside the British in the Helmand Task Force. In January 2008 they set up a base called FOB Armadillo, from which they sallied out to try and dominate the countryside around. Lately, though, the small area of control they had established was shrinking as the Taliban pressed back. "Every time they went out they got into a fight," said Williams. "They were really struggling." The Danes had lost three soldiers in clashes with the Taliban in March, as well as two more killed in a suicide attack on a convoy in Gereshk. The new operation, code-named Oqab Sterga (Eagle's Eye), was intended to clear the insurgents from the area and allow the construction of another base, which would be manned by Afghan troops. It was to be called FOB Attal, Pashto for "hero".

The number of British troops in Helmand had been growing steadily and there were now nearly 8,000 soldiers in the Task Force. Carleton-Smith commanded two battlegroups. The first, which had at its core the second and fifth battalions of the Royal Regiment of Scotland, was based in Musa Qaleh at the limits of logistic sustainability. The other was formed around the Second Battalion of the Parachute Regiment, 2 Para, who were 3 Para's next-door neighbours at the headquarters in Colchester. Their commander, Lieutenant Colonel Joe O'Sullivan, initially based himself at

Bastion but soon moved to Sangin, the centre of their area of operations. This added up to a considerable increase in resources compared to 2006. But the fact remained that, as one Para officer said in what was an expression of universal opinion, "troop levels are ridiculous for what we are being asked to do." Carleton-Smith's "deep not broad" approach was dictated by the severely limited means at his disposal.

Oqab Sterga would involve both Para battalions as well as the Danes and troops from the ANA. The plan was for the Danes to launch out of Armadillo and push the Taliban northwards. At the same time 2 Para would advance from the south down the eastern bank of the Helmand river. The forces would form a vice to squeeze out the Taliban from the upper Gereshk valley.

3 Para was tasked with taking on the Taliban in Qal-e-Gaz on the western bank of the river. It was an area of cultivated land, about seven or eight kilometres long and over a kilometre wide, crisscrossed with watercourses. It was typical "Green Zone" territory, lush, fertile and densely planted, which made it heavy going for the hunter and excellent cover for the hunted. The Taliban who lived there had been left alone until now. The British troops who had come and gone since 2006 had been too preoccupied with other dramas to disturb them. Carleton-Smith's thinking was that if the Taliban were forced to defend their haven in Qal-e-Gaz they would be unable to move reinforcements out to counter the push northwards from Gereshk when it came.

The place was important to the insurgents. It gave them a logistical centre from which they could support operations up and down the Sangin valley. Intelligence reports said that Taliban high command, over the border in the Pakistan town of Quetta, had ordered the local commanders to fight hard to prevent it being taken.

3 Para were arriving in force with two complete companies and their support elements, the battlegroup headquarters and a company of ANA soldiers. At the beginning of May they started moving from Kandahar to Bastion, west of Gereshk, to prepare to launch. Before they did so one of the crises of nerves that regularly shook the province flared up. Disturbing reports arrived from Musa Qaleh claiming that the Taliban had appeared in strength in the area and were threatening to take the town. The British had learned not to jump when the local security forces sounded the alarm bells. Information about insurgent numbers and the ground they had seized was assumed to be exaggerated, inflated by "Afghan arithmetic". The reports, though, were too persistent to be ignored. Carleton-Smith detached "B" Company from the 3 Para Battlegroup and sent them to reinforce the Scots in Musa Qaleh. "A" Company, together with Patrols Platoon and Huw Williams's Tactical HQ, headed off to start the operation without them.

Williams decided to base his men in a "leaguer" in the desert to the west of the Green Zone. Desert leaguers had many advantages. They were easy to defend as no one could get near without being spotted.

This did not mean that they were beyond the reach of indirect fire, as the Paras were soon to discover. They were also relatively easy to resupply by air or land. From a leaguer the Paras could launch patrols and probing missions into areas where the Taliban were thought to be lurking. They also had their disadvantages. Living conditions were harsh even by Helmand standards. The soldiers spent days sitting on treeless, flat expanses of gritty ground, pounded by the heat. "You're absolutely at the mercy of the sun," said Tosh Suzuki. "If there's no breeze it's unbearable. You put your poncho up and all you've created is a greenhouse effect. It looks like it's shade but the heat comes in and it doesn't come out again."

On 7 May, Patrols Platoon set off from Bastion to recce a suitable spot. They settled on a bare patch of undulating, stony desert halfway down the Qal-e-Gaz district, about two kilometres to the west of the Green Zone. "A" Company were in place by the following morning, accompanied by a supply convoy loaded with ISO containers carrying enough food and water to sustain them for several days. With the lorries was a mechanical digger which was used to gouge out rudimentary trenches known as shell scrapes.

Just before 10 a.m. the men were taking a break, eating a ration-pack breakfast and watching the digger as it scooped up dirt and rock, when their meal was interrupted by a flash, a thump and a plume of smoke. A mortar had landed right by their location. It was swiftly followed by several more. "At first it was on the flanks," said Captain Mike Thwaite, the company second-in-command. "Then it got closer and closer." The mortars started landing fifteen to twenty metres away from the WMIKs, the stripped down Land Rovers, bristling with weapons, which the Paras used to get around on the ground. One exploded close to the signals team as they set up their position. Up on the high ground to the rear of the leaguer, Private Liam Walsh and two others from 1 Platoon were filling sandbags to build up a sentry position, when a round burst on the hillside behind. Mortar bombs make no noise as they drop to earth. The first Walsh knew about it was a heavy blow to his backside, and he was thrown to the ground. The other men were showered with dirt. Walsh had been hit in the buttocks. His injury was not life threatening but it was bad enough to need proper treatment, and a helicopter was summoned, which arrived two hours later to lift him out.

The bombardment continued all morning. Now there were RPGs streaking in as well as mortars. The fire was coming from the Green Zone, but well inside it so it was hard to pinpoint exactly where. Jamie Loden pushed out a patrol to see whether they could get "eyes on" the Taliban mortar team. It took more than an hour before they were able to identify their likely location and an air strike was called in. Ten minutes later a 500-pound bomb erupted in the target compound. But by early afternoon the Taliban mortars were back in action, lobbing bombs around the desert leaguer and forcing everyone to take cover in the shell scrapes.

There was one sure way of identifying the enemy firing points. The brigade was equipped with Light

Counter Mortar Radar (LCMR), which was able within a few minutes of an incoming round being fired to estimate the mortar's location. The Paras had asked for the kit before setting off but had been turned down on the grounds that it would probably not be necessary. It was certainly needed now. The following morning at first light a helicopter dropped one off.

That afternoon, just before 3p.m., another mortar round dropped into the leaguer. The LCMR computer picked up the trajectory and the mortar team ranged eighteen high-explosive rounds on to the target. There was no more fire that day. Later a Predator drone sent back images which showed the dead bodies of the operators scattered inside a compound.

The Qal-e-Gaz Green Zone was a "vipers' nest", according to the intelligence briefing, but that was as far as the information went. No one knew how many insurgents were inside it or how well prepared they were to defend themselves when the Paras went in. Williams decided to proceed with caution. On the morning of 10 May he tasked Patrols Platoon with conducting a recce along the edge, probing inside occasionally to gauge reactions. "I said . . . I want you to poke it. The hornets' nest analogy. Just trying to get enough to see what is happening." They were also expected to scout locations from which the Fire Support Group could watch over the incursions into the Green Zone when they came, and to look out for possible points of entry.

Nine WMIKs set off from the desert leaguer southwards over corrugated desert and numerous wadis. The ground looked innocuous enough. But everyone was well aware of the potential dangers hidden among the dirt and rocks. There were "legacy mines" scattered everywhere in Afghanistan, left over from the time of the Soviet occupation. They posed a remarkably durable threat, and could still be deadly decades after they had been planted, as 3 Para knew from the previous tour. And now, increasingly, there were the Taliban IEDs to worry about. The likelihood was that the insurgents would have laid IEDs to protect the western approaches to the stronghold. The WMIKs were fire support and reconnaissance vehicles that were tried and tested in this sort of terrain, having first been used in the 1990–1 Gulf War by SAS units operating behind the lines. They were basically stripped-down Land Rovers, fitted with roll bars and the Weapons Mount Installation Kit from which they took their name. They could carry a .50-cal or a Heckler & Koch Grenade Machine Gun (GMG), a new addition to the Paras' armoury, on the back and had a GPMG bolted in front of the passenger seat. They were robust and manoeuvrable but could not handle very steep gradients. It would not be difficult for insurgents to identify their likely routes into the Green Zone and up and down its fringes, and place bombs accordingly.

The battalion and brigade intelligence teams had worked out the likeliest mine sites. The platoon's commander, Captain Andy Mallet, a veteran of 2006, had seventy-five danger points logged on to his Global Positioning System computer within one five kilometre square area. He remarked to his men that the experience was "like being a World War Two destroyer, negotiating through the sea with all these mines bobbing about".

At 11.40 that morning they were moving slowly around a plateau that dominated the Green Zone for several kilometres north and south when there was a thunderous explosion and one of the WMIKs flew into the air. It flipped over, turned around and landed on its roof, belching smoke and fire. It looked, thought Mallet, "like a Coke can that had been ripped open". The driver, Private Luke Van Der Merwe, was lying face down, half hidden by the wreckage. The commander, Corporal Neil Sant, and gunner, Lance Corporal Duncan Armstrong, had been thrown clear. Sant picked himself up and staggered over to Van Der Merwe. "At first I couldn't see his legs," he said. "I thought they had been chopped off. There was blood all over his face and it looked pretty bad." Both of Van Der Merwe's legs were broken and his nose was smashed but he would survive. The others were shaken but had no broken bones. The front wheels and engine of the WMIK had been blown right off. The three men had been saved from likely death by the vehicle's armour plating. Sant and Armstrong pulled Van Der Merwe free. But where there was one mine there would be others. They had to wait for a passage to be cleared to the vehicle before they could be extracted and helicoptered out.

There was no point in recovering the WMIK. Early the following morning a Harrier jet destroyed it with a 500-pound bomb to prevent the Taliban from salvaging anything of worth. The Paras had been lucky with the first mine strike. Their luck held that same afternoon when Fire Support Group WMIKs twice struck mines and came through unscathed. There were another two mine strikes the following day. All the explosions seemed to have been caused by the detritus of the Soviet era, but it was difficult to be sure. There were plenty of IEDs in the area, as later events were to demonstrate.

Just before the first explosion Mallet had received an intelligence warning that the Taliban were watching the patrol. Reports had continued to arrive, advising the Paras that a mortar attack was imminent. Once the helicopter carrying off Van Der Merwe, Sant and Armstrong for treatment was safely away, Mallet decided to take the initiative. "I said, right, fellas, we have lost a vehicle and we have lost a crew but we have a job to do and we are going to have to saddle up and get on with it." The decision was in keeping with an established Para drill, which ordained that an engagement was not to be broken off simply because casualties had been sustained.

His men "were fantastic . . . they were champing at the bit to get back in". They set off towards the Green Zone. They were moving across bare, rolling ground, dotted with a few compounds and sliced by wadis. There were four vehicles at the front and two on each side. One WMIK would probe forward then stop while the one behind moved past it. The idea was "to try and make the Taliban have a go at us". A new intelligence report suggested that an ambush was being prepared. Mallet decided to drive into it. "I thought, bugger this. Right, let's see what you are made of, then."

They were on their third approach towards the Green Zone when "all hell broke loose". The Taliban were firing with everything they had, RPGs fused to burst in the air blasting red-hot shrapnel downwards, heavy machine guns, AK47s and mortars. "There were RPGs flying over and rounds smacking into the ground next to the WMIKs," said Mallet. Between them, the platoon's WMIKs carried four .50-cals, four GMGs and nine GPMGs.

All their firepower was needed now as the Paras began to pull back, following a "pepperpot" drill, with each vehicle covering another as they withdrew, and WMIKs on the flank pouring down suppressing fire. There were "vehicles driving everywhere, commanders screaming at one another". After several hectic minutes they managed to manoeuvre into a line abreast so they could bring their guns to bear. They poured a concentrated stream of fire against the Taliban positions. "Everything was shooting in unison," said Mallet. It was "massively impressive, horrendously noisy". Eventually the shooting from the Green Zone stopped. The Paras pulled back behind the cover of a hill, caught their breath, then set off patrolling again. The firefight had lasted twenty long minutes. The images from the UAVs suggested that the Taliban had lost five or six men and other casualties were seen being carried away.

It had been a busy day but the real work had not yet started. The Paras were trying to do something new. Their job was to keep the Taliban preoccupied, to divert their attention and resources away from the operation that was taking place across the river in the upper Gereshk valley. That did not mean taking them on in a full-blooded battle. Carleton-Smith was more concerned with converting civilians than killing insurgents. In an all-out attack, there was a strong possibility that property would be damaged and innocents killed and maimed, which was unlikely to win the government any support among the inhabitants of Qal-e-Gaz. It had been made very clear to the Paras that they were not there to "mow the grass". The intention was to demonstrate to the Taliban the power of the force they were facing in the hope that they would back away. The Paras would then move into the area in strength to make contact with the locals and try to persuade them of their good intentions.

Over the next two days "A" Company patrolled up and down the edge of the zone in what was effectively a show of force. The plan, said Jamie Loden, was "to adopt an approach that would allow us to get the enemy out of there without razing the place to the ground". They made no attempt to hide their movements, and in the end the insurgents felt compelled to respond. Towards the end of the morning of 11 May the Paras were perched on high ground watching a compound that overlooked a route into the Green Zone when a mortar round landed near by. It was followed shortly afterwards by four more. Loden said later that "it would have been very easy to have continued moving towards them and to end up assaulting the compound". Mindful of the new, subtler approach, however, he kept his men where they were and requested a fire mission by the rocket battery situated at the nearest FOB. The missiles were fused to burst in the air rather than smash into the compound. It was just as well. The Paras later discovered that there were ten civilians inside along with the Taliban who had taken it over. No one was hurt but buildings were damaged and the Paras ended up paying compensation to the owner.

The following day they went up to the plateau that dominated the area and detonated smoke grenades to let the insurgents know they were there. Intelligence reported that some of the fighters were eager to start an engagement. Their commander ordered them to hold their fire. The message, it seemed, was getting through. The following day the Paras made a short foray inside the Green Zone. They were watched all the way. They saw one dicker observing them from the roof of a building and fired warning shots in his direction to scare him away. He stayed put. Under the rules of engagement, anyone who was believed to be directing operations against "friendly forces" was deemed a legitimate target. When, forty-five minutes later, the dicker was still in place, a sniper shot him dead.

Steve Boardman, the battalion influence officer and head of "Team Pink", was with the patrol, and eager to meet local leaders. In the first village they entered, the interpreters found an elder who was prepared to meet the strangers. Boardman asked him to point out the mosque, which he did. Boardman then enquired about the name of the mullah. The elder turned to take advice from a mysterious younger man who had appeared. This seemed odd. "Obviously, as the elder of the village, he would know everyone and he would certainly know who the mullah was," Boardman said. His interpretation was that the new arrival was a Talib and that the elder was signalling to him "that there were other people in the village than the people who should be there". The conversation ended. But as they were leaving, the old man reappeared. Speaking through the interpreter, he said he had not been able to talk freely before and passed on a warning that IEDs had been planted near by. As they left, Boardman felt greatly encouraged. "It seemed a sign that people wanted peace and stability and that they wanted us to remove the Taliban," he said.

The display of might appeared to be having the desired effect. Williams had sent the ANA troops up to penetrate the northern end of Qal-e-Gaz. "I said to them, keep going until you get a contact. They went in quite a way and had no contact but they did have a chance to speak to the people." The impression they formed was that the Taliban had been sobered by the sight of their enemies. There were reports that some insurgents were already pulling out.

Williams decided it was time to patrol Qal-e-Gaz in force. "B" Company had now rejoined the battalion after an uneventful tour of Musa Qaleh. The Taliban assault on the town had failed to materialise and Stu

McDonald and his men had spent their times tabbing around the villages to the south, meeting the locals and gleaning what information they could.

Just before dawn on 14 May the whole battlegroup began a sweep through the area. They entered the Green Zone in the south, pushed into the middle of the cultivated strip, then swung northwards. The pattern of life seemed tranquil and unthreatening. There were workers in the fields and children scampering around the compounds. The people they encountered were reserved but not hostile. They picked up information as they went. In one settlement they were told that the local Taliban commander was in the next village along. But as the day progressed there were no signs of impending ambush. The patrol finally ended sixteen hours after it began. No shot had been fired at the battlegroup and no IED had been detonated.

Two days later the Paras returned to Qal-e-Gaz, this time to stay there. At first light the rifle companies crossed into the Green Zone. Their initial task was to find bases from where they could operate in the days ahead. They needed a presence on the edge to watch over the supply routes between the desert leaguer and their area of operations and to prevent IEDs being planted. Even so, four bombs were found along the main route. Several resupplies would be needed. Keeping the soldiers hydrated was a major task. Each man required 12 litres of water a day and the companies had only a few quad bikes each to tote the cases in.

"A" Company found an empty compound which suited their needs and settled in. The owner, it turned out, was a Talib who was away fighting and was subsequently killed near Gereshk. The compounds were easily turned into temporary forts. The thick walls of sun-baked mud and chaff provided excellent protection from bullets and shrapnel. The company groups posted sentries, set up their sleeping pods and prepared to get their heads down. The Taliban were lying low. They had not disappeared completely, though. On the third night, a sentry with "A" Company saw through his night sights the ghostly green outline of four men carrying a mortar barrel and rifles, and drove them off with his Minimi light machine gun.

For six days the battlegroup worked its way methodically through the fields and compounds. It was clear that the Taliban were well embedded in Qal-e-Gaz. The soldiers discovered seven bunker complexes, simple but efficient strongpoints solidly constructed with earth-filled rice sacks to provide overhead cover, and commanding good fields of fire. The engineers blew them up with bar mines. The searches also turned up small caches of weapons, ammunition and bomb-making equipment, and resulted in the arrest of two suspects.

These were minor successes. The bigger prize was supposed to be the goodwill of the local people. One of the main tasks of the operation was to carry out a survey of the population, a Domesday Book that would detail family structures and ownership of property and that would identify the men of influence in the area.

Steve Boardman and his NKET team, together with interpreters and Afghan troops, split into two groups and worked methodically through the villages. Before they could ask their questions they had to deal with their subjects' grievances. In the mortar exchanges that preceded the incursion, buildings had been hit and crops destroyed. Once compensation had been paid, the atmosphere improved. Elders were willing to have their photographs taken for ISAF records and to air their opinions.

In Boardman's view the locals were remarkably understanding about the trouble the ISAF soldiers had brought in their wake. Most of the damage had been done to buildings from within or near which the Taliban had chosen to mount attacks. "The feedback from the locals was that they didn't want the Taliban there," he said. "They knew exactly why ISAF had to respond the way that they did and also appreciated that ISAF go out of their way to avoid any collateral damage and if we do cause it . . . to repair it or give them recompense."

It seemed true that there was little obvious support for the Taliban. The soldiers heard many complaints of violence, intimidation and extortion. But that did not translate automatically into support for the foreign soldiers. Huw Williams found that the prevailing condition was fear, both of the insurgents and of the trouble that invariably followed when ISAF came to fight them. "Most people were too frightened to speak to us," he said. It was not difficult to understand why. The inhabitants' chilling dilemma was spelled out in a conversation Williams had with the owner of a compound the Paras had taken over. "I paid the bloke some money and he was very friendly. His kids were there. He made us some tea." The man told him that the Taliban "would kill me" if they knew he had offered the soldiers tea voluntarily. "As he happily served us he said, 'But I'll just tell them you forced me. What could I do?' " It was, Williams noted, the same line that was given when the soldiers asked villagers why they gave the Taliban shelter and sustenance. It was also, Williams believed, no more than the truth. "It wasn't that we had forced him. But he was frightened of us. We were five hundred men with guns. What was he going to do?"

At the end of six days, the battlegroup pulled out. Oqab Sterga was judged a success. The Danes, with the support of the Paras, managed to push the Taliban back five kilometres and the ground they had retaken would now be easier to hold. The new patrol base, FOB Attal, was set up and ANA troops installed to man it. So the fighting north of Gereshk had achieved an enduring effect.

The 3 Para operation had contributed to that achievement. Whether their presence in Qal-e-Gaz had made any difference was harder to answer. The Taliban had been forced out, but for how long? There were not enough men or resources to allow the troops to remain in the area. By stepping on the insurgents, said Williams, they had only "squirted them somewhere else". Within a few days of the Paras' departure, the fighters were sure to filter back to the Green Zone. It would not take them long to rebuild their bunkers and tighten their grip once more on the inhabitants.

On the other hand, some good things had happened and bad things had not. There had been no "mowing of the grass". No British or Afghan soldier or civilian had been killed and the waste of war had been minimal. The coalition now had a detailed social picture of the area that could form the basis for future efforts to bring good governance to the place. "It certainly wasn't fruitless," said Jamie Loden, "but there was a degree of frustration." And frustration, as everyone was learning, was a natural part of counter-insurgency operations.

CHAPTER SEVEN

IED

The initial operations had shown 3 Para how the nature of the fighting had changed since their last tour. Their encounters with the Taliban so far had been fleeting and inconclusive. The insurgents no longer stayed around to get killed after launching an attack. They had learned to behave more like orthodox guerrillas, avoiding direct encounters and living to fight another day. The main development in their evolution was their increased use of IEDs and suicide bombers. The tactical switch meant they were able to inflict a steady stream of casualties while preserving their own numbers. They were still, on occasion, willing to take suicidal risks and to demonstrate great bravery. But in general the Taliban now favoured a tangential approach which kept their enemies preoccupied, while avoiding heavy damage to themselves.

The changes were apparent in the pattern of death and injury to British troops. In the two years to June 2008, the rate of fatalities caused by enemy action had stayed fairly constant, fluctuating between zero and six a month. What was different was the way in which soldiers died. Of the twenty-one men who lost their lives as a result of enemy action in Helmand in 2006, all but five of them were killed by bullets, grenades or missiles. There was only one instance of death by IED and one as a result of a suicide bomber. The other three were caused by mine strikes or friendly fire.

In the spring of 2007 the shape of the Taliban campaign began to shift. On Monday, 28 May, Corporal Darren Bonner of the Royal Anglian Regiment was driving in a Viking armoured vehicle through the desert near Hyderabad in the Gereshk area with his company commander. Two vehicles passed the bomb, which lay buried at the side of the road, before it went off. The explosion caught the middle of Bonner's vehicle, sparing those in the cab. Corporal Bonner, thirty-one, who was in the back, was killed instantly, the fiftieth soldier to die since British troops went to Afghanistan. His death marked a new phase in the conflict. Henceforth it was IEDs which caused the most bloodshed. For the remainder of the year roadside bombs accounted for eleven of the twenty soldiers killed in action. At the beginning of June, as 3 Para prepared for their next operation, all eleven deaths in action that year had been the result of bombs or mines planted by the Taliban. The shift affected everybody. In 2008 the insurgents carried out 3276 bomb attacks, killing 161 American and ISAF soldiers, compared with 75 in 2007.

The Taliban had shifted the emphasis of their tactics rather than changed them completely. All soldiers who served in the front line in southern Afghanistan in 2008 were certain to experience a "contact" during their tour, as well as come under mortar and rocket attack. The insurgents would still attempt conventional frontal attacks. The most notable were an ambush of French troops near Kabul in August 2008 and an ambitious attempt to seize Lashkar Gah in October. The first was a spectacular success for the insurgents, in which ten French soldiers were killed. The second was beaten back easily with heavy insurgent losses.

In general, though, the Taliban had relearned the truth that their mujahedin predecessors had demonstrated so effectively. This was that insurgencies succeeded by killing and maiming a few soldiers on a regular basis rather than inflicting the occasional massacre. The Taliban's means might be predominantly military, but their objectives were moral and political. The point of the violence was no longer to drive their enemies out. They had tried that in 2006 and they had failed. The strategy now was to persuade the foreigners that their presence in Afghanistan would bring only blood, sweat and tears, with nothing to show for the sacrifice. IEDs were an effective means of inducing such a mood among soldiers, the public and politicians.

The insurgents had been remarkably slow to turn to the tactic. It was an obvious means of hurting the enemy with relatively little risk to themselves. There were few roads in Helmand and the lack of support helicopters meant that British troops were forced to use them. The scarcity of "lift" had cramped the soldiers' freedom of movement from the outset. In the spring of 2008 the situation was as acute as ever. Britain had eight heavy-lift CH-47 Chinooks in service in theatre at any one time, the same number as two years before. This was despite the fact that troop numbers had doubled in the meantime. The Chinooks were old now. Some had been flying for twenty years and they looked and felt their age. The government had been under sustained pressure to act. Commanders whose demands for kit were usually restrained and tempered by realism abandoned their reticence when it came to Chinooks. Stuart Tootal had raised the subject with the Prince of Wales when he visited in the summer of 2006. The story had been picked up and amplified by the media and politicians.

The public prodding had accelerated efforts to get more helicopters to Afghanistan. But the process of procurement was long and complicated and resistant to hurry. A crash programme was under way to refit eight Chinooks earmarked for special operations for general use, but the first was not due to arrive until the end of 2009. Media reports cast doubt on whether they would be sent at all. Several Sea Kings, the venerable Royal Navy all-rounder which Westland had stopped making in 1990, had been refurbished and switched from Iraq. They were much smaller than the Chinooks and could carry only ten passengers. To deal with the extra numbers, resources were juggled and training intensified to increase available flying hours by 33 per cent compared with March 2007.

These improvements did not compensate for the lack of airframes. All commanders could always do with more kit. But in the case of the Chinooks, the absence was particularly keenly felt. They were the workhorses of the battlefield. The soldiers called them "cabs". They whisked troops, up to thirty-six at a time, with all their kit from base to FOB and back again. They kept them resupplied when they were there and flew them out when they were injured or sick, saving many lives. The question was how many more lives they could save by sparing the troops the need to move by road. The matter got a frequent airing in Parliament. It was raised again in the Upper House in the summer of 2008 by Lord Astor of Hever, who asked Baroness Taylor, Under-Secretary of State at the Ministry of Defence, about plans for additional helicopters for Afghanistan. He pointed out the recent high incidence of deaths by roadside bombs and maintained that "the families of these casualties are entitled to ask whether lives are being lost because of a chronic shortage of helicopters leading to the use of high risk vehicles on the ground".

The minister did not deny the shortage, but claimed that there was no link between helicopter numbers and the use of vehicles to get soldiers where they needed to be. Helicopters could not be used for every troop movement. They would not, for example, "be the appropriate means of transport for people engaged in patrols or dealing with local communities".

It was true that it was hard to influence local opinion from a helicopter. Nor was it possible to wins hearts and minds from behind a pair of sunglasses, encased in body armour, from the back of an armoured vehicle. But the truth was that shifting troops around the battlefield was best done by helicopter. It was a point that the Paras made repeatedly to higher-ups when they passed through southern Afghanistan. "More helicopters means less road movement which means less death," said one senior officer. "It's as simple as that."

The shortage also hampered the Paras' overall effectiveness. Most of the time the support helicopters were humping supplies out to the forces in the field. There was only limited space in their programme to whisk troops around the battlefield to fight. "[This] denied us the ability to move rapidly throughout the battlefield, thereby preventing us from being deployed in a timely fashion to where we were most needed," said another Para officer later. "There were times when we were sat in a benign area achieving very little when our presence could have been used to better effect elsewhere . . . with more helicopters we could achieve more with fewer troops."

The increased reliance on road movement stimulated a parallel debate on the armoured vehicles in use in Afghanistan. Soldiers got around in a range of transport of varying quality. The Paras were happy enough with their WMIKs and Jackals, a new-generation, all-terrain armoured patrol vehicle. But the Snatches and Vikings used by other units were widely criticised for being under-armoured and underpowered. The Snatch, so called because it was originally used to grab rioters in Northern Ireland, was particularly inadequately protected. By the end of 2008 thirty-seven soldiers had died of injuries sustained in them in Iraq and Afghanistan. The Defence Secretary, John Hutton, announced a programme to replace them in time with an up-armoured, improved version called Vixen. The Viking tracked vehicle had first been deployed in Afghanistan only three years previously. Several had been lost to Taliban mines, and plans were in place to replace them with the better-protected Warthog. Again the process would be painfully slow. Not all the new kit would be in-theatre until the end of 2009.

In the spring of 2008, therefore, the threat from roadside bombs was the predominant danger facing British troops and seemed set to remain so. The Taliban knew all the routes habitually taken by British vehicles. Patrols tried to vary their travel patterns, but the virtual absence of roads and the dictates of the rough terrain meant a certain amount of predictability was unavoidable. The arrival of IEDs in southern Afghanistan was surprising only in that it had taken so long in coming.

IEDs were simple to make, hard to detect and devastatingly destructive. The explosive usually came from the old artillery shells left behind by the Russians, or was home-made from fertiliser. Lately the devices had grown more sophisticated. Some were now detonated by radio, others by electric pulses sent down a command wire by a watching insurgent. But the majority were "victim operated", set off by simple pressure plates. The weight of a vehicle passing over them, or a heavily laden human, brought two wires into contact, completing an electric circuit and sparking the explosion.

Newcomers to theatre did a mine awareness course at KAF. A stretch of stony sand was mocked up to show vulnerable points where bombs might be planted. Pupils were drilled to look out for telltale signs but the anonymity of the desert made them extremely hard to detect. Somehow, the survival instinct kicked in, and after a while soldiers developed an extrasensory ability to spot trouble. Finding a bomb did not necessarily mean the end of the immediate danger. By watching disposal teams at work the Taliban had developed nasty new surprises. Two counter-IED experts had been killed by a booby-trapped device.

The outbreak of roadside bombs was accompanied by another development that confirmed the shift towards "asymmetric" warfare. At around 11a.m. on Sunday, 8 June, soldiers from "B" Company of 2 Para were returning to FOB Inkerman, a fort just north of Sangin, after a routine foot patrol. It had been a quiet morning. The pattern of life seemed normal and there was nothing to alert the soldiers to what was about to come. As the lead section from 4 Platoon headed for home, a man emerged from a compound and approached them. He was called on to stop but kept coming. There was a flash and a blast knocked the first four Paras off their feet. When the dust and smoke settled, three of them lay desperately wounded in the dirt. The medics with the patrol worked to stem the men's bleeding while they waited for the evacuation helicopter. Shortly after arriving at the hospital at Camp Bastion they were pronounced dead. Private Daniel Gamble was the patrol linguist. He had studied Pashto before the deployment and was proud of his grasp of the language and the ability it gave him to engage with the local farmers and their children. He was twenty-two. Private Nathan Cuthbertson and Private Dave Murray were both nineteen.

Dan Gamble came from Uckfield in East Sussex, which marked him out for some teasing in the ranks of the Paras, where Northeners tend to predominate. He was one of ten private soldiers selected from the battalion to take the forty-week-long language course. At the end of it he had impressed his mates during the Helmand preparations by delivering a presentation on Pashtun society. "Not only did he understand the language, he also tried to understand the culture and empathised with the people of Afghanistan," said his friend Lance Corporal Alan Farmer. [He was determined] to make a difference to this country. "Nathe" Cuthbertson came from Sunderland and was sixteen when he decided to join the army, following in the footsteps of his father, Tom. He started off at the Army Foundation College (AFC) in Harrogate, where school leavers interested in soldiering start their careers. Cuthbertson thrived there. He met his best friend Lee Cunliffe when they were both raw sixteen-year-olds at the AFC and, when it came to choosing a unit, they both applied for the Paras. They went to the Infantry Training Centre in Catterick, then underwent the intensely testing ordeal of "P" Company, which recruits have to pass through before their first jump. "I remember on 'P' Company he would always be at the front of the 'tabs' or helping someone else keep going," Lee said. "When we joined 2 Para we were put into the same platoon and shared a room together. We became the best of friends. When we went to Brize Norton to do our parachute jumps course, we shared the same room there as well. I can remember on our first jump, when he was on the starboard side of the plane and I was on the port. We were both to be the first ones out of the door on either side. I remember we both looked at each other and he laughed and shouted 'Yeehaa!' "

Dave Murray, who was born in Dumfries, also came from a service family and his father, grandfather and uncle had all been soldiers. He was slight but exceptionally fit, even by Para standards, and an outstanding sportsman, representing the AFC during a tour of Australia.

He, Nathe and Lee Cunliffe had arrived at the college together and formed a tight trio, on and off duty. "We near enough did everything together," Lee remembered. They had teamed up to go to Cyprus the previous summer. "That was the best holiday I ever had [and] I am sure it was Dave's too. We were planning another holiday when we got back."

The loss of three members of one platoon in a single incident was a ghastly first. The emotional impact rippled through the battalion, emanating outwards so that it touched every British soldier in Afghanistan. Mark Carleton-Smith flew to Inkerman to see his men. The Para tradition was to leave your grieving until the fighting was over, but what had happened was a test of any soldier's resolve. They stood in the FOB compound and listened to Carleton-Smith as he told them that the sacrifice had meaning. "He reminded them they were part of a great tradition," said one soldier present. "That when they pulled on the maroon beret they were linking themselves with the men who jumped at Normandy and Suez and who took Goose Green and Mount Longdon."

Among the listeners was Captain Brett Jackson, a Fusilier who was attached to the Paras as "B" Company's second-in-command. "He was very inspirational," he said. "He knew what he was talking about and the people he was talking to. He really lifted the spirits of the troops."

Jackson had been even more impressed, though, by the attitude with which the Paras went back to work. The following day they had to return to the scene of the attack with an investigation team from the Royal Engineers and Royal Logistic Corps. The patrol included 4 Platoon, to which Gamble, Cuthbertson and Murray belonged.

"You would expect them to go out trigger happy and wanting to have revenge," he said. "They didn't. They never came close. They were just as professional as ever. They went back and they moved on. It's very much the soldier's creed that there is a time for grieving but that time is later and we stick to it."

The deaths were also felt deeply by 3 Para. The two battalions lived side by side in Colchester. They shared the same messes and drank in the same pubs. The Para spirit ensured that there was rivalry. 3 Para derided "Shiny Two" for their alleged neatness and respect for the rules, which they regarded as counter to the regimental spirit. 2 Para mocked "Gungy Third" for their affectation of slackness. Sometimes, downtown, after closing time, if there was no one else to fight, they would fight each other. But the competition was a pose, designed for laughs. When any Para was hurt, everyone bled.

That they had died at the hands of a suicide bomber was another dark development. The threat had been there from the beginning. Many suicide bombers had blown themselves up in Kabul and a British soldier, Private Craig O'Donnell, had been killed in one attack. But until now there had been only one suicide operation in southern Afghanistan, twenty months previously. On 19 October 2006, in Lashkar Gah, a man had stepped out into the road between two passing Snatches and detonated a bomb-belt. Marine Gary Wright of 45 Commando was manning the gun on the back. Shrapnel hit him in the neck and head and he was killed.

The conflict seemed dirtier now and uglier. In 2006 the combatants had fought each other face to face. They could think of each other as warriors. Some of the 3 Para battlegroup had respect for their enemy and even felt a rueful sympathy for them when they paid the price of throwing themselves against superior weapons. Those emotional subtleties had gone. No one spoke about "Terry Taliban" any more. The Taliban now belonged in the place in the Paras' psyche that was once occupied by the IRA. They were an enemy to be treated with caution, but not with respect.

The new development not only added another peril. It made the job they were there to do much harder. It was difficult to interact easily with the local population in the constant knowledge that one of them might be wearing a bomb-belt. The suspicion was not confined to young men. A woman, or what appeared at first glance to be a woman, could also turn out to be a suicide bomber. Later that summer soldiers in Lashkar Gah shot dead a female figure who ignored warnings and rushed towards them. It was a ghastly decision to have to make. The victim was dressed in a burka and had fetching pink nail varnish on. When the veil was lifted the corpse had a bushy beard and was strapped with explosives. Even children came to present a threat. In December a thirteen-year-old boy detonated a bomb in the middle of a patrol near Sangin, killing three Royal Marines and himself.

3 Para heard the news about the deaths at Inkerman several days into an operation that had been presented as an opportunity to disrupt Taliban IED operations. The mission was code-named Janub Zilzila (Southern Edge), and it was focused on the Mizan district of Zabul province, an area that ISAF troops had barely set foot in before. It was a big effort. The Paras were working with Task Force Zabul, which was based on a company from the small Romanian contingent in Afghanistan, supported heavily by the Americans. The force was bolstered by an ANA unit which operated under American mentoring.

Zabul was a remote and mountainous area north of Kandahar and south-west of Kabul. It had no electricity and war and drought had ravaged its rural economy. Government control extended no farther than the district centres and the Taliban could roam the villages without fear of harassment or disruption. The limited intelligence available suggested that several senior leaders returned to homes in Mizan. The insurgents were also thought to have IED workshops there, the products of which were planted on Highway One, which ran through Zabul connecting Kandahar and Kabul.

The operation was supposed to demonstrate to the insurgents that they had no sanctuary in southern Afghanistan. ISAF troops were going to comb Mizan, sowing fear and uncertainty. At the same time, the show of force would help persuade local people that it was ISAF and the government in Kabul which held the most power and would eventually prevail.

The Paras arrived in Mizan on 3 June. The task was split between the two rifle companies. The only government presence in the area was a small garrison of Romanian and ANA troops holed up in a fort called FOB Masoud, which lay along "Route Chicken", a gravel road connecting the district centre at Mizan to Highway One. Chicken was intersected by numerous culverts which funnelled away water from the mountains during the rainy season. They also provided perfect hiding places for Taliban bombs. "A" Company's job was to secure the route while "B" Company roamed an area 20 kilometres further into the mountains to the west, challenging the Taliban to come out and fight.

From the beginning it was clear that the mission would have little long-term effect. The Paras were to stay only three weeks. They would come and they would go. The Romanians had nothing like the capacity to dominate the area and the Americans were to play only a supporting role. The show of force might impress initially. But the effect would fade almost as fast as the throb of the helicopters bearing the foreigners back to their bases. "Lots of people have said what was the point of you going," said Huw Williams. His answer was "we go where we're told to. It wasn't our idea, it was RC South's."

The Paras arrived to a sceptical reception from the local people. Williams's first impression was that though he "didn't think they necessarily wanted to support the Taliban [. . . they] just felt the government wasn't an option for them". Central authority barely had a toehold in the place. Only one of the eight districts of Zabul had a leader. You had to be very brave to want the job. The district leader of Mizan had been assassinated four days before 3 Para got there. Muhammad Younis Akhunzada was a man who gave substance to ISAF claims that their presence was welcomed by ordinary Afghans. In April 2007 he had spoken to an American journalist, Michael Fumento, who was visiting with American forces. He told him that local people accepted that the disruption caused by Afghan and ISAF operations in the area was a necessity, caused by the activities of the Taliban. Fumento was sceptical at first, thinking that he was "saying what we wanted to hear". But "over the course of lengthy conversations . . . I realised he was quite straightforward".

This attitude marked the district leader down for death. On the evening of Friday, 31 May, Akhunzada went to answer a knock on the door of his home. His visitors shot him and another man present in the house. They were taken to the hospital in Qalat, where they died early the next morning. A Taliban spokesman, Qari Yousaf Ahmadi, contacted news agencies to claim the credit for the murders. The district leader's death presented the Paras with an unscheduled task. They now had to help provide the security for the shura that, two weeks later, would appoint the local police chief as successor.

The assassination was characteristic of Taliban methods. They established themselves in an area by a mixture of menace and persuasion. They were parasitical, demanding food, shelter and tithes. They were bullies, but they brought with them a degree of order, offering to impose a rough, Islamic justice on thieves, rapists and murderers which was suited to the peasants' harsh world. There were policemen in Zabul, but like Afghan policemen everywhere in the region they were often feared and despised. Many lawmen were drugged-up predators, extorting "taxes" at roadblocks, carrying off any young man or woman, some of them no more than children, who took their fancy. Rapists in uniform had little to worry about. The justice system in Zabul was nominal.

Whatever the inhabitants might think about the sincerity of the newcomers they could be sure of one thing. Their arrival meant trouble. The Taliban were certain to regard the Paras' presence as a challenge.

They would fight them. The British would fight back. And the peasants, who wanted only to be left alone to work the land, would be caught in the middle.

There were signs from the outset that local reactions to the presence of foreign troops were more complicated and changeable than the murdered district leader's assertions might suggest. As always, the Paras' first task on arriving in the new location was to find a base. The practice was to locate a compound big enough to accommodate them then offer the owner cash to vacate it for as long as it was needed. Normally, despite the dangers of reprisals from the Taliban, money talked. The rent was generous and farmers could usually be found who were willing to move their family and livestock away to stay with relatives in return for a sum of money that could amount to a year's income. Mizan was different.

In his dealings with the local people Williams found that, unlike in Qal-e-Gaz, there was no one who was prepared to stake his life on his ability to persuade the insurgents that when he handed over his property he was doing it under duress. "It was the first place where people wouldn't talk to us," he said. "We were offering lots of money to take over a compound and the owners were refusing, saying that if they did so the Taliban would kill them."

The Paras identified one compound, halfway along Route Chicken, which was ideal for their needs. The owner refused all inducements to leave. In desperation Williams offered $50,000 a week, a colossal sum of money to a poor farmer. "He said even if you offer me double that I'll not do it because [if I take it] the Taliban will kill my children." His conclusion was that "the grip of fear that was felt up there was not going to be overridden by a transitory few weeks' operation".

Jamie Loden was present at the negotiation and was impressed by the terror that the Taliban could induce in the population. "The wife came forward carrying a baby and the baby was screaming and she was screaming at her husband," he said. "Any idea of Islamic modesty went right out of the window. She made no attempt to veil her face. It was made quite clear to us . . . that these people really are significantly intimidated." Eventually they found an abandoned compound a little way off the road and settled in there.

The reaction of the local population to Taliban brutality, though, took different forms. The reception was not uniformly hostile. Lieutenant Fraser Smith, a reservist who in civilian life worked as a corporate lawyer in Edinburgh, found that as a rough rule it was the wealthier peasants who were the least friendly. In Mizan, as in the rest of Zabul, society was stratified. Some families owned sizeable farms growing almonds, apricots and wheat as well as poppy, which gave them a degree of prosperity. In the middle were tenant farmers who leased land from the big landowners, and, at the bottom, landless labourers who worked the fields for cash and a roof over their heads.

"There was a contrast," he said. "Certainly [in] the poorer villages people were more willing to come right up to you and speak to you." In the more prosperous villages, however, "people wouldn't speak to you or they would say they didn't know anything. Then eventually they would say, look, we can't tell you anything because if we do then they [the Taliban] will come and cause trouble." Eventually an elder informed him that "yes, they did come here and they take a break and take water but his attitude was, well, we've got a wealthy village. We grow enough wheat and almonds that we can feed ourselves and sell the rest for a profit. He said, so why should I jeopardise that and make my life difficult with the Taliban by telling you everything?" Smith sympathised. He countered, however, with the standard ISAF argument. "I said I understand what you are saying but if you tell us more about the Taliban we can remove them completely." It was, he admitted, "a big ask". Until now all they had seen of ISAF was the occasional American patrol.

It was the peasants with the least to lose who gave the most. Some of them were "quite happy to tell you how many [Taliban] there were, what they were wearing, if they spoke Pashto or whether there were foreigners among them". In some cases it was hatred which had driven them to take such an appalling risk. The insurgents' cruelty towards anyone they thought might oppose them had made them some bitter enemies. In one village Smith noticed a distraught girl weeping at the edge of a group of women and asked what was wrong with her. He was told that "the Taliban had killed her mother and her father so she was scared of soldiers". One fourteen-year-old boy came forward to volunteer information and Smith was soon told why. "The Taliban had killed his mother because they thought that she had helped the ANP, providing information on one of their own . . . so the boy was more than happy to tell us what he knew and was saying, I'll keep my eyes open, I'll tell you if I find [out] anything more if you come back."

The first two days were quiet. "A" Company began securing Route Chicken, searching the compounds on either side and trying to establish friendly relations with the locals. They carried out their tasks under the eyes of Patrols Platoon, positioned on the high ground overlooking the Green Zone. There was not much for them to do except sit in the sandbagged observation posts (OPs) they had dug in the hillside, and look down at the farmers and their families coming and going from fields and compounds. They had a fine view. From their position, about 600 metres up, they could see the whole valley. The Patrols Platoon commander, Andy Mallet, had set up three OPs, all facing southwards, in a line about 180 metres in front of his HQ location. From there they could look down on "A" Company's base, Route Chicken and the Green Zone. It was from the Green Zone that any attack was most likely to be launched. Behind Mallet's position were only bare hills, which appeared to provide no cover for the enemy.

At 8p.m. on 5 June the sun was sliding fast behind the mountains and new sentries had taken over in the OPs for the first stretch of the night watch. Down in the valley everything seemed quiet. Then, as Mallet was settling down for what seemed like another uneventful night, "the whole world opened up". The dusk was streaked with "red and green tracer fired from AK47s and PKM heavy machine guns. It was firing straight at our position". Bullets smacked into the sandbags stacked up around him and spattered the quad bikes parked near by. The fire streamed onwards, bouncing into the three OPs to the south, piercing the ponchos stretched out to provide some shade. Mallet was a veteran of 2006 and had been in the thick of the Sangin fighting. But it seemed to him that "this was the heaviest rate of fire I had ever seen".

For a few moments there was confusion. The fire was coming from behind them, from the north, where the threat was meant to be negligible. Mallet admitted they had been taken by surprise. "For the first minute or two it was horrendous," he said. All their guns were facing down the valley. Now they had to swing them round 180 degrees to bring them to bear on the attackers.

Mallet realised what had happened. The obvious explanation was that the Taliban had waited until dusk cast the folds in the hills into darkness to infiltrate and take up their positions. There seemed to be at least four firing points, well chosen to provide good cover yet give the attackers clear sight of their target. It was a carefully thought-out and professional operation.

They kept up a heavy stream of fire as the Paras struggled to turn their guns around. One minute passed, then two, then three, an eternity in a firefight. Mallet was kneeling by the radio, trying but failing to raise Corporal Jack Russell in one of the OPs that was getting pasted by the incoming fire. "The rounds were coming past my face and I could hear the zip and crack and see the distortion of the tracer," he said. "I knew it was missing me but hitting the guys behind."

One of the GPMGs was finally lined up facing the enemy and began firing, short bursts that streamed away into the darkness towards the muzzle flashes flickering from the hillside. Another joined in but it was not enough to suppress the enemy. Corporal Neil Sant scrambled over open ground with bullets kicking up dirt around him to reach the Javelin in one of the OPs. The missile was designed to knock out tanks but had been used in recent years to hammer Taliban firing points. Sant ranged the sight over the hillside behind and soon picked up the heat signatures of four men. He moved the cross-hairs on to them and pressed the trigger. A fiery ball raced out across the shallow valley and almost immediately there was a flash and a crack as the Javelin hit the target. As the noise of the explosion died away it was replaced by the cheers of the Paras. "I can't say I didn't enjoy firing it," Sant said later. One insurgent position had been dealt with. But the others were still banging away.

Bullets were now whacking straight into Mallet's position, the closest to the insurgents. The Paras had grown used to being able to "overmatch" the Taliban in any clash, with their superior weaponry and ability to call in artillery and aeroplanes to bomb them out of trouble. But they were beyond the range of the nearest ISAF battery and it would take time for air support to arrive. On their own, Patrols Platoon did not seem able to muster enough fire to suppress the Taliban attack. Salvation was at hand in the shape of the mortar team who were down in the valley in the "A" Company compound. But they needed to have an accurate idea of where to aim. Mortar-fire missions were directed by a grid system. The controller sent back a map reference and the team adjusted their barrels accordingly.

Mallet was the closest to the action. But as he hugged the ground beneath a low parapet of sandbags, it was impossible for him to observe the enemy positions. An approximate location was no good. If it was wrong, the bombs could end up blasting the Paras. Jack Russell's OP was also under fire. He could see that Mallet and the others in the forward position were in a desperate situation. They needed a plan but the radio link between the OP and Mallet did not seem to be working. The only way to communicate was face to face. Russell got to his feet and scrambled over the parapet, running as fast as his body armour allowed into the darkness filled with skidding tracer trails and the buzz and crack of bullets. It was a distance of about two hundred metres across open ground. He arrived to ask an astonished Mallet: "Right, boss, what do you want me to do?" He was told to bring up a GPMG to try to get a better fix on the enemy firing points. Then, he "ran back all the while under fire, rounds striking the ground by his feet".

Russell was joined by Patrols Platoon's Sergeant Phil Manning and a young newcomer, Private Scott White, and they set out on another high-risk dash. They scurried forward until they found a fold in the ground from where they could see the enemy firing points. They set up the machine gun and sent the first burst of tracer floating up the hill. "Until [Russell] did that we were totally pinned down," said Mallet. "There was very little we could do. We needed something to happen quickly. The mortars weren't firing because I couldn't get forward and give an accurate grid."

Mallet now had the chance to pop up from behind the sandbags and dart forward for a quick, anxious scan, before scampering back. His comms with the mortar team were working and he was able to pass over the coordinates. Then he waited for the sound of the rounds rushing overhead before jumping up again to see where the bombs had landed and calling back adjustments.

According to Huw Williams the 3 Para mortar team were the best in the British Army. "They are absolutely incredible," he said. "All COs would say that, wouldn't they, but they are just unbelievable." That night, from the "A" Company compound where the barrels were bedded in, he watched them justify their reputation. The compound walls shook with the concussion from the outgoing rounds flying north into the hills. Mallet was watching the stuttering spurt of yellow as automatic fire continued to pour from one of the Taliban positions. Then it was obliterated by a flash of light as the first mortar landed. "I have never been so pleased to hear or see mortars ever," he said. Almost immediately, the insurgents' fire slackened. Then it stopped altogether. An intelligence report came over the radio. The Taliban teams were pulling back.

It was some time before the adrenaline subsided and the Paras started to believe that the crisis was over. The platoon had been pinned down for forty-five minutes. Even for Mallet, the experience had been "tremendously scary . . . it was the most sustained barrage of fire I have ever been involved in". The mortars had done the Taliban some damage. A patrol the following day found bandages littering one of the firing points. But the insurgents of Zabul had shown they were skilful and determined. As they picked over the clash in the following days, Mallet and his men could not quite understand how they had come through the fight without any of them receiving a scratch.

Mortaring was a local military skill. It had been honed by the mujahedin in the long war with the Soviet invaders. They used to operate them from folds in the hillsides, waiting for the unsuspecting Russians to appear, then nailing them. Return fire was unlikely to be effective as the mujahedin were firing from 4 or 5 kilometres' distance.

"B" Company, who were operating 30 kilometres to the west of "A" Company, were to discover that the Taliban had inherited the mujahedin's skills. They were stationed in a small cluster of houses in a patch of Green Zone with mountains on either side. The area was meant to be the fiefdom of a Taliban leader whom they were hoping they could entice to come out and fight. At the same time they would try to add to the meagre store of information on the area. They were operating on foot and constrained by the amount of water they could carry. They also had to contend with the knackering effects of altitude. "It was something like twelve hundred metres above sea level," said

Private Scott Milton, one of the new boys who had been inspired by 3 Para's deeds while in training in 2006. "It was a lot harder breathing-wise because we'd not been up so high before." Nonetheless, Stu McDonald's intention was "to cover as much of the terrain as we could, to search some compounds, to try and find some arms caches, to speak to the locals hoping that the longer we were on the ground [the more] intelligence would come in". The presence of the Paras would also cause the Taliban communications to "light up like a Christmas tree".

They had set up their base in one of the best-appointed compounds in Mizan. Unusually for the area, the main building had two storeys, an indication of wealth and status. Inside the walls there were orchards and lawns. A river ran through the property which had been dammed to form a reservoir that was wide and deep enough to swim in. "B" Company had the Fire Support Group and a mortar team with them. They had settled in nicely, setting up defensive sangars on the corners and an OP on a slope above the compound and digging shell scrapes. For the first two days nothing much happened.

On the third night they were settling down under the fruit trees when a warning came that the period of calm was about to come to an end. Dusk was the nicest part of the day. The big orange ball of the sun slid behind the mountains and the heat slowly leaked from the earth and the air. The mountains of Mizan were cool by Afghan standards, and the temperature was only 40 degrees, 10 degrees less than the scorching summer heat of the plains. The nights were pleasant. You needed your sleeping bag, a welcome contrast to lying sweating on your roll mat as you did in Helmand. It was something to look forward to. But before night fell came the time of greatest danger. Even with the night vision sights and goggles that the British were equipped with, the dark brought the Taliban a degree of protection, and it was at dusk that many attacks were launched.

Just before seven o'clock, the hour at which Stu McDonald gave his officers and senior NCOs their orders for the following day, reports started to come in that an insurgent team was moving a mortar barrel up to target the compound. The Paras were used by now to intelligence false alarms. The Taliban's approach to communications was extremely casual. Security was so lax that it reached the point where the information gleaned from it could often be as much of a hindrance as a help. They often seemed to use their radios as a morale-boosting instrument, ordering ambushes and attacks that never materialised and calling for the deployment of weapons that they did not have.

The orders group went ahead. Sergeant Chris Prosser, the Fire Support Group second-in-command, was sitting to one side of the gathering, chatting with some signallers, when a rocket fizzed over the compound. The meeting disintegrated, with everyone running to the sangars. The rocket had exploded next to the OP overlooking the camp. The dusk was split by flashes of fire that seemed to be coming from the fields and compounds to both north and south. Within a few minutes all the Paras' guns were pumping in the direction of the enemy's muzzle flashes. Private Vinny Hutton in one of the sangars saw a man dodge out from behind a compound wall with what looked like an RPG on his shoulder and fired a burst of GPMG in his direction, sending him scurrying back into cover.

With all the sangars manned, there was nothing for Lieutenant Tosh Suzuki's platoon to do. They were receiving a ball-by-ball commentary on the Taliban's activities as they prepared to launch their mortar attack, from an interpreter who was listening in to the radio traffic. From what they were saying, they seemed to be able to look down into the base. Jokiness and nonchalance were de rigueur among the soldiers in these circumstances, but the tension inside the compound was rising. Then a shout of *"Allahu Akhbar!"* announced the launching of the first mortar and everyone dived for the shell scrapes. The first one landed short. The second burst some distance behind them. As they waited for the next round, the interpreter passed on the adjustments he was picking up from the Taliban team. "They were saying, 'Right three hundred paces and one to the left,' " Suzuki said. "So everyone is calculating in their heads — and miraculously everyone comes to the same [conclusion] — that's right on my shell scrape." He found it "a horrible experience but surreal at the same time in that you're hearing it on the radio".

Suzuki had never been under fire before. Chris Prosser had, many times, yet he too felt the brush of fear. "They obviously had some form of eyes on [the target] because they were making the adjustments. So you just sat there waiting for the fourth one to come in, not knowing whether it was going to hit us, mortars or 'B' Company."

But soon the Para mortars were firing back. The FSG were able to identify the enemy launch point and passed on the grid. Rounds started exploding on the target. The FSG had a Javelin missile in their OP, which they added to the barrage. The incoming fire appeared to die away. Suzuki climbed out of his shell scrape. He was standing talking to another officer when a final round landed, sending shrapnel zipping past his head. It was the last shot of the exchange. It had lasted three-quarters of an hour.

As soon as calm had returned Stu McDonald ordered Suzuki to take his men out to investigate the firing points and see what they could find. It was pitch black now. There was no sign of the Afghan moon that, when full, shone so bright it cast shadows. The thickly planted fields surrounding the base looked threatening and sinister. "I was not the most popular man with my platoon," said Suzuki. They pushed out, into the blanket darkness. The use of torches, "white light" in military-speak, was out. They had to rely on their night vision goggles. Suzuki found it hard to coordinate his three sections as they blundered, weighted down with weaponry and equipment, through the fields. "There were all sorts of obstacles, irrigation ditches, wadis, low compound walls, high vegetation and uneven ground," he said.

Eventually, though, they stumbled on the mortar position. The Taliban had chosen it well. It was on the reverse face of a slope, which meant they were hidden from the Paras while they could look down from the top into the compound and adjust their fire. "It had an excellent ingress route and an excellent escape route with vehicle access," he said. "They obviously came in there with a Toyota Hilux or whatever, set up, fired and disappeared in the vehicle along the track."

Dawn was coming up when 4 Platoon struggled into the compound, nine hours after setting off. Suzuki and his men were shattered, but there was little chance of a respite now. The Taliban had decided to rise to the challenge. The insurgents' decision to initiate an attack had delighted Stu McDonald. He combined a genial manner and a sensitive streak with a warrior mentality and made it clear that his doctrine was to fight the enemy whenever and wherever he could. McDonald was happy with the mission's intent. "It was about denying them safe havens," he said. "It was about taking the fight to them and showing them that it didn't matter that they were in the mountains where they thought they were inaccessible, we can strike wherever we want."

A medieval compound, in the remoteness of the southern Afghan mountains, was not a natural place for Suzuki's background and upbringing to have led him. He was the son of a lawyer and the grandson of a Japanese soldier who had fought in Burma against the British. He had gone to Oundle public school then Leeds University, where he studied Mandarin and

Economics. He chose the course because it seemed the perfect entry to a richly rewarded job in an investment bank. When the time came to decide on his post-university career, he looked at the door of the gilded cage and paused. He had already joined the Para territorials, "thoroughly enjoyed that", and decided to carry on.

Three nights after their nine-hour patrol Suzuki and the men of 4 Platoon were tasked with a silent patrol. Given the near-impossibility of keeping movement secret, the exercise was in the nature of a provocation. The calculation was that the insurgents would find the presence of British soldiers on their turf an intolerable affront. They would then come out to fight, but on ground that the Paras had chosen. The exercise looked like a mere excuse for a scrap. It seemed to sit uneasily with Mark Carleton-Smith's assertion that the British Army was not in Afghanistan simply to kill insurgents. There was another way of interpreting the tactic, though, which invested it with a higher purpose.

One of the structural aims of the overall mission was to demonstrate to local people the military superiority of the Allies and so to plant the idea that the Afghan government and its foreign backers held the balance of power. They would turn out to be the winning side and it would be sensible to join them now. Skirmishes like the one that was to follow were supposed to contribute to the creation of that perception. The plan was for 4 Platoon to set off at last light to a cluster of compounds on the edge of the Green Zone. The area was overlooked to the west by a range of hills where a

140

Taliban presence had been reported. A patrol had been fired on from the hillside two days previously. It was decided to go out late in the day because that was when the insurgents liked to operate and it would provide the best chance of a clash. Suzuki wanted to find a spot where he could see any movement on the mountain and react quickly to it. As they were tabbing along, looking for a likely spot, a local man approached an Afghan officer who was attached to "B" Company. The officer belonged to the National Directorate of Security (NDS) intelligence service and he came from the area. The local man knew him and had come with a warning. He advised against going down a wadi that lay ahead because the Taliban had set up an ambush. The Paras' enthusiasm for provoking a fight did not extend to walking into a trap. Suzuki had already seen what looked like a good location, off to the west, in which to lay up.

They got into position and Suzuki deployed his men. He put two of his sections facing the mountain, from where the insurgents had opened fire two days previously. The other covered the Green Zone behind. With the Paras' arrival the landscape emptied. The farmers picked up their tools, untethered their donkeys and trudged back to their compounds. Such departures were a reliable "combat indicator". British soldiers were always being urged to "develop their tactical aware-ness", seeking a heightened sensory state that would alert them to all the physical factors around that might have a bearing on survival. After decades of conflict the peasants of southern Afghanistan had developed a better tactical awareness than any soldier or insurgent. Their senses were tuned to register every coming and going in their domain. The presence of a group of armed men alone was not enough to get them to leave their fields. There was work to be done, and once they departed they would be unlikely to be able to return that day. But on this evening the locals had noted two armed bands in the area, and did not have to guess what would happen next. As they watched the exodus, the Paras stiffened for imminent action.

There was a while to wait. When the first volley came it took Suzuki by surprise. Instead of coming from the mountainside it swept in from the fields to the east, the Green Zone, where the defence was thinnest. Suzuki speculated later that the men preparing the ambush had got tired of waiting and had gone forward to try to engage the Paras wherever they found them. He ordered one of the sections facing west to move south to support the men taking the incoming fire. As soon as they got out of cover, the hillside began to crackle with fire. There had been insurgents there all along. They were hidden behind an outcrop of rock that gave excellent cover. The platoon had sniper teams attached, led by Sergeant Ray Davis. He could glimpse the Taliban among the jagged rocks but never for long enough to get a shot in. After ten minutes the shooting stopped. The Taliban, it seemed, had run out of ammunition. They sank back into the shadows and Suzuki and his men tabbed back to the compound. No one was hurt. But nothing had been achieved either. It was just another of hundreds of encounters that moved the war neither forward nor back.

Over the days that followed, Op Janub Zilzila soaked up an enormous amount of energy and resources. The Paras conducted dozens of long patrols, made all the more gruelling by the high altitude, which more than compensated for the cooler temperature. They also carried out several "strike ops" intended to seize important Taliban targets.

Tracking insurgents at any level was extremely hard work. Capturing or killing the leadership was even more problematical. The small numbers involved in special forces operations allowed a degree of stealth. But it was impossible to move company-sized groups around without alerting the entire neighbourhood. On many occasions the soldiers arrived in villages to be told that the men they were seeking had left by motorbike for a new location a few hours previously. Chasing them was pointless. The chances of finding them in their new refuge were nil. Identifying targets was fraught with difficulties. Often soldiers felt sure that the diffident, blank-eyed men denying all knowledge of Taliban activity were the very insurgents they were seeking. The early, naive belief that the enemy identified themselves by helpfully wearing black turbans turned out to be mistaken. The Taliban looked like every other male. And, to Western eyes, all the men looked pretty much alike.

The problem was apparent in the descriptions issued to the Paras as they hunted their quarry in Mizan. On one occasion "B" Company were sent to search for a deputy Taliban commander armed with the knowledge that he had "black hair and a beard and no distinguishing features". Sometimes the brief tried gamely to provide more detail. On a later date they were sent after another senior figure described as "very pale, bushy long black hair combed to right hand side. Full black beard with 'tache and squinty eyes, very long nose that turns up at end". The presence of an NDS officer improved the chances of success a little. Stu McDonald admitted that he could walk around Mizan "for a month, I could bump into a member of the Taliban every house I go into and I simply wouldn't know. I'd be polite, I'd say hello, have you seen any Taliban? He would smile at me and say no and on I'd go". Having an NDS officer meant he could at least report his suspicions. It was "something to go on and something's better than nothing".

After ten days in which no one of significance had been captured, "A" Company was launched on another arrest mission. There had been repeated intelligence reports of a strong Taliban presence in a village called Takir. By now, the Paras were likely to question the reliability of the information coming down from Task Force Zabul, but they were assured that the operation would definitely be worth it.

It got off to a bad start. The helicopters carrying them were delayed and the soldiers did not lift until an hour after first light. They were put down a kilometre to the east of the objective on the far side of a hill. By the time they had tabbed down a wadi and reached the village any insurgents present would have had ample time to depart. There were a few people in the fields but it was a Friday and most were at home. The busiest location was the mosque. Steve Boardman had been in Takir a week before with "A" Company and had met the chief village elder. He sought him out again and together with some Afghan soldiers settled down for a shura.

The company was under the temporary command of Major Adam Wilson, as Jamie Loden had just gone back to KAF prior to returning to Britain to take up a promotion. Wilson was normally OC of "D" Company, whose assets had been divided among the two rifle companies. He was anxious to make the most of his opportunity, and while Boardman took tea and embarked on another long, slow discourse, he took his men off for a look around. The patrol soon discovered the entrance to what seemed to be a tunnel system close to a nearby village. Inside they found some British Army-issue high-frequency batteries. The engineer party collapsed the tunnel with a plastic explosive bar mine and then tabbed the three kilometres back to Takir.

By now it was clear there were no Taliban there. It emerged later that a commander on the Paras' target list had left forty-eight hours before. But there was some intelligence to compensate. Information came through that a number of insurgents were still in the village near the tunnels that they had just left. Among them was Mullah Sadullah, a medium-value target thought to be heavily involved in IED-making.

Wilson headed back there. He had decided to use guile rather than intimidation and took only twelve men, an interpreter and a visiting journalist, Thomas Harding of the *Daily Telegraph*. The villagers had seemed friendly enough earlier in the day. When they entered the village now Wilson found that "the whole dynamic had changed . . . nobody was around. It was completely quiet, completely dead." In the mosque they came across a group of fourteen males who looked at them warily. Sergeant Major Steve Tidmarsh came up with a ruse to explain their reappearance. The story, relayed by the interpreter, was that they had left a "daysack" backpack behind and were anxious to retrieve it. Anyone who helped them find it would be given a cash reward. The interpreters were immensely valuable in such situations, spotting clues and giveaway signs where the soldiers saw none. Wilson's interpreter was soon confident that he had identified Sadullah. Tidmarsh asked whether he could speak to him on his own and they went outside. As they moved away from the mosque, the tension in the air thickened. Some of the men in the mosque had followed them, watching from a distance and clearly unhappy with what was happening. Tidmarsh noticed some dickers on high ground overlooking the village and an intelligence report came in that a Taliban mortar team had arrived near by.

The operation had been watched over by a Dutch F16 jet, which at the Paras' request now swooped down to deter any would-be attackers. It raced in at 60 metres, pumping out flares and shaking the mud walls in a powerful show of force. When the Paras were a safe distance from the village Sadullah was searched and formally detained. "He did nothing, he said nothing, offered no resistance whatsoever," said Wilson. On closer inspection he stood out from the rough farmers of the village. "He had very manicured hands, really good teeth with fillings and proper crowns and very good skin for an Afghan." Sadullah retained his composure for the rest of the time with the Paras. It was three days before they could hand him over to the Afghan NDS in KAF. When the Paras extracted to the American base at FOB Mizan the prisoner shared a room with Wilson, Captain Ian McLeish of the Army Education Corps, who was attached to the battalion, and Corporal Lee Hall of the Royal Military Police. They took it in turns to guard him but he was a model prisoner, posing no threat, saying nothing and calmly munching the muffins they fed him from the American canteen. He was imprisoned after trial for five years.

It was a result, but hardly on the scale that the Paras had been led to expect their presence would achieve. The arrest was more through luck than planning. Once again the intelligence had been found to be wanting. The truth was that there was a dearth of hard information to underpin company-sized strike operations aimed at the Taliban leadership. The methods that the intelligence collectors and analysts employed were of limited use in a society where much communication was still by word of mouth. The solid information they did manage to glean was gold dust and priority went to the British and American special forces units that roamed southern Afghanistan. As the capture of Sadullah had shown, the Paras, as Stu McDonald said, were really "just following our noses".

It was with few regrets that the Paras heard that their mission in Zabul was to be ended a week early. They were needed for an emergency. More than a thousand prisoners had broken out of Kandahar prison and rumours were rife that the city was about to fall to the Taliban.

CHAPTER
EIGHT

The Stadium

The jailbreak was the most impressive feat to date of the Taliban resurgence. It demonstrated not just daring but skill and a high degree of organisation. The coup added to the growing perception inside and outside Afghanistan that the rebels now posed a genuine threat to the government of President Karzai.

The drama began at about 9p.m. on the evening of Friday, 13 June, when a water tanker drove into the entrance of Sarposa Prison on the edge of Kandahar city and exploded, demolishing the gates of the jail. At the same time, a pedestrian suicide bomber blasted open a door in the back wall. As the smoke cleared thirty Taliban fighters perched on small motorbikes poured through the breaches, shot down the guards and opened the cell doors. All the 1100 prisoners inside escaped. They included murderers, robbers and thieves and women who had been locked up with their children. The 450-strong Taliban contingent among the prisoners were identified, shepherded through the holes in the walls then whisked away in a fleet of waiting minibuses. Twenty-four hours later only a handful had been recaptured. The rest were absorbed into the homes of relatives or supporters in the surrounding area.

Nothing boosts the morale of an insurgent movement like a successful jailbreak. It demonstrates the rebels' ability to reach into the citadels of their enemies. It also has the reassuring effect of suggesting to activists that if they are captured they will not be forgotten and every effort will be made to rescue them. The hyperbole that came naturally to the Taliban spokesmen who channelled insurgent propaganda to the Western news agencies and local media was, for once, justified. "This was our first attack in the very heart of Kandahar and this is a signal to the puppet government of Hamid Karzai and the infidel governments of the West that they should not forget the Taliban," exulted Qari Yousaf Ahmadi, their voice in southern Afghanistan.

The episode was a severe embarrassment to the Canadian force in southern Afghanistan. They led the military effort in Kandahar province. They had just poured $1.5 million into sprucing up Sarposa Prison, training the guards to treat their charges humanely and kitting them out with new uniforms. The Chief of the Canadian Defence Staff, General Rick Hillier, said that the horde of insurgents now on the loose constituted only "a small splash in the pond".

The Afghan authorities, however, did not bother to hide their alarm. Ahmed Wali Karzai, the head of Kandahar's provincial council and a brother of the president, claimed that among the escapees were some experienced commanders, trained assassins and volunteers who had been psychologically programmed for suicide missions.

The incident also reinforced a mood that was starting to infiltrate the upper levels of the Alliance. The feeling was growing that the war in Afghanistan was faltering. A few days after the jailbreak the outgoing US military commander in Afghanistan, General Dan K. McNeill, said he was disturbed at the increase in violence in eastern Afghanistan, bordering Pakistan, where most of his troops were based, and described the Taliban as "resurgent in the region". He blamed their vitality on their ability to operate from havens inside Pakistan, unmolested by the Pakistani security forces. He produced figures showing that in April attacks in the area had gone up 50 per cent compared with the same period the previous year. The increase, he said, was "directly attributable to the lack of pressure on the other side of the border".

The perception that Pakistan, through political and military weakness, the machinations of elements of its intelligence services or a mixture of both, was sustaining the Taliban campaign was felt strongly by the Afghan government and its foreign supporters. It came from the very top. Two days after the jailbreak, President Karzai threatened to send Afghan troops across the border into Pakistan to deal with the insurgents if the government did not act firmly to dam the flow of fighters and supplies from bases in the mountainous frontier regions of the north and west. It was a statement that showed more anger than intent.

The Afghan army was in no shape to mount offensive operations into its neighbour's territory. The Americans, however, were, and had shown their willingness to launch air strikes on targets in Pakistan regardless of any diplomatic damage that ensued. Only the previous week they had bombed areas on the border, in strikes which the Pakistani authorities said killed eleven of their paramilitary troops.

It had always been clear that what happened in Pakistan would have an important bearing on any plan to overcome the Taliban in Afghanistan. As time went on it was glaringly apparent that Pakistan's role was not merely important but crucial. Unless the Taliban were defeated or neutralised in Pakistan there was little chance of smothering the insurgency in Afghanistan. The ISAF forces were treading on the tail of the Taliban. The head of the snake was across the frontier in Quetta, where the high command were able to deliberate and issue orders to their men on the ground without fear of assassination or arrest.

In public, ISAF had downplayed the threat posed by the jailbreak. Behind the scenes there was alarm at what the reappearance of several hundred gunmen might mean. Intelligence reported that the "Quetta Shura" — the military's term for the insurgent leadership — were ordering the escapees to team up with local rebel forces to launch an attack on the governor's compound and the Afghan army and police bases in Kandahar. The newly arrived ISAF commander in Kabul, General David D. McKiernan, ordered Major General Lessard to move his Canadian troops to the west of the city to block a possible move from the Taliban stronghold of Panjwaii. At the same time an Afghan army *kandak* (battalion) was sent in to reinforce the local security forces in the city. The Paras were to be moved to the Sarposa football stadium south-west of the city centre, where the governor and UN agencies had their compounds, to "enhance security and limit enemy freedom of movement".

"B" Company arrived by helicopter from Zabul at 1 p.m. on Tuesday, 17 June. They had had only a few hours for preparations, which included an intelligence briefing that led them to expect trouble. The Paras were psychologically prepped. "We always hope for the worst-case scenario," said Stu McDonald. "We'd all convinced ourselves there was a very high chance of a fight, which naturally lifts your adrenaline levels." There was an extra frisson as the Chinook skimmed over the streets of the city and dipped into the bowl of the stadium. There were reports that the insurgents had got hold of Misagh 1 man-portable infrared guided ground-to-air missiles, an Iranian version of the American Stingers that had downed dozens of Soviet helicopters during the war with the mujahedin.

They touched down safely, set about fortifying the stadium and within a few hours of landing had pushed out the first patrol to feel the ground truth. The stadium was in an upmarket neighbourhood which had been colonised by the UN and other agencies for offices and accommodation. The city was rippling with panic. Four days after the breakout, many Kandaharis were convinced that the Taliban were massing and

153

about to retake the city where their swift march to power had begun. Women and children were starting to leave, businesses and cafés were pulling down their shutters and the UN were talking of moving out. There were reports that some mullahs were prudently preparing for regime change, preaching sermons that lauded the city's former masters.

Kandahar was a good place to monitor the attitudes of ordinary Afghans towards the Taliban. The city was sometimes referred to as the "crucible" of the movement, the iron bowl in which it had been forged. The insurgents' foundation legend went some way to explaining their initial appeal to the local people. The story was that in the spring of 1994 two teenage girls from the village of Sang Hesar outside the city were abducted by a band of former mujahedin and taken to one of their checkpoints, where they were raped repeatedly. Their violators would have had little fear of retribution. In the swirling anarchy that followed the overthrow of the Soviets, the strong did as they pleased and the weak trembled and submitted. But retribution came. Living near by was a man called Mohammed Omar, himself a former mujahed who had lost a leg fighting the Soviets. He had retired to deepen his knowledge of Islam and was studying at a local madrasa. When the news reached him he gathered thirty of his fellow students (*taliban*) and set off to rescue the girls. After they had freed them the men hanged the mujahedin commander, slowly, from the gently rising barrel of a tank.

154

From this episode, bursting with symbolism, the Taliban were born. Mohammed Omar became Mullah Omar, who fourteen years later, despite all the efforts of the Americans to kill him, continued to lead the movement from Pakistan. Most of the men with him that day had been mujahedin themselves. They had been driven to revolt by the cruelty and decadence of the warrior bands that, once the Russians were beaten, had dragged the country into anarchy.

The Taliban were motivated by a primitive sense of justice and a yearning for order. Order would rest on the word of God, as expressed in sharia law. There could be no exemptions from, or dilutions of, the code. If necessary it would be imposed by force. They were harsh and inflexible but upright, and, initially at least, there were few in and around Kandahar who objected to the Taliban manifesto. Western journalism had painted a romantic picture of the mujahedin as tough, resolute and colourful, noble in their own primitive way. But after their victory Afghans had more cause to fear them as murderers, rapists and robbers than they had to celebrate them as liberators from the rule of the communists. The Taliban offered a simple remedy to the years of terror and injustice, one that was not jarringly discordant with prevailing values and beliefs. The rebels' village mores chimed with those held by many in Southern Afghanistan, especially the majority who lived in the countryside. They believed in piety and in respect for traditional codes of behaviour enshrined in the Pashtunwali, the honour system of rights and obligations that had been the basis of society for

155

centuries. Women had their place within it. They were protected, but at the price of what to Western eyes was slave-like subservience. There would be no freedom for women, no chance to go to school or to follow a career. But for many, the only freedom that mattered in the years of anarchy was freedom from murder and molestation.

To the small middle class in the big cities, and to those Afghans who did not share their Pashtun blood or the Sunni tradition of Islam, the Taliban were as cruel and oppressive as the warlords. But in Kandahar and the south there were many who regarded their rule as an improvement. Mullah Omar had been acclaimed by some as a saviour. The story went round that after the Taliban took Kandahar he visited a royal mausoleum in the city looking for a sacred relic. The cloak of the prophet Mohammad was said to be stored there, inside a nest of chests that could be unlocked only by the hand of the true "Amir ul Momineen" or Leader of the Believers. At Omar's touch the chests sprang open. He donned the cloak and displayed it to an awestruck city. Omar uses the title "Amir ul Momineen" today.

Years of Taliban rule had rubbed the shine off the attractions of puritanical zealotry even in the southern heartland. Kandaharis liked their music and their kite-flying as much as other Afghans. When Omar and his followers fled in December 2001, the population was telling media visitors that they were the victims of fanatics preaching a distorted version of Islam. They seemed reluctant, however, to talk about the mass attendances at public executions, carried out at the football stadium, where six years after the last shots rang out, the Paras were now setting up camp. The Taliban hated display and persecuted those seeking pleasure in even its most innocent forms. They did, however, promote fiestas of public violence and death, and the pre-match entertainments had been popular events. These carnivals of bloodshed usually started with amputations. Minor miscreants, thieves and swindlers, were led in by soldiers and made to lie face down with their arms tied behind their backs. Penal "surgeons", suitably dressed in white coats, then appeared and cut a hand or a foot off each offender. Then it was the turn of those condemned to die. Death was the penalty for men who killed or raped or blasphemed. It was also the sentence for women accused of adultery, or prostitution. In the case of a murderer, a relative of the victim was given the chance to carry out the punishment. If the offender was a man, the amateur executioner was given an AK47 and invited to riddle him with bullets. Adulteresses and women who had killed their husbands were sometimes stoned to death, though there exists no record of this having taken place in Kandahar stadium.

These spectacles took place in front of large crowds. Many approved of rough justice and the taste for it did not fade with the coming of elections, a constitution that stressed human rights and female equality, and President Karzai and his Western backers. In the autumn of 2008 there were calls for the reintroduction of public executions from religious councils and a Kabul women's group. The relief and gratitude felt by

157

many Afghans towards their deliverers was eventually eroded, however, by the Taliban's bullying zealotry. When America launched its offensive, aided by the Taliban's unreconciled enemies among the warlords, there was no popular resistance. The regime collapsed within weeks. The new order promised security, and in its wake peace and economic progress. Over the years that followed the invasion, the failure of the government and the West to deliver these benefits, especially in the south, was disillusioning. It did not create sufficient anger to sustain a popular uprising such as had originally brought the Taliban to power. It did, however, leave a vacuum into which the insurgency could seep. When the Taliban began filtering back into Afghanistan they were not returning as saviours but as subversives, and instead of primitive righteousness they brought cruelty, exploitation and coercion.

The Taliban had launched their second insurgency without concern for the lives of the ordinary Afghans in whose name they claimed to be fighting. In 2006, according to a report by the American independent organisation Human Rights Watch (HRW), they killed 699 civilians, the highest death toll since they were removed from the power five years before. Nearly five hundred of the Taliban victims died in bomb explosions. As the report noted, even when targeting security forces, "they generally kill many more civilians than they do military personnel". This was particularly true of suicide bombs, the use of which rose dramatically in 2006. In 2003 there were only two suicide attacks in Afghanistan. In 2006 there were at least 136, six times more than the year before. Eighty of these were aimed at military targets, but killed eight times as many civilians as they did soldiers or policemen. The rest were directed indiscriminately at schools, buses and bazaars with no military value and appeared, said the report, "to have been primarily intended to cause terror among the civilian population".

Among the dead were 177 victims who had been deliberately singled out for the challenge their existence posed to the Taliban's psychotic values. They included humanitarian aid workers, doctors, teachers, education officials and journalists. The insurgents had copied some of the shock tactics used by al-Qaeda in Iraq, filming the decapitation of an Afghan journalist, Ajmal Naqshbandi. The number of civilian deaths at the hands of the Taliban and their al-Qaeda allies rose substantially again in 2007, when at least 950 were killed.

The Paras were arriving in Kandahar while the memory of a recent atrocity was still raw. On Sunday, 17 February, at least a hundred people were killed when a suicide bomber blew himself up in the middle of a crowd of men who had gathered to watch dog fights at a picnic site on the outskirts of town. Among the dead was Abdul Hakim Jan, leader of a local militia who had been fighting alongside British and NATO forces. He may have been the target, although there were other possible motives. Dog fighting had been banned under the Taliban, as were all forms of entertainment.

But if the Taliban killed innocent civilians so did ISAF and the Americans. The Allies boasted of the technical intricacy of their weapons. Their sophistication, though, did not prevent them from being aimed regularly at the wrong targets. Most of the casualties were caused by bombs. According to HRW's meticulous accounting, civilian fatalities nearly tripled from 2006 to 2007, when 321 ordinary Afghans were killed. Air power was notoriously indiscriminate even in a high-tech age. ISAF's excuse was that it was forced to rely on aircraft to make up for the shortage of ground troops. Other blunders were blamed on faulty intelligence or the fact that the aircraft were responding to emergency calls from soldiers on the ground which reduced planning time and increased the risk of mistakes.

The context mattered little to the families of the men, women and children who died as a result. The feeling inevitably grew that, for all their talk, the foreign soldiers cared no more about their lives than did the Taliban. The impression that the rhetoric cloaked a granite pillar of self-interest was intensified by the Americans' habit of responding to each report of civilian deaths with a denial followed by an unconvincing investigation and finally a grudging apology.

The frequent protests from President Karzai pushed the Americans to take more care, especially when launching air attacks, but the deadly cock-ups continued. In February 2009, the UN Assistance Mission in Afghanistan reported that 2118 civilians had been killed in fighting the previous year, the highest number since the Taliban were ousted and a rise of 39 per cent on 2007. Their investigation found that the insurgents had caused 55 per cent of the deaths. Pro-government forces had killed 828 innocent Afghans, many of whom died in air strikes aimed at militants and often mounted at night. Another 130 had lost their lives in crossfire incidents. The report was rejected by NATO, which said its forces were responsible for 237 civilian fatalities. Whatever the precise figures, the blunders mocked the efforts of the soldiers on the ground to persuade locals that their presence was a good thing. Witnessing the side-effects of the conflict was a harrowing experience that no one forgot. One Pashto-speaking soldier described being in an FOB when the victims of a crossfire incident arrived.

A mortar had landed in their compound. The family consisted of a man with two wives, which was normal practice, and he had children from both . . . one of the wives was killed with her son and [another] son aged five was brought in . . . the boy was badly injured. The doctor started to work on him but after five minutes he shouted over to me to tell the father that the son had passed away. When I told him he crumpled to the floor in tears and yelling . . . later on in the day we had to hand over the boy's body to the village elder . . . that memory has not left me.

Another described being confronted with a family who had lost their father, killed during a firefight between soldiers and insurgents. "The massive and long-lasting effect of this loss was so clear to see, and the depth of feeling of the uncle charged under the social code with the care of all his brother's children was huge . . . we were able at least to engage him in conversation but it doesn't change the fact that [the death] will make for a hard winter for that family and some of the children may not survive it."

As the Paras' 6 Platoon, made up of soldiers on attachment from the Brigade of Guards, set out on their first patrol in Kandahar, the streets were almost empty and there was sense of foreboding in the air. It was a test of the Paras' ability to stay flexible. "One minute you're in the mountains," said Colour Sergeant Mark Kennedy, Commander of 6 Platoon, "the next you're in the city having to deal with cars driving past that might be carrying a suicide bomber." The ANP had been asked to spread the word among local people that the British were there to protect them. The message did not appear to have got through to a large group of youths who gathered outside the stadium and threw stones at one of the sangars mounted on the walls, refusing to disperse even when the soldiers fired warning flares in their direction.

The following day the mood had changed. The previous evening, the ANA and the Canadians had pushed out to engage Taliban bands lurking in the fertile area along the Arghandab river to the west of the city. The crisis seemed to be passing. The UN abandoned their evacuation plans and decided to stay put. During the day the streets began to fill up again and the shops to open.

When the patrol set out next morning the people of Kandahar were pleased to see them. "We were welcomed with open arms," said one soldier. "Smiles, handshakes, gifts and offers of cups of tea." Stu McDonald went to lunch at the home of the president's younger brother, Ahmed Wali Karzai, to "keep things warm and fuzzy". The warm reception was an indication of relief rather than affection, and it would not take long for the mood to change once again.

There were still security concerns that prevented the Paras from relaxing. Intelligence reports warned that the threat from suicide bombers remained high. Some spoke of the likely use of water tankers to mount the attack, the method used to trigger the jailbreak. As it happened, the sentries in the stadium had noted a tanker driving past the entrance twice during the course of Wednesday, 18 June, the day after they arrived. By the evening, the Paras were convinced that the driver was carrying out a recce, just as the prison suicide bomber had done. The stadium was an obvious target for a Taliban attempt to pull off another "spectacular". Inside, all personnel were ordered to wear helmets and body armour. The Afghan army were tasked with intercepting any suspicious-looking trucks in the area. At 8.30p.m. an ANA patrol stopped the driver of the water tanker that had been seen earlier as he cruised once more around the streets next to the stadium. After a few tense minutes the soldiers relaxed. He was, it turned out, a farmer who had been ferrying water back and forth from a well in the city to a patch of green south-east of the stadium.

Earlier the Paras had been worried about the throng of people, most of them young boys, who had abandoned their initial hostility and were now hanging around the stadium watching the comings and goings with friendly interest. If the Taliban had attacked, the youths would have been the first to die. The company's interpreters broadcast megaphone warnings to the crowds to keep their distance. The message soon became spectacularly garbled. It was picked up by the local ANP and ANA and amplified. By the time it reached the Canadians at the Kandahar Provincial Reconstruction Team, the British were reported to be urging the locals to evacuate the city before it was devastated by a wave of suicide bombers. The Canadian commanding officer did not try to contact McDonald to seek clarification, even though "B" Company was technically under his command and they shared a radio net. Instead he passed his anxieties up the line until they reached Major General Lessard at RCS. Nerves were taut at Kandahar PRT headquarters. It was, after all, on their watch that the prison break had happened. Lessard calmed his fellow Canadians down. He gave immediate backing to the Paras and called Stu McDonald to emphasise his support. The incident nonetheless caused some friction between the Paras and their parent formation and was an indication of the potential for misunderstanding between supposedly close and like-minded allies.

The following day the Canadians and the ANA clashed with the Taliban in the Arghandab valley and inflicted heavy casualties. There were reports that a hundred insurgents had been killed or wounded. As the threat faded, so too did the initial enthusiasm of the locals for the Paras' presence. "The first day we arrived we were like heroes," said Williams. "And within a space of five days they wanted us out."

Their presence had become an irritant. "It doesn't take long," said Matt Cansdale, the new OC of "A" Company, which had replaced Stu McDonald's men on the morning of 19 June. "As soon as people feel safe they start to moan about the things you are doing. When you first go in and stop the traffic it's, oh, thank you very much, because you're keeping the bad guys away. Then . . . it flips. We're fickle beasts us humans. All of a sudden you're disrupting my route to work or my business or whatever."

The tension caused by the suicide bomb threat sparked a shooting incident that accelerated the change of mood. On the morning of 22 June a patrol was checking traffic near the stadium when a car pulled out of the queue and moved towards them. They shouted at it to stop, fired warning flares and eventually put four bullets through the windscreen. It came to a halt 20 metres from the soldiers. When they approached they found a man and a young boy inside. Mercifully they had suffered only cuts from flying glass. They were treated on the spot by company medics then sent by taxi to hospital. It was the second shooting episode in three days. Shots had also been fired at a three-wheeler van, this time without causing injury. The incident provoked another encounter between the Canadians and the Brits. The commanding officer of the Kandahar PRT descended on the stadium and told Matt Cansdale that "this had got to stop. You've got to get the judgement right". The criticism was unfair. Such errors were inevitable given the risk posed by suicide bombers and impatient and erratic Afghan driving habits, as the Canadians knew from their own experience. They had been involved in a similar incident only a few days before. The genuineness of the threat was underlined six months later when a Toyota Land Cruiser pulled out from a traffic queue at a Canadian checkpoint and ignored warning shots. The Canadians opened fire, killing the driver. The car was crammed with 600 kilos of explosives.

Huw Williams was reaching the conclusion that the Paras were wearing out their welcome. He ordered patrolling to stop. The decision was made to vacate the stadium as soon as possible. The Paras' presence was clearly now doing more harm than good. Their occupancy of the stadium was causing resentment. The toing and froing of the Chinooks had not improved the structure's shabby and neglected fabric. Their typhoon-force downdraughts had shattered a few windows and blown over a large billboard bearing a portrait of a local mujahedin hero. These mishaps caused another flurry of complaints from Ahmed Wali Karzai and the Canadians.

Despite the friction, Williams felt that the Paras had "achieved a lot in those five days. We proved ISAF had the flexibility to respond to any situation, that it had troops available as a reserve [and] that we could surge and dominate any area we wanted to", he said. Most importantly, they had shown "the people of Kandahar City that they were not on their own". Lessard agreed. He cited the Paras' ability to move from the mountains of Zabul to the streets of Kandahar as an admirable example of their flexible approach and can-do attitude.

The Paras left late on the evening of 22 June, five days after they had arrived. Before departing they organised a handover ceremony with the ANA to mark the restoration of the stadium to the Afghan people. It was the midpoint of the tour. The companies were now heading off for two weeks of R&R. Herrick 8 had so far delivered more frustrations than satisfactions and less action than most of the Paras would have liked. That was about to change.

CHAPTER
NINE

Facing the Dragon

Throughout the tour 3 Para had been watching with concern the progress of their sister battalion in the Sangin valley. 2 Para were having a hard time. They were manning forts to the north and south of Sangin town, clashing with the Taliban daily and taking heavy casualties. Since the triple deaths on 8 June they had lost four more paratroopers. On 12 June Lance Corporal James "Jay" Bateman and Private Jeff Doherty were killed in a firefight near FOB Gibraltar, just south of Sangin. A fortnight later, Company Sergeant Major Michael Williams died in an ambush. The same day Private Joe Whittaker, a member of the anti-IED team, was blown up by a roadside bomb.

The affection in which the men were held poured out in the tributes that followed their deaths. "Jay" Bateman was twenty-nine, and according to his company commander, Major Adam Dawson, "hard working, fit and keen, a source of inspiration and a man with a light heart and a sensitive touch". Jeff Doherty had just marked his twentieth birthday two days before his death. His platoon sergeant, Chris Lloyd, described him as "the main deliverer of morale in the platoon".

Michael "Mark" Williams was a forty-year-old veteran who, in the opinion of his friend Sergeant Major Karl Mitchell, "was a classic case of short of height but tall in stature. A man who was larger than life". His company commander, Major Mike Shervington, regarded him as "one of the fulcrums of the battalion". Everyone knew Williams. His death brought home the fact that the best-known faces were as vulnerable as anyone to the swing of the scythe. "When he died," said Shervington, "people were going, 'bloody hell, this is really serious'."

Joe Whittaker was just starting his army career. He was twenty years old and a 4 Para reservist who was going to Sandhurst for officer training the following year. In the short time he had known Whittaker, Shervington marked him down as "great for morale, always upbeat and optimistic".

When talking about the dead everyone emphasised the passion they had for the job they did and the pride they felt in being a Para. "I know he loved the Parachute Regiment," wrote Jay Bateman's wife Victoria, whom he had married the year before. "And I draw comfort from the fact that he died doing the job he loved, for the country he loved, with the friends he loved."

The Paras had expected losses but that did not diminish the emotional impact when they came. "Everyone anticipated losing guys before we deployed," said Shervington. "It's easy to say that and to tell your guys 'we won't come back with everyone' when you're briefing your soldiers. To actually have to deal with it

169

there and then is a different proposition." But after the initial shock, the instinct was to intensify efforts to prevent further losses. "You became even more determined to bring your blokes back alive," said Shervington. "You thought even deeper about tactics and deception and how to outwit and outthink the enemy."

3 Para were eager to support their mates. When the soldiers of "B" Company returned from their break, Huw Williams told O'Sullivan that if he wanted to use them they were his for the asking. Stu McDonald was only too pleased to help out. "It was a natural reaction given that so many of them were our friends," he said. Shiny Two and Gungy Third would be fighting together. 2 Para was in the middle of its own R&R cycle, with the companies leaving theatre for their mid-tour two-week break. The battalion needed reinforcements in both its main locations. Half of "B" Company went to Gibraltar. McDonald took the rest to Inkerman on 19 July.

FOB Inkerman overlooked Route 611, which wound up the Sangin Valley parallel with the Helmand river. It was unpaved, like most roads in Afghanistan, dusty, rock-strewn and potholed. It was nonetheless an important commercial artery along which the farming communities who inhabited the broad cultivated strip that bordered the river could move their goods to Sangin market. It was also a vital logistical route for the Taliban who lived among them. The fort loomed directly above the road. Sangin was seven kilometres to the south-west. To the north was the Kajaki Dam, home of the hard-pressed hydroelectric plant that sent a meagre supply of power down the valley, providing settlements with a few hours of electricity a day. On the far side of the road, a band of Green Zone several kilometres wide ran down to the Helmand river, overlooked by a rampart of cardboard-coloured bluffs which turned pink in the rising and setting sun. To the left, there was the village of Jusyalay, a jumble of mud-brick compounds planted on lunar clinker. The desert spread out behind the fort like a carelessly unrolled carpet, nondescript, featureless and neutral.

Heat pressed heavily on the land. The men and women scattered around the fields moved slowly as they worked. The deep quiet was disturbed now and then when a moped puttered past or a pick-up truck with a couple of bearded and turbaned men on the back, who looked up at the soldiers in the sangars with blank, unreadable expressions. The sound of gunfire shattering the tranquillity seemed shocking and incongruous when a newcomer first heard it. To the farmers in the fields and the children who played round about them, it had become part of everyday reality.

The violence had forced many of the population out of their compounds in the Green Zone, and they had shifted to the Jusyalay area under the walls of the fort. When 2 Para arrived in the spring they began an intensive patrolling programme, spreading the ISAF message among the locals and listening to what they had to say in return. It was the middle of the poppy season. Brett Jackson, "B" Company's second-in-command, found them polite but also distrustful.

171

"They would talk to you but they were very cautious of you as well because they know that the drugs are something that we don't see as a good thing. They know that the end state of development here will hopefully mean the eradication of the growth of poppy and encouraging the locals to grow something else . . . the people will talk to you and say the poppy is our livelihood." The message Jackson heard was "if you don't want us to grow poppy you must get rid of the Taliban".

That goal, however, was still far away. The base was under mortar attack when McDonald and his men flew in. It was a routine event at Inkerman. The fort had been hit every day for the previous two weeks by indirect fire, small arms or rockets, and the Hesco wall was cratered with explosions. Every patrol that left the gates was attacked. The area was jumping with Taliban. Intelligence estimated there were about seventy in the immediate area of the FOB. "They were well armed and if they wanted to, they could put up a significant fight," said McDonald. "The realisation dawned on me that we would have to become very much more robust in how we dealt with them."

Brigadier Carleton-Smith's desire to keep "kinetic" activity to a minimum could not apply in Inkerman. The soldiers were there to fight. The FOB was a breakwater, designed to block the flow of insurgents down the valley to menace Sangin. The town was the nearest there was to a success story in Helmand. If the fragile security that had been established in Sangin was shattered, the whole British effort in southern

Afghanistan would have been thrown into reverse. The soldiers manning Inkerman had arguably the toughest job in Helmand. Lieutenant Wes Smart, a descendant of the legendary Big Top entrepreneur Billy Smart who joked that he had "run away from the circus to join the army", commanded a 3 Para platoon which spent the whole summer alongside 2 Para at the FOB. "Firefights were the norm," he said. "Until October, every time a company patrol stepped out we were contacted."

With the danger came extreme discomfort. The FOB was two years old but felt to those visiting for the first time as if it had been thrown up a few weeks previously. There was little or no fresh food and the cooks struggled heroically to wring some variety out of the ration packs that provided the basic diet. When the bottled water ran out the soldiers drank warm chlorinated water. It was only halfway through the tour that a fridge-freezer arrived which provided a meagre supply of cooled drink. The camp was spartan and unsanitary. The latrines were essentially plywood planks suspended over stinking holes in the ground, permanently enveloped in a cloud of flies. Despite a rigorous hygiene regime, there were constant cases of diarrhoea and vomiting. D&V could cripple the fort's fighting strength. At one point twenty-seven people had gone down with it in one day. It sounded innocuous enough, but it was not merely a question of a touch of biliousness and regular runs to the latrines. Those afflicted by it suffered agonising stomach cramps and were laid low for days. They called it "Inkerman Fever" and no one who got it ever wanted to suffer from it again.

Surviving life inside the FOB required deep reserves of stoicism. Operating outside its walls required a different kind of fortitude. The fighting had a strong psychological element to it, for both the British and the insurgents. Each was trying to impress on the other the depth of their determination. The potential practical benefits of the patrolling were likely to be fleeting. The soldiers might push the Taliban back a kilometre or two. In the process they might uncover a small-arms cache or a bunker which they would then blow up. But they did not stay to hold the ground. They trekked back to base and the Taliban crept in again, a few steps behind them. The lost weapons and explosives were easily replaced and it was a few hours' work to build another bunker.

It was, in some ways, a macabre game, but a game with a serious intent. The regular patrols were a demonstration to the Taliban of the strength of the soldiers' resolve. The message was that no matter how many times they were shot at or blasted by IEDs they would carry on, constantly challenging and probing, refusing to accept the insurgents' claim to ownership of the fields and compounds. Eventually, the Taliban would be forced to decide it was time to cut their losses and depart. 2 Para were playing the game not just in Inkerman but from a string of FOBs that stretched from Kajaki to FOB Robinson, just south of Sangin. The outgoing RSM of 3 Para, John Hardy, called it "facing the dragon" and they were doing it almost every day. It placed a huge strain on the soldiers and the commanders who led them out of the forts. They had to believe the risk and effort had some value. "I would never take my company out on patrol unless I thought it was worth it," said one major. "[If] a soldier got injured badly or lost his life, I could then look the parents in the eye and say that patrol had a purpose . . . I had to go and do it and I would do it again tomorrow."

But the insurgents showed the same grim purpose. They knew that every time they fired an RPG or machine gun they could expect to be hammered by mortars, shells, missiles and bombs. Yet it was a rare day when they did not rise to the challenge. The soldiers and the insurgents were trying to impress each other. But they were also signalling something important to themselves. The routine tests of courage were essential to maintain morale. It was a struggle of wills that would end only when one or other side left the field. Until that happened the game would go on, exhausting, nerve-racking and deadly.

The players had an audience. Their clashes were observed by the people in the fields and compounds whose active or passive cooperation, according to counter-insurgency doctrine, was the prize both sides were struggling over. The population of southern Afghanistan felt a natural and understandable suspicion of outsiders who, experience taught, brought trouble. The local insurgents were mainly Afghans and Pashtuns from the surrounding area, and claimed to be fighting a war of liberation. Yet the farmers and their families did not seem to feel any reflexive loyalty towards them. "They don't give a rat's arse about the Taliban," said a member of the intelligence cell. "They just want to get on with their lives. If we help them, they help us. If the Taliban help them, they help the Taliban."

The British, though, were not in a position to offer much help. Reconstruction was impossible while the fighting went on. Nobody appeared to be planning any. "I never once saw a civilian aid rep at Inkerman," said an officer who spent six months there. In that time "no-one even came to do a feasibility study. Civil servants need to have a cultural understanding of the place which they can't get if they don't visit. If someone's taken the trouble to find out what is going on it speeds things up when you are in a position to do something."

And speed was crucial if the object of influencing the population in favour of the government was ever to succeed. "People will accept a certain amount of trouble if what follows is some sign of progress," the officer said. "But it has to follow quickly, because the enemy is moving faster than us." The soldiers knew better than anyone the dangers of the environment. They would like, however, to have seen more evidence of "bottle" on the part of their civil servant partners.

On the afternoon of 24 July Stu McDonald led a patrol through the rusty sheet-metal gate set in the west wall of the fort and out on to Route 611. They turned left and followed the road for a kilometre past Jusyalay before crossing west into the broad, tree-lined fields that stretched across the Green Zone. They were heading south, to an area where there was thought to be a strong concentration of rebels. "Primarily it was to have a disruptive effect," McDonald said. "It was to search compounds, looking for weapons caches that we believed were there." He had arrived at Inkerman with about sixty men, one platoon of his own company, a dozen members of Patrols Platoon, plus some signallers, a Joint Tactical Air Controller (JTAC) to coordinate helicopter and fast jet support and an extra medic. The reinforcements were very welcome. There were three resident platoons at Inkerman, two from 2 Para, plus Wes Smart's platoon from 3 Para. But the depletion caused by R&R and the ravages of D&V meant that lately they had been able to put only small forces into the field.

As the column trekked towards the first compounds, the locals stopped work, collected their tools, unhitched their donkeys and made their way to safety. The patrol was about seventy strong, split into two platoons. The standard manoeuvre was for one to push forward, then go firm and provide overwatch to cover the second one as it made the next tactical bound to join them. The lead platoon had reached a kilometre into the Green Zone and the second was halfway across an open field when the Taliban opened up. Most of the soldiers raced forward and made it safely to the other side. The others were forced into cover. The firing was coming from the west. The first group engaged them and quickly won the firefight. "We cleared through the ambush quite successfully," said McDonald. "The enemy chose to flee in the face of superior numbers rather than stay and fight." The second platoon then bounded forward to conduct the next phase of the patrol.

They were now just over a kilometre inside the Green Zone. On the far side of a canal a series of compounds straggled off to the south-west. There was another line of buildings that ran parallel, 200 metres to the north. Between the two lay fields, planted with maize which had grown to the height of a man. 6 Platoon led by Lieutenant Tom Coke-Smythe of 2 Para took the nearest corridor of compounds. The other was allocated to 5 Platoon, the resident 3 Para platoon. McDonald went with them. The idea was to comb through the kilometre-long line of dwellings and storehouses, then reorientate and head back to the FOB. There were slim pickings. After an hour the haul amounted to two old rifles. It was getting late now and the land was throbbing with heat. Searching was hard work, even though there was an established way of doing things.

It was quiet. The buildings seemed all to have been abandoned. Then, when they had pushed about four hundred metres from the canal, they heard a ripple of gunfire from the south-east. 6 Platoon was under fire. Almost immediately, 5 Platoon was also attacked with small arms and heavy machine guns. McDonald was "not overly concerned by this. It was nothing new. The platoon commanders knew their jobs and for me it was very much about giving them the space to work out what they're facing and to fight the immediate battle." The drill then was to go firm, and call in mortar or artillery fire on the enemy firing points. McDonald's main preoccupation was keeping track of where the front man in each platoon was and transmitting their locations to the mortar and gun lines at Inkerman to reduce the risk of "fratricidal" casualties.

Then the radio squawked and the atmosphere sharpened. Normally there was an information gap while details were verified before the announcement of bad news. This "came across incredibly quickly," said McDonald. "'We've got one times KIA [killed in action].'" McDonald had a hurried consultation with Sergeant Gaz Marshall of 5 Platoon. Bullets were now cracking and buzzing around their own position and the soldiers on the compound roofs barely dared get their heads up to shoot back. "We were getting hit very hard by the enemy but we couldn't identify their firing positions," said McDonald. All they knew was that the Taliban were very close. The enemy were also making use of the roofs to fire down on the soldiers on the ground. But crouching in the tall maize, it was impossible to make out exactly where they were. Now another message came through from the southern platoon. There were more casualties. One soldier had been shot in the foot and one or two others were bleeding from shrapnel wounds.

The situation had taken a dramatic turn for the worse. McDonald made a quick calculation. Extracting the dead man and the gunshot victim would create a big hole in the platoon's manpower. Carrying the victim's body armour and weapon, toting the stretcher and providing a degree of protection could require up to eight men. It sounded as if at least two stretchers would be needed. McDonald's first thought was to attempt a flanking movement and attack the Taliban from the side. But the ambush had been mounted from straight ahead. To work round the enemy and open fire on them carried a high risk of sparking a "blue on blue" in which 5 Platoon would end up shooting their own comrades. "It became quite clear I couldn't go to their assistance," said McDonald.

He radioed Coke-Smythe, telling him that if he could break contact with the enemy and fall back a little he would bring his men down to join 6 Platoon and they could withdraw together. Alternatively, if Coke-Smythe felt confident enough, he could make his way back to the canal 400 metres to the rear and they could meet up there and organise evacuation of the body and casualties. The young lieutenant "was absolutely outstanding", said McDonald. "He's got a guy dead, he's got a guy shot . . . he was as calm as you like. He said to me no, I can do this, I can manage on my own. I thought, yeah, good on you." Both platoons began to withdraw to the canal. They had been fighting at a distance of only 20 to 50 metres from the Taliban, too close to call in indirect fire. As they fell back the mortars and artillery began crashing into the Taliban compounds, allowing the Paras to retreat in good order.

By now darkness had fallen. The soldiers donned their night vision goggles but it was still hard to see anything thanks to the high crops. They reached the canal and waded through the chest-high water holding their weapons over their heads. Everyone was tense and anxious. They were not out of danger yet. They had broken off one engagement but there could be no certainty the Taliban had given up for the night. "I'm not saying we were twitchy but we'd been in a fight and we were perhaps expecting another one," said McDonald.

The two platoons eventually joined up in a field on the north side of the canal. McDonald put the casevac operation in the hands of Gaz Marshall. Having been alongside 2 Para since the beginning of the tour, he had become well versed in the drill to remove dead and wounded from the battlefield. The procedure was for the platoon that had been hit to extract its own casualties while the other provided protection. But 6 Platoon was exhausted from carrying the corpse and the injured man under fire across ditches and walls.

The dead man was Corporal Kenneth Rowe, a dog handler from the Royal Army Veterinary Corps and one of 16 Air Assault Brigade's explosives search experts. He had worked with the Paras many times, taking part in dozens of patrols. He had been in the rear section of the group crossing open ground when he was caught in a volley of RPG and small-arms fire which killed him instantly. Sasha, the dog he was working with, also died, and was lying alongside him on the same stretcher.

It was decided that 5 Platoon would do the carrying. The question now was which route they would take to return to base. Intelligence reported that the Taliban were planning another ambush as the Paras withdrew. Normally the insurgents preferred not to operate in darkness, but the latest information was that they too were now equipped with night vision goggles. There

181

was only one easy route out of the Green Zone, as the Taliban well knew. That was the one the Paras had come in on. Striking out across country would have taken hours and everyone was approaching exhaustion. There was another solution. There was a narrow lane that ran off the 611, which was used by local traffic. Normally there would be no question of moving down it without first carrying out an IED sweeping operation. McDonald said "Right, get onto the road and just go for it,"

They picked up the stretchers and resumed their trek. First an Apache helicopter then an F16 criss-crossed overhead, scanning the ground for thermal images which would reveal the presence of rebels. The Taliban, though, appeared to have had enough for the night and left them alone. The platoons arrived at the junction with Route 611 at about 10p.m. Vehicles had been sent out from the FOB to pick up the body and the casualties. The remaining troops trudged the last kilometre back through the gates of Inkerman and collapsed. It was a little while before McDonald and Company Sergeant Major Martin Thorpe from 2 Para noticed the absence of the dog. Somewhere between the canal and the fort Sasha's body had gone missing. "We looked at each other as if to say 'bloody hell, what more can go wrong tonight'," said McDonald. But they both "agreed instantaneously that it was the wrong thing to do to leave the dog behind".

If it had been daylight, he "would not even have contemplated it". But the Paras were comfortable operating in darkness and reckoned the risk was worth it. The problem was that the dog could be anywhere between the fort and the canal. Then someone remembered having seen what looked like an animal carcass by the side of the road as they trekked back. He had assumed it was one of the stray dogs that roamed the Helmand countryside and had thought little of it at the time. It was dark and Sasha was blonde. But Sasha's coat had been soaked in blood. It would have looked black in the dense darkness. It was definitely worth checking out. It was nearly midnight when the search party set off. They did not have to go far before they found Sasha's corpse, put it into a bergen rucksack and trudged back to Inkerman. They arrived as the helicopter came in to take Corporal Rowe and the injured Paras back to Camp Bastion.

Sasha was not Corporal Rowe's regular dog. She belonged to Marianne Hay, a fellow RAVC handler. Hay had known Ken Rowe well. "He was always full of confidence," she said in a tribute. "He was popular with the ladies and he always made me smile." Stu McDonald had met him first on the Hutal operation, then again in Qal-e-Gaz, and had been out with him twice before on patrols from Inkerman. "He was an absolutely outstanding young kid," he said. "He was bubbly, he was incredibly professional, a thoroughly decent guy, massively up for the job."

Ken Rowe's dedication had cost him his life. He had been due to leave Inkerman on 23 July, the day before he died, and return to the safety of Camp Bastion. But he was worried that his departure would leave his comrades without adequate explosives and ammunition search cover. He had lobbied his unit to be allowed to stay and his stint had been extended to 10 August.

His popularity gave an extra jolt to the news of his death. "The guys were chinned," said McDonald. "There were a lot of people mourning privately until the early hours of the morning . . . people were standing round having brews. They were gutted. They were still somewhat subdued the following morning but very quickly they appreciated that you have to continue, you've got to crack on."

Cracking on would have to wait a while, however. July 24 had been a heavy day in which the Paras had effectively been forced to retreat. Patrolling with two platoons and attached elements, "company minus" strength in army-speak, brought them perilously close to being overmatched by the Taliban. The latest estimates were that there were now up to 180 fighters in the Green Zone opposite. The build-up in numbers suggested that a major move on Sangin might be in the offing. That was McDonald's belief. He told his men that "the enemy is having a pop at us to eventually allow him to go down and infiltrate Sangin".

The fact was that there was little at that moment that they could do to prevent it. After taking the fort's protection requirements into account the Paras could muster only sixty men to go out on patrol, and then not on a regular basis. "It's all very well for a day," said McDonald. "But you can't do it again the next day without severely degrading the blokes, and when you consider that they're here for six months then you've got an issue." Inkerman housed a battery of 105mm light artillery pieces and 81mm mortars, and they could call on lavish air support from Apache attack helicopters and jets. But these were resources to get you out of trouble once you had fallen into it. To beat the enemy you needed boots on the ground. Fortunately, more were on the way.

Two Chinook-loads of 3 Para reinforcements were due to arrive soon. The boost to Inkerman's numbers would allow McDonald to take the robust approach that he believed was needed. The Taliban were dictating events on the ground. They had killed a man, the fourth to die from Inkerman within seven weeks. It was time to take the initiative. McDonald began planning a surge operation to swamp the area where they had clashed with the insurgents. It was scheduled for the morning of Sunday, 27 July.

Helicopters carrying the reinforcements took off from KAF at midday on Saturday, 26 July. The airframes showed every one of the hundreds of thousands of flying hours they had notched up in their long years of service. The soldiers filed in to squat down on bum-numbing canvas seats that lined the fuselage. The metal was scarred and pitted and the quilting that was supposed to muffle the noise from the two engines that drove the huge rotors hung down, revealing skeins of wires and hydraulic lines like the sinews and arteries of a great metal beast.

The helicopters flew low for the first few miles, skimming over the desert that stretched beyond the camp fence, stirring up plumes of dust in their wakes.

The RAF loadmaster sat perched on the tail ramp, silhouetted against the sky, swivelling a GMPG back and forth. The shadow of the Chinook slid over the ground, across the bands of fields and orchards that bordered the waterways. From the air everything looked neat and orderly. The compounds were laid out in disciplined squares and the fields were marked out with ruler-straight stands of grey-green trees. Then the farmland shaded into semi-arid scrubland where a scattering of goats cropped the bushes that clung to the dirt, watched over by young boys who glanced up as the helicopters whop-whop-whopped over them.

The Paras sat facing each other in silence. Everyone wore earplugs against the din of the engines and conversation was impossible. Then the loadmaster was signalling five minutes to landing and the pilot took the helicopter down to a few hundred feet, swerving it left and right along the contours of the wadis, minimising the target that it would present to the Taliban, who were always ready with machine guns and RPGs to have a go at an arriving or departing Chinook.

Landing and take-off were always times of danger. The Paras were on their feet, hauling their huge bergens on to their backs before the wheels were down. Then it was "go! go! go!" and they bounded off the back and into a swirling typhoon of dust and dirt. They scurried forward over the stony ground and crouched down in firing positions, facing outwards, weapons trained on the miserable-looking compounds dotting the hillside. Fifty metres away the back gates of FOB Inkerman were open and quad bikes bounced over to the helicopters to pick up the supplies that the loadies were bundling off the back. Then the engines throbbed faster and the engine pitch rose to a manic whine and the Chinooks were lifting, tilting and heading skywards in an apocalyptic cloud of khaki dust.

For those seeing it for the first time, Inkerman looked like a stockade from the frontier wars of the Wild West. The walls were made out of 3-metre-high Hesco Bastion, steel mesh containers lined with thick brown polypropylene fabric and filled up with stones, sand and gravel. Hesco had originally been designed to protect riverbanks and shorelines from erosion. It was even better at stopping insurgent rockets and bullets. Now it could be seen everywhere that the British and Americans went in Iraq and Afghanistan.

The gates opened into a big compound. In the middle were two low buildings that had been adapted to make an ops room and an aid post. To the left was a large cookhouse and canteen. Placed at regular intervals around the walls, sangars looked out over desert and river valley. Inkerman was an important link in the chain of FOBs that stretched up the Sangin Valley. They were designed as platforms from which ISAF could project its power into the surrounding countryside. They were also intended to proclaim the authority of the Afghan government in the area. The Afghan flag hung limply over the ANA accommodation at the front of the fort. But the thick walls and the guns jutting from the sangars made it clear that Kabul's rule was asserted more than it was exercised.

The garrison gave the newcomers a warm welcome. They distributed brews and passed on the latest news. There was never any shortage of incident at FOB Inkerman. That morning there had been a deadly mishap at a vehicle checkpoint. A minibus had pulled out from a line of cars at a barrier set up by the Paras on the 611, just north of the fort. The driver had ignored shouts to stop and warning shots. When it was 30 metres away the soldiers had fired for effect, killing four passengers. The men in the car were all cousins. The driver, it was said, had been out of his head on opium. It was one of those things that happened in Afghanistan but in a struggle where "influence" was crucial such incidents eroded the credibility of the outsiders' claims to be a beneficial presence. The incident had provoked a deputation of elders to seek a shura with a local Taliban commander, who went by the *nom de guerre* of "Saddam". Whether it was to ask him to punish the British for the deaths or to demand he and his men leave the area was unclear.

The new arrivals were going straight into action the following morning. At 6p.m. they were briefed on the mission. It was going to be a "surge" operation, a positive-sounding term that the British had learned from the Americans in Iraq. The Paras had the numbers now to swamp the Green Zone and punish the Taliban. The patrol added up to a "company plus". The two platoons from 2 Para were boosted by a platoon from 3 Para and elements of the battalion Fire Support Group. Altogether there would be more than 120 soldiers on the ground. McDonald described the purpose as "denuding the enemy's capability . . . trying to hit them where it hurts . . . it's about mustering as many troops as we can as part of a demonstration of force just to show the enemy we still have the ability to punch in there and assert our influence over them and take the battle to them".

The officers and senior NCOs stood, squatted or sat on the few rough benches available, gathered in a courtyard sleeping area that doubled as a briefing room. The meeting opened with an intelligence read-out. An informant had tipped them off about a plan to send a bomber on a motorbike to launch a suicide attack. Despite the events of the morning, McDonald's instructions were icily clear. If a suspicious person had not heeded the escalated warnings, "if he's not stopped at the twenty metre mark, kill him. It's as simple as that".

Then he began a detailed explanation of how the operation would unfold. McDonald stood in front of the briefing board, a slight, smiling figure in baggy shorts. He spoke in a soft Scots accent, his bright blue eyes moving around the group, shifting from face to face. He radiated a natural, easy authority, glowing with confidence and relish for the fight. He started off by defining the greater purpose of the mission. The surge was part of the plan to maintain Sangin's security.

"This is us taking the fight to them," he said. "If we can control the Green Zone it prevents reinforcements coming from the north to the Sangin area." There were important potential prizes. The fierce resistance put up by the Taliban two days before suggested the patrol might have been about to stumble on Saddam's headquarters compound. There were also persistent reports that there were significant weapons and logistics caches in the area.

The plan was to return to the same spot. They would use the same tactics, moving forward on two fronts down the parallel lines of compounds, with one group securing and searching a building then providing overwatch while the next "echeloned through". Then the rear group would leapfrog forward and the process would begin again. The difference was that they would now be patrolling in force. There was to be no stopping for heat exhaustion victims, who would be put to one side to recover. Nor would more serious casualties hold up the momentum of the operation. "Nothing will be allowed to divert us," he declared. The Taliban would soon learn that the Paras meant business. Any male tracking the patrol's progress on behalf of the insurgents was in trouble. "If the situation dictates it, dickers will be shot," McDonald told them. The key verbs for the operation were "dominate, disrupt, find and destroy and defeat". The OC's cherubic face glowed with cheerful aggression as he assured his men, "We have massive combat power at hand. We can smash through anything we come up against."

McDonald had painted a lurid picture of what the next day might bring. But the soldiers conscientiously scribbling in little notebooks seemed serene and unperturbed. They were as broad an assortment of British manhood as you could assemble. They ranged from stunted, bullet-headed musclemen covered with tattoos to floppy-haired Hugh Grant lookalikes. They all had one thing in common. They were up for the fight ahead. That was why they were soldiers.

"The mission of the infantry is to close with and kill the enemy," said McDonald afterwards. "It's that simple. If I wasn't prepared to do that or genuinely didn't enjoy doing that, then I'd be in the wrong profession. That isn't bloodlust. It's just professionalism and I think that's what keeps people going out."

In his view, the love of risk and the urge to test oneself were not confined to the Parachute Regiment. "It's the fighting spirit that's instilled in British soldiers generically. I wouldn't even confine it to infantry soldiers because a lot of the attachments that come out with us such as the dog handlers . . . are very keen to get out and do their bit and perform just as well as our guys." Nor was it just guys. Female medics and dog handlers were on most patrols these days. "I think the common theme is the belief that you should never let your friends down and if someone else is going out, then why aren't you?"

There were more, specialised briefings before the evening was over. No detail was left to chance. The sleeping area was busy with men checking their kit and making final adjustments to the plan. Their head torches flickered over the smiling, big-breasted pin-ups torn out of *Nuts* magazine and stuck on the walls. By nine everyone was stretched out in their cots and zipped into their mosquito nets. The absolute silence of the Afghan night filled the space, interrupted now and then by the odd beep and chirp from the radios next door.

Six hours later the sleepers stirred, yawned, farted and emerged from their cocoons. The patrol was due to leave at 3.30 in order to get into the Green Zone under cover of darkness and to lie up in the fields until dawn. The soldiers seemed in good spirits, checking their radios and trading banter. It was as if they were off on a day's orienteering rather than going out to tangle with the Taliban. Someone switched on an iPod hooked up to some speakers and stadium rock washed through the courtyard, a reminder that the soldiers were just young men. It was midnight on Saturday in Britain. As the soldiers were starting their day, their contemporaries back home were finishing theirs, spilling out of pubs and clubs, queuing for a kebab or waiting for a minicab to take them home.

They picked up their weapons and padded down through the velvety darkness to the gate set into the west wall. There was a short delay while they waited for one of the "terps" to appear. He arrived wrapping a keffiyeh round his head before strapping on his helmet. The gate swung open with a rusty screech and they stepped out on to the soft, thick dust of the road.

By dawn they were 500 metres inside the Green Zone and about a kilometre south of the fort. A string of compounds ran off to the north and it was there that the search would begin. The first two hours were uneventful. They moved methodically through. The sniper pairs scrambled up scaling-ladders on to the roofs, one to observe, one to engage. Down below, others pushed in doors and picked through the musty rooms and storehouses.

A kilometre away, every movement was being scrutinised through high-powered binoculars by the sentries in the sangars, who radioed the patrol details of the slightest movement that might indicate trouble. There was little to see, it seemed. The fields were empty except for a man and a boy. The odd pick-up truck trundled along the 611 and there were men moving slowly back and forth on small motorbikes on a lane that led north from the road, in the vicinity of a low-built mosque known as the Four Arches. They could be dickers. There could be a suicide bomber among them. Or they could merely be innocent young men, whose curiosity was stronger than their sense of danger. The sentries in the sangars watched them intently. Behind them the gun line and mortars were primed, ready to unleash a bombardment as soon as a target was identified.

The patrol was working its way northwards along a line of six compounds. To the right lay a wide stretch of open ground. It was here that the Taliban were most likely to strike. Corporals Jay Steed, Paul Scott and Matt Williamson of 2 Para watched their progress from the main sangar overlooking the road. Their senses were tuned to every shift in the scene before them. Steed was famous for his "times twelve eyes". He was able to pick things out that the others could only see with the aid of the binoculars.

The lead section of the patrol reached the last compound. There was no more cover now for several hundred metres. Half a kilometre away a man in a black turban was standing on a rooftop watching them, a walkie-talkie in his hand. There was a burst of static on someone's radio. The Taliban radio traffic indicated that the insurgents were preparing to open fire once the patrol moved into the open ground. The insurgents had given away their position. The Inkerman artillery and mortars laid on to the targets. So too did the Guided Multiple Launch Rocket System missiles standing by in the area. They were the latest addition to the British armoury, which could land a 200-pound high-explosive warhead within a few inches of a target from a range of 70 kilometres.

The ambushers were in for an unpleasant surprise. A few seconds later the air in the fort wobbled as the first mortars and shells flew towards the Green Zone. There was a brief, surreal silence, then a ripple of flashes marched along a treeline 500 metres beyond the compounds. Banners of smoke and dust climbed upwards, staining the startling blue of the sky, followed by a succession of flat bangs. The dicker was still on the roof. "Fuck me, he hasn't even flinched," said someone. Then there were more stuttering white flashes, more smoke, whiter this time, and sharper, louder bangs as the rockets landed.

It was quiet again. "Look at that donkey standing there on its own," said Jay. "It hasn't moved." There was indeed a donkey immobile in the field in front. "It's been there a while," said Paul. "I think it's a cardboard cut-out." The donkey seemed to resent this for it suddenly twitched its tail. The only sound was the buzzing of flies. The patrol was reaching the end of the line of compounds, moving slowly in the mid-morning heat.

Jay was on the giant binoculars. "He's popped up again." The man in the black turban was back at his post. Each compound in the Green Zone had a number. The dicker's location was radioed to the mortar line. A few minutes later there was a flash and the compound was smothered in smoke. "Right on target," said Paul.

Once again the quiet rolled back. Then in the treeline a few hundred metres beyond the compounds something twinkled and an RPG flew out accompanied by the popping of small-arms fire. The insurgents were finally launching their ambush. The RPG landed 20 metres from the middle section of the patrol and the Paras hugged the compound walls, bracing as several more crashed in. Corporal Mike French felt a thump in his ribs and looked down to see a lump of red-hot shrapnel skittering across the dirt. The grenade had hit the wall right behind him but his body armour saved him from serious injury. The attackers did not have a chance to get off a second volley. Mortars and artillery shells were already hurtling towards the insurgents' firing positions. On the sangar the .50-cal was chattering, sending glittering flecks of yellow tracer curving towards the treeline. In a few minutes the attack had fizzled out.

The patrol pressed on. The lead section cleared another compound and was starting on the next when the Taliban returned to the attack. Stu Bell was

195

crouched behind a broken wall with Sergeant Chris
Prosser when "all of a sudden they opened up with
PKM, RPG and AK47, directly at our position". They
could see the enemy firing points on the roof of a
compound 70 metres away. Stu Bell was a veteran
mortar man, who had stepped down for a few days
from his post as sergeant major of Support Company to
volunteer to come to Inkerman to do a corporal's job as
a mortar fire controller. He reported back the insurgent
positions via the OC to the mortar line in Inkerman
and moments later rounds exploded in the compound
where the Taliban had been spotted. Another volley
landed on the ground behind. Chris Prosser had the
light 66mm anti-tank rocket he was carrying propped
on his shoulder. He pressed down on the trigger bar
and the missile streaked away and exploded in the
compound, generating whoops of delight. Then the
firing stopped. "It was all over fairly short and sharp
but it was the most intense contact we had that day,"
said Bell. The Taliban had seen the size of the force they
were facing and decided against a head-to-head
encounter. What had ensued was a display of the
bravado they possessed in spades, rather than a serious
military effort.

The Paras headed for home, strung out in a long line
as they moved slowly across a broad open field, the last
danger point before they reached the FOB. They passed
through the hole in the wall and flopped to the ground,
gratefully gulping down water from the jerrycans
waiting for them. They were caked in dust and bathed
in sweat. "I think we definitely won today's

proceedings," said Ben Harrop, the 3 Para FSG commander.

In Stu McDonald's opinion it had been "a good warm-up, a chance to give the new group a feel for the ground", even though the results of the searches had been disappointing. They turned up some sundry documents, Pakistani ID cards, religious leaflets including instructions for ritual bathing prior to prayers and some texts that would be sent away for analysis, and had uncovered some weapons storage pits but no weapons. On the other hand the Taliban had suffered for their bravado. Intelligence reports said one of the local commanders, named Hajji Akkar, had been wounded and six of his entourage killed.

McDonald felt that the events of the day had taught the Taliban a lesson. "It says to them . . . they don't dominate the area of operations, they can't dictate our actions or restrain us." That may have been so, but as everyone accepted, killing large numbers of insurgents was not the way to go about winning the war. The prize, the endlessly repeated mantra emphasised, was the hearts and minds of the people.

The problem was that the very presence of the fort sucked insurgents into the area. That meant that every time the Paras emerged from the FOB they were almost certain to clash with them. The constant fighting had forced families out of their homes. There was a dwindling population with whom the soldiers could interact and no security within which the smallest reconstruction work could take place. The only long-term benefit of the day's events, McDonald thought, was that it sent "a message to the locals that we can inflict defeat upon the Taliban". He was determined to look at the bigger picture and what was happening down the road in Sangin. "We appreciate that we will never physically defeat the enemy," he said. "We can't kill them [all]. That's simply an unrealistic goal. But we're creating the conditions for Sangin to thrive as a showcase to [demonstrate] what can be done. And then hopefully more people will jump sides. They will become a little bit more ambivalent towards the Taliban presence, a little more accepting of ISAF. They [will] realise that we can change their life. It seems like an idealist's view, but if we didn't have that, then what are we doing?"

It was true that the Taliban appeared to have been checked by the show of power the Paras had mustered. The following day there was another company-plus-strength patrol. This time the insurgents failed to rise to the bait. The commanders watched the patrol from a safe distance and ordered their fighters to hold back. The Paras had demonstrated that with a large enough force they could dominate the ground, go where they wished and do what they wanted. But the truth that patrols of this size were exceptional and the boost to numbers that 3 Para had provided was only temporary. Two days later they were off.

On Tuesday afternoon they boarded the helicopters that would take them back to KAF. They were sad to leave 2 Para, but not to leave Inkerman.

2 Para were bearing the brunt of the fighting and fighting was what Paras were supposed to do. But no

one in 3 Para would have swapped their role for life in the FOBs. It required extraordinary inner resources to cope with that existence. The men in the forts knew that when they walked through the gates for the first time they were going to be staying there for virtually the whole of their six-month tour. Life was harsh and physically degrading. The soldiers left, on average, two stone lighter than when they arrived. Every time they went out on patrol they faced the prospect of death. There was a reminder of that in the stone cairn raised in the middle of the camp commemorating five of the Inkerman dead from previous tours. The names of the four who had been killed on Herrick 8 so far had yet to be added.

Morale is hard to define and harder to quantify. But three months into their tour, the inhabitants of Inkerman seemed remarkably relaxed and good-humoured. "It all goes back to *esprit de corps*," said Brett Jackson. "It's a privilege to command these soldiers." To sustain morale, though, it was important to believe that the sacrifices, the discomfort and the unrelenting effort were worth it. And for that, there needed to be signs of progress.

CHAPTER
TEN

Sangin Revisited

The most obvious place to measure progress, or lack of it, was Sangin. The town had played a central role in the history of Britain's Afghanistan adventure. It was where the British had fought their first prolonged battles with the Taliban. It was here that the insurgents had suffered their first major tactical defeat. And now, two years on, it was in the vanguard of the stabilisation and reconstruction effort.

The base had expanded from the clutch of dilapidated government buildings where the 3 Para Battlegroup held off constant Taliban attacks in the summer of 2006. In Helmand terms it now counted as a pleasant posting. There was a feeling of space and solidity. It sat on the edge of the Green Zone, and there were trees, shrubs and a small garden where sunflowers nodded in the breeze coming in from the river, replacing the marijuana plants that had once flourished there. The main attraction of Sangin was the irrigation channel. It was fast flowing, deliciously cool and milky green. It was channeled in from the Helmand river, which irrigated the thickly planted fields around the fort. It was deep enough to swim in. It was where the soldiers went to relax when they came off duty. You could wash in it, do your laundry, or jump in from the 4.5-metre-high concrete wall that dammed one end and let the current whisk you downstream. There were fish in the canal, which were easily hooked on ration-pack processed cheese. The anglers handed over their catch to the ANA, who grilled them on open fires on the canal bank while listening to CDs. In the evening, with the smell of cooking and the high, sweet voices of the Afghan pop divas drifting over the water, the sound of splashing and laughter and a big half-moon hanging in the sky, it was easy to think that there were worse places to be in Afghanistan.

Sangin was where 2 Para had their headquarters. It was also the home of Ranger Company of the Royal Irish Regiment, which was attached to the battalion. The Paras were deployed at the FOBs and patrol bases to the north and south. The Royal Irish were responsible for local area security and also mentored the ANA. One part of the camp was occupied by a company of US Marines, who also patrolled and supervised the Afghan troops. There was a sizeable police presence. They were members of the Afghan National Civil Order Police (ANCOP), replacing the local police contingent who had been sent to Kandahar for retraining. The programme had not got off to a good start. The routine drug test that all trainees submitted to before the course began revealed that twenty-nine out of thirty-eight of them were chronic opium users. The ANCOP were a different breed. They were a multi-ethnic force from outside the area. About

201

two-thirds of them were literate and they had a discipline and *esprit de corps* that were notably lacking in the regular police.

The base also housed a civilian Stabilisation Adviser (Stabad), charged with coordinating the reconstruction effort. The UK mission in Helmand was a joint effort. The soldiers shared responsibility with civil servants from the Foreign Office, DfID and the tri-departmental Stabilisation Unit. Despite their overwhelming numbers, the military did not have first place in the bureaucratic pecking order. That went to the Foreign Office representative, Hugh Powell, who presided over the mission in Lashkar Gah. In the protocol firmament Powell had "two-star" status, the equivalent of major general rank. Mark Carleton-Smith was a brigadier and only a one-star. The military had no problem with the way the hierarchy was ordered. It reflected a truth that everyone recognised. Afghanistan's problems would ultimately be solved by civilians, not soldiers.

For the moment though it was the troops who were, overwhelmingly, doing the bulk of the work. The division of labour was not reflected in the living conditions. The civil servants fared much better. The senior officer in Sangin, Lieutenant Colonel Joe O'Sullivan, slept in a stiflingly hot Hesco shelter, the same as his men. The Foreign Office was arranging for three air-conditioned Portakabins to be moved up to the base for its use. One was an office, another a bedroom with en suite bathroom for the senior representative, while the third was intended for guest accommodation for visiting colleagues and technical experts.

Whitehall rules prevented civilian officials from moving outside the base limits. The Stabads worked in six-week stints. Security concerns constrained their movements outside the base and most of their encounters with local people took place inside the walls.

Much thought had been applied to the question of how to drag Helmand out of backwardness and chaos. In the process, some of the basic assumptions that underpinned official thinking when the British first arrived had been thrown out. The initial impulse had been to go for "quick-impact projects" — small-scale, essentially symbolic works such as digging wells and repairing roads that would persuade the locals that the newcomers were there to help. These would be followed, as soon as security allowed, by a much more ambitious public works programme, building clinics and schools and essential infrastructure. By 2008 the policy was discredited. For one thing, the rising level of violence did not allow serious building programmes. Over time, the PRT experts in Lashkar Gah and Sangin had rethought the whole approach.

"What really matters to people?" asked Tim Foy, a senior Stabilisation Unit official and deputy head of the Helmand Provincial Reconstruction Team at their headquarters in Lashkar Gah. "It isn't schools, it isn't clinics in the first instance. This is a fragile state, one that can't deliver the basic functions of [government] to its people." Before any development could begin someone would have to establish the vital conditions of "human security freedom of movement, basic justice and rule of law". Outsiders could help create them. But the essential work would have to be done by Afghans if it was to have any lasting value. The soldiers were always mindful of putting an "Afghan face" on operations. What was needed in the long term was an Afghan hand.

"Us doing it doesn't do . . . any good at all," said Foy. "[It] has to be seen in terms of the Afghan government providing something that actually means something to the people . . . building institutions that are capable of delivering some form of good enough governance that will allow people to connect with the state rather than the opposition."

Helmand, as the PRT officials were the first to accept, was a very long way from this condition. The emphasis now was on building governance rather than classrooms. "Us cutting about the place, whacking stuff up . . . measuring success in terms of how much we've spent or buildings that we've built is absolutely meaningless."

Developing good government was certainly a harder option. There were virtually no institutional foundations on which to base progress in southern Afghanistan. In Helmand, only six of the twenty districts had officially accredited leaders. What bureaucratic resources there were in Afghanistan were centred in Kabul. The ambition was to spread the network of authority through the districts, appointing officials and medical workers, teachers and agricultural experts, in places that had been secured. The first problem was finding people who had the training or qualifications to fill these posts. The second was persuading them to accept the job. A government job came with a death sentence from the Taliban.

To take on the task required a profound selflessness and sense of mission. These were hard to find, even in the upper reaches of the government. There were notable exceptions. The latest governor of Helmand, Gulab Mangal, was a model of diligence and courage. He was appointed in March 2008, replacing Asadullah Wafa, whose relations with the British had deteriorated after he complained about the activities of two EU diplomats who had been holding secret meetings with Taliban figures in Helmand. The officials, one British, one Irish, were subsequently expelled. Mangal was a Pashtun from Paktika province in the south-east and unencumbered by the tribal affiliations that complicated and obscured Helmand politics. He had worked for the Soviets in the 1970s before turning against them and joining the resistance. He was head of the committee that drafted Afghanistan's new, progressive constitution and had served as governor of first Paktika then Laghman province before arriving in Helmand.

Mangal was energetic and resolute. He moved around the province, meeting elders, promoting education and development and trying to generate a climate of responsibility and self-sufficiency that would allow Afghans to take advantage of the opportunity that the resuscitation of democracy and the West's surely finite largesse offered. He took enormous risks doing

205

so. The governor was top of the Taliban's hit list and numerous plots were hatched to assassinate him. In May the Chinook taking him to inaugurate a new mosque in Musa Qaleh was hit by an RPG but managed to land safely.

Mangal's qualities won him the respect and admiration of ISAF and the outside world. "He's bright and he's sharp and he wants to make a difference," said Colonel Neil Hutton, Deputy Commander of the Helmand Task Force, who saw the governor regularly. "There is a chance for Helmand with this bloke." He did not seem to be as well appreciated by his own government. President Karzai had never visited him in Lashkar Gah. The dismal record of central government in publicly associating itself with the international effort in southern Afghanistan was a constant source of annoyance and dismay to Regional Command South. "There is too little attention [paid by] the central government to the south," said Brigadier Harme de Jonge, the deputy commander. "We have not seen the president visiting one of the provinces in the last year. Most of the ministers don't come down south . . . if you have the luck to have a courageous governor with some kind of vision who wants to give his utmost to improve the situation in that province on behalf of the president of the republic then you would expect that this man would receive a lot of political empowerment . . . that is not the case."

Four years after riding to power on a wave of high hopes, Karzai was proving a disappointment to his Western backers and increasingly to his own people.

Despite constant urging he had made no concerted moves to unseat corrupt officials, ministers and security chiefs or to go after the opium oligarchs who stood behind them. Some of the biggest offenders were said to be members of his own family. His brother, Ahmed Wali Karzai, the head of the Kandahar provincial council, was regularly the target of American allegations that he was a major player in the drugs trade. Kim Howells, who served as Foreign Office minister with responsibility for Afghanistan between 2005 and 2008, told the House of Commons in December 2009 that he believed that "institutionally Afghanistan is corrupt from top to bottom, and there are few signs that the chaotic hegemony of warlords, gangsters, presidential placemen, incompetent and under-resourced provincial governors and self-seeking government ministers has been challenged in any effective way by President Karzai."

Howells said later that when he tackled the president on the subject "he became very angry." Karzai's argument, with which it was possible to have some sympathy, was that the British and Americans simply did not understand the complexities of Afghan tribal structures and local ways of doing things. Sometimes control could only be exercised via unsavoury strongmen and "if you've got to use bad guys, you've got to use bad guys".

In the summer of 2008 the Americans began to make public their disillusionment with Karzai and by 2009 the incoming Obama administration in Washington let it be known that Karzai could not rely on their backing in the presidential elections scheduled for later in the year.

But Karzai represented the summit of the problem. The British were struggling in the foothills, and Sangin was the highest ground they had scaled so far. Despite the shift of emphasis towards governance, some reconstruction was going on in Helmand where circumstances allowed. Medium-scale refurbishment projects had been finished in Lashkar Gah, Musa Qaleh and Garmsir. In Sangin, the British had spent money building a new mosque, repairing and equipping a school and improving a stretch of road that ran through the bazaar. Bigger schemes were in the pipeline. The work had been made possible as the soldiers broadened the security footprint around the district centre, pushing the Taliban back into the Green Zone so they were no longer able to use the streets and alleyways of the town to launch attacks on the base. The main sign of progress was the increased commercial bustle. Streets that had once been battlegrounds were busy again. One road leading away from the north side of the compound had been known in 2006 as "the pipe range" and had been the scene of a suicidal Taliban head-on assault. Now, looking down its tranquil, tree-lined length, it was hard to imagine it strewn with burning vehicles and dead bodies. It had been renamed the "Avenue of Hope". The bazaar was heaped with goods and twice a week the wadi beneath the west wall of the compound filled with the sound of bleating goats and the shouts of traders at the livestock market.

But the sense of safety was fragile and the security bubble the soldiers had created did not extend much beyond the tight boundaries of the town centre. On the morning of Sunday, 8 August, a Royal Irish patrol set off from the base to follow a route that would take them from the north to the south of Sangin, passing all the points of interest and importance. They included two vehicle checkpoints at the entrance and exit to the town. These were fortified structures built to protect the ANA and ANP who manned them from routine shoot-ups by passing insurgents. The soldiers were also intending to visit the three mobile phone masts on surrounding hills which the Taliban were bent on destroying. The patrol included Captain Phil Owens and Major Jim Castle of the civil-military cooperation team (CIMIC), who wanted to check on the progress of development projects. We left at 8 a.m., turning right out of the gate and moving along the wadi to the "flyover", a narrow concrete bridge supporting Route 611 which ran through the town.

The scene outside the walls looked tranquil and unthreatening. With the arrival of the soldiers the atmosphere changed. Their appearance seemed to increase rather than reduce the prospect of danger. We passed a bearded man sitting on a moped. His young daughter in a sky-blue burka was perched on the pillion. Her mother, enveloped in black, squatted in the dirt a few paces away. The man wore a skull cap decorated with sequins that sparkled cheerfully in the sun. There was nothing friendly about the empty stare that he turned on the soldiers as they smiled and nodded at him. We reached the flyover and started to cross the wadi. A motorbike puttered out of a side alley and the interpreter, who went by the nickname "Rock", shouted at the driver to stop. The soldiers tensed, then relaxed. He was an old man, too old to be a suicide bomber. It was the young, with all their lives before them, who were impatient to get to paradise. The elderly man obeyed dumbly, waiting obediently until the column had filed past.

We turned left into the area known as the garages. It was a row of mud and breeze-block hole-in-the-wall workshops, metal-bashing establishments that repaired cars and motorbikes. Men and boys were squatting in front of them in the narrow band of shade. Phil Owens called out "*salaam aleikum*" as we passed. One or two raised a hand in greeting. Most just looked back blankly, hostile or indifferent, it was impossible to say. The "terps" claimed to be able to identify a man's affiliations at a glance. To the outsider, the Afghans' body language was untranslatable. The men and boys could have been Taliban sympathisers, or off-duty Taliban gunmen, or simply peasants too wearied by experience to pretend they were pleased to see the sweat-shined faces of the soldiers who were eager to be their friends.

Beneath the surface bonhomie the soldiers were taut and wary. The sections moved methodically forward. As the tail of the patrol entered the garages there was a sudden loud burst of gunfire off to the left. The soldiers froze for a second then ducked into the cover of the workshop walls. All the radios buzzed into life. A few

210

hundred metres away, an ANA patrol was under attack. The patrol was ordered to go to their aid. We set off jogging down a wide street lined with empty storehouses towards the sound of the shooting, and turned left into a path that led into a field. The word swept down the line. We were going forward to flush the gunmen out. Faces emptied and hardened. The bursts of fire got louder as we doubled forward down a muddy path that ran along a maize field flanked by a drainage ditch. It was easy to slip and I tumbled into the water and had to be hauled out by Rock. The path led to a bridge spanning a wider and deeper waterway. If you fell into that wearing body armour you would have a job getting out. We swung to the left and the section went firm, taking up firing positions in a broken-down compound with all-round arcs of fire. But the drama seemed to have subsided. The firing faded out and the soldiers prepared to resume the patrol.

It was led by Lieutenant Peter Franks, a young Irishman from just outside Dublin. Before setting off he ordered a search of a compound by the edge of the field. Two men had been seen running into it during the shooting. They turned out to be a father and his young son, who had been working in the fields when the rounds started coming over and had run home to take cover. One of the soldiers ducked through the gate, followed by two interpreters. As well as the Afghan terps there was a British linguist in the party, Corporal Bev Cornell from Derby. Pashto was just one of seven languages that she spoke either fluently or well. Corporal Cornell's ability to communicate with the women who were usually found inside the compounds made her an invaluable asset.

This morning the women of the family had clustered together in a room in the main dwelling. The sight of soldiers framed in the doorway started them screaming. When the situation calmed, the man of the house gave Cornell permission to enter and she walked out of the bright sunlight into the dim and musty interior. The women were sitting on the floor in varying states of distress. "There was an old woman, the grandma, I guess, and four daughters plus their mother," she said. "The mother in particular was quite emotional." The daughters were hanging back, waiting to see what happened next. Bev Cornell is slender and petite. But she must still have seemed threatening in her helmet, encased in body armour and carrying a rifle. She went over to the mother. "She was in tears, absolutely uncontrollable, and I hugged her. And as I was hugging her, the daughters came forward and we started to talk."

The tension was broken. The woman poured out her misery at the anarchy that was wrecking their lives. They told her that they blamed the Taliban for the violence. Bev was soothing and sympathetic. Gradually the woman calmed down. Everyone relaxed. They started to see her as a female rather than a soldier. "The mother actually touched me, and I was like, yes, I'm black . . . and she said, I can't believe you're doing this . . . why are you putting yourself through this? I said, it's not putting myself through [anything]. It's something I love doing. I'm a soldier like anyone else but obviously I'm a female." The woman started asking her, "Are you married, do you have kids? I was conscious of the fact that I've got to get 'int' out of her rather than tell her my life story but you have to balance it, you can't have a one-way conversation." While they talked some of the women took off their headscarves. It was rare to see a woman unveiled even inside her own home and Cornell was fascinated. She had not known what to expect but "the women I saw there were beautiful." They had little to tell her in the way of hard "int". The male translators, though, had more luck. They had moved to a separate room to talk to the men of the family. They blamed the shooting on the Ishakzai tribe, Taliban allies and rivals of the Barakzai to which they belonged, claiming they had been responsible for a number of shoot-and-scoots aimed at the ANA in recent days.

There was one more excitement before the episode was closed. Just as Franks was about to resume patrolling he was told to stand by. The gunmen were believed to be lying up in the maize fields west of the patrol's position. The ops room at Sangin had come up with a plan for the patrol to push the insurgents northwards, to where the ANA had set up an ambush. As Franks was only too aware, this was easier said than done. The maize stalks were two metres high and densely planted. Nonetheless, he gave the order to fix bayonets and the soldiers moved in an extended line into the enveloping greenness, blades at the ready. It was a dashing move but quite impractical. "We abandoned it after about eighty metres because you couldn't see a foot in front of you," said Franks. "If the enemy had been there and heard us coming we would have been in trouble." They retreated, and tried another approach, moving along a path firing flares to try to get the gunmen to react.

There was no response. We moved back in the direction of Sangin, crossing the road where the ambush had taken place. ANA soldiers were crouching behind the walls, weapons trained on firing points that had probably been long abandoned. Later the story of what had happened emerged. The soldiers had been travelling in a pair of pick-up trucks driving along a road from Sangin to their base just to the north. They were returning from a shopping expedition to buy chicken in the market. The gunmen opened up from a field to the west. The ANA jumped down, took cover behind a wall and a firefight ensued. There were a number of civilians on the road. Two men were caught right next to the ANA truck and threw themselves on the ground. There was a gap in the wall where it opened on to a track, which exposed them to the gunmen's fire. One man was hit in the head and killed instantly.

All that was known about the victim was that he was youngish, in his thirties, and came from a village just north of Sangin called Tughay. He was killed by a 7.62mm bullet from a PKM machine gun, the insurgents' equivalent of the GPMG. While the soldiers were hanging about, the normal life of the countryside rolled back, resuming its natural rhythm. Women balancing shopping on their heads glided past, trailing a troupe of children, and tiny donkeys laden with sacks, or ridden by boys who beat them monotonously, raising puffs of dust from their long-suffering hides. There was nothing to show that a short time before a man had been lying dead on the road.

The incident illustrated a point that had struck almost everyone involved in the enterprise. Security meant different things to the different players in the Helmand drama. Westerners measured it by their ability to move around and carry out their duties without being shot at or blown up. To the local population, it was the freedom to go to their fields or visit the bazaar without fear of getting caught in a firefight or bombardment. By trying to establish security for themselves, the soldiers were jeopardising that of the people they had come to save. The soldiers excused themselves to the locals for shattering the calm of any area they entered by explaining that it was the Taliban who started the trouble. But the obvious response was that if the soldiers had not been there the Taliban would not have attacked them.

The great task facing those involved in CIMIC and all the other toilers in the propaganda effort was to persuade local people by words and deeds that the destruction and disruption were worth it and the removal of the Taliban was the price they would have to pay for a better life and broader opportunities. Not only would they have to endure, they would have to cooperate, by essentially acting as informants with all the risks that involved. Some people were prepared to give general information about personalities, leaders and even potentially lifesaving specifics such as the whereabouts of IEDs.

To actively support the allies, however, required not only courage and faith in the newcomers' good intentions but signs that life was getting better. There was no doubt that things had improved since the worst days of 2006. People seemed more likely, though, to look back to the situation before the British had arrived.

A snapshot of life at the start of the mission emerges in the diary of Major Will Pike, the officer commanding "A" Company of 3 Para, the first troops to garrison the town in June 2006. On 22 June he recorded his first meeting with the area's notables. "The Shura started with me giving them a chat on what we were doing in Sangin and why, very much emphasising that we were there to help, initially with security, then paving the way for reconstruction." The locals, however, were unmoved. They told Pike "that they would rather we went away, since our presence would guarantee a fight with the Taliban, which would affect business in the bazaar. They would rather live under the coercive terror of the Taliban than actively help us, or the Afghan Government". Pike countered by saying that the British presence was proof of the government's commitment to reconstruction in the area. He noted: "This didn't seem to convince them, with some justification, since the Afghan Government has done basically nothing for these people in four years and is seen to be largely corrupt." He concluded with the thought that "the lesson is clear — we must demonstrate a tangible benefit of Afghan governance to the people".

After the shura, Pike did a tour of the town, accompanied by the district chief, Haji Khan Mohammed, and the Regimental Medical Officer, Captain Harvey Pynn. The bazaar was "quite small but with wide dirt streets, hundreds of stalls lining the streets selling or making more or less anything. Lots of people were about either among the stalls or sitting in groups on carpets drinking 'chai'." The mood was "guarded rather than openly hostile, though there were a few rather menacing groups around". They visited a hospital "run by a Pakistani and with a female doctor which was unusual". The doctors both spoke English and soon established friendly relations with Pynn. It seemed "OK", though the government-contracted Afghan Ibn Sina organisation, which was supposed to support the hospital had not been seen for two years. They made their way back to the base across the wadi where every week "Kuchi nomads with their hardy sheep come into Sangin from the West, from the grazing by the Helmand river, over the rickety straw/stick footbridge that is washed away by the floods in winter and into the . . . livestock market".[1]

Shortly after Pike's diary entry, the fighting the elders had predicted broke out and Sangin became a ghost town. The effort and sacrifice of the intervening

---

[1] Quoted in Hew Pike, *From the Front Line, Family Letters and Diaries — 1900 to the Falklands and Afghanistan*, Pen and Sword, 2008, pp. 194–5.

217

two years had got it back to a semblance of its former self. But the "tangible benefits" of the ISAF presence were hard to discern at first sight. The goal of security seemed as far distant for the soldiers as for the local population. The Taliban were as vigorous as ever. The heavy losses they had sustained over the last two years did not seem to have deterred them. Nor did the special forces-led campaign of "decapitation" to assassinate the top commanders appear to have the devastating effect on organisation and morale that was hoped for. The Taliban leader in Sangin, Mullah Sazhaddin, had been killed at the very start of the fighting in 2006 in a special forces strike that left two British soldiers dead, but his removal made very little difference.

Like the Taliban everywhere, the Sangin insurgents had adjusted their tactics, stepping up their use of IEDs and suicide bombers. They were still willing to ambush patrols wherever and whenever they could, however. Much of the violence seemed pointless and instinctive. It had an atavistic feel that did not appear necessarily to have anything to do with the stakes of the conflict as defined by the Afghan government and the West. The farmers questioned by the Royal Irish patrol that Sunday morning did not think of the gunmen as "Taliban". In their minds, their chief characteristic was their membership of a rival tribe, one that had a grievance with the "government". The government in this case was less likely to mean President Karzai than a local official with whom they had fallen out over a promise not honoured or a disputed drug deal. That the

218

soldiers were government employees was reason enough to shoot at them.

Whatever their motivations, the insurgents around Sangin were energetic and resourceful. It was hard not to reflect that the place would have been transformed into a showcase of prosperity in a few weeks if the rebels had applied the same industry to construction as they did to destruction. Keeping the peace in Sangin was the responsibility of Ranger Company of the Royal Irish Regiment. Their job was to maintain the security bubble within which development could take place. It was led by Major Graham Shannon, a charismatic thirty-five-year-old Ulsterman who had long experience of Iraq and thought deeply and imaginatively about his task. The main security threat in the town was IEDs. A team of experts was operating in the area, constantly testing the army's counter-IED specialists with their ingenuity. "[We] have the whole gambit in Sangin," he said cheerfully. "Remote control, pressure plates, command wire. There's a little bit of everything here. It makes life entertaining and you need to be on your toes."

Shannon had spent a year in Iraq with the Americans, serving with the Second Brigade of the 101st Airborne Division. Their area of operations lay south of Baghdad, in the farmland between the Tigris and Euphrates bounded by the capital and the towns of Mahmoudiya and Latifiya. It was known, without hyperbole, as the "Triangle of Death". It was infested with Sunni diehards who had allied themselves with al-Qaeda outsiders who were waging an asymmetric war against the invaders with IEDs and suicide bombs. The American approach had been to first identify the areas that seemed to be most important to the insurgents. This was determined by the amount of effort they put into defending them when the US forces arrived. From their review of the rebels' tactics they were able to identify their main lines of communication, in particular the route between the bomb factories and Baghdad, their target destination. Over a year they managed to squeeze the insurgents back, creating security zones inside which reconstruction could begin. "The brigade fought hard and spilled a lot of blood," Shannon said. "At the end it was considered that al-Qaeda had been defeated in that area."

The experience had convinced Shannon that the same approach could work in Sangin. "You really see the enemy snap when you get to the right place," he said. "It will take a while . . . there are times when you stumble backwards a little bit." But he was convinced that military victory was possible, "as long as we continue to identify these enemy sanctuaries, these enemy facilitators, and we keep striking at them".

Ranger Company was in the middle of an operation aimed at disrupting the activities of just such a facilitator, believed to be behind the spate of IED attacks in Sangin. His name was Mullah Kadhoos, and he operated out of a compound near the 611, south of the district centre. His motivations were, as was often the case, mixed. He was thought to be an important figure in the opium trade. There was an obvious convergence of interests between the drug lords and the

Taliban in maintaining a climate of lawlessness. Where security was established, the poppy eradication programme was supposed to eventually follow. The opium barons were fighting to protect a business that brought them wealth, power and status. This made them allies in anarchy with the Taliban. How long the alliance would survive should the movement ever come to power was anyone's guess.

On the night of Friday, 8 August an ANA force, watched over by Royal Irish and US Marine mentors, had raided the compound of Kadhoos. He was not at home but, judging by the attack that was launched on a nearby patrol base the following day, the operation had caused him some annoyance. For half an hour the midday quiet was shattered by RPG blasts and the throb of machine guns as the insurgents pounded patrol base Armagh, a Royal Irish position south of the district centre.

The location had once been a no-go area but was now dotted with mini-forts, of which Armagh was one. Shannon had led the move into the area. He remembered an early shura. "The local elders came down to have a chat wondering what we were doing down there," he said. "They said, the most dangerous place in the world is Afghanistan, and in Afghanistan the most dangerous place is Helmand and in Helmand the most dangerous place is Sangin and you're sitting in the most dangerous place in Sangin!"

There were nine patrol bases dotted around the district centre manned by the Brits, the Afghans and the Americans. In Armagh they mounted patrols twice daily and a Royal Irish platoon left the district centre regularly to roam the length and breadth of the 80 square kilometres of their area of operations. The patrols could take three hours or a whole day and night. Sometimes the effort was rewarded. Shannon had recently gone out to search an area where an IED had detonated, mercifully without causing casualties, and discovered five more. One of them was a booby trap, wired to an abandoned motorbike. They were ambushed on the way back and an outing that was supposed to take two hours had ended up lasting twelve. It was exhausting and it was nerve-racking. The IEDs, said Company Sergeant Major Frankie O'Connor, were "very unsettling for the boys. It's like having a sniper out there". You couldn't see the threat but you could never ignore it. Everything and everyone presented a possible mortal danger, even the most harmless-looking individual, as Ranger Company had seen in the first days of the tour.

They had gone out in strength with the ANA to dominate the Green Zone south of the district centre, moving through the poppy fields along a canal, stopping to chat to anyone who was prepared to talk to them. As they turned northwards back to the base they got an intelligence warning that an attack was imminent. They moved forward cautiously. The lead section was walking up a track parallel to the canal path when they saw a young man in a ragged brown dishdasha such as the field workers wore, squatting on the ground ahead. "He was hunkered down, looking down at the ground, sort of playing with the gravel," said Shannon. "He didn't look out of place. He was just like anyone else sitting in the fields." He appeared to be ignoring the advancing soldiers. When they were 20 metres away he stood up and looked towards them. Then "he exploded, just detonated. There were eight soldiers in the formation and all of them were blown on their backsides". All that was left of the suicide bomber was his legs, which landed on the canal path. The explosion was the signal for some gunmen to pop up on rooftops and engage, and a firefight developed.

Shannon got on to a compound roof to join in. He looked down to see a donkey tied to a tree nuzzling one of the bomber's legs. The other was being examined by an Afghan soldier. "It was one of those completely bizarre moments [when you think] what is going on!" said Shannon. "This donkey is nibbling on a leg and an ANA soldier is playing with the other one and there is shooting and shelling going on all over the place." The suicide bomber's post-mortem indignities were not finished. The body parts were brought back to the district centre and handed over to the Royal Military Police. Then an order came through that an attempt should be made to identify the corpse. There were no fingerprints to be had. Perhaps toe prints would do. The task fell to Corporal Bryan Maddison, a Royal Irish intelligence specialist, and Corporal Don Lane of the RMP. The limbs were then taken away to be burned in the base rubbish pit. Two days later breakfast was in full swing in the open-air cookhouse when someone noticed Sandbag, one of the camp's pet dogs, chewing what looked like a large bone. When Maddison went over to investigate the object looked all too familiar. It was the leg's final appearance. It was taken off and given a supervised cremation. The incident, though, lived on in the Sangin black comedy repertoire.

Patrolling was only partly about subduing and disrupting the enemy. Shannon's formula placed equal emphasis on nurturing the confidence and goodwill of the local people. "It isn't a great science," he said. "It's getting off your arse, going into town, talking to people and treating them like human beings." If the soldiers could not only provide security but make some practical improvements to local life, "then people start to understand that you are there for some tangible benefit and then they start providing information against the people who are taking away [those] benefits".

Shannon found that despite the dangers of being identified as an informant, local people were regularly tipping off the soldiers about the presence of IEDs. Their motives were mixed. Some were repaying a favour from the soldiers. Others were doing it for the small rewards that were given for useful information. There were also those who were driven by "an absolute, inbred hatred of what the terrorists are doing . . . they want to give you what information they can because of what the Taliban have done to them and their family".

Delivering the "tangible benefits" that both Will Pike and Graham Shannon had identified as essential was an arduous business. The process seemed weighed down by a mass of bureaucratic machinery and hedged in by thickets of procedure. The fact that the Stability

Advisers who led the effort did only six-week tours before taking a break did not help continuity, nor did the fact that they kept changing. In 2008, Sangin had four separate Stabads in six months.

The Stabads' main point of contact with the Afghans was via Governor Isatullah, the district leader, who had his home and office inside the base. It was there that local representatives came to talk. Isatullah was a former mujahedin fighter who had given up the relative safety of Lashkar Gah to come to Sangin. But even he did not venture out much more than once a month to check on progress in his domain. This prudence was completely justified. In the eighteen months to August, forty-three policemen and members of his bodyguard had been killed by the Taliban. Isatullah, who like some Afghan males went by a single name, seemed to understand the purpose of the huge effort going on around him. He told visitors that his greatest desire was to see Afghanistan become "a good democracy".

His methods, though, seemed closer to those of a medieval magnate. Isatullah was protected by his own militia. They dressed in police uniforms and roamed the bazaar and the goat market and the local shops in ANP vehicles collecting "taxes". The CIMIC team had alerted the PRT in Lashkar Gah to the situation in July and were told that the activities were illegal. It was some time, though, before the situation was resolved.

The most obvious sign of returning normality was the goat market that took place on Monday and Thursday mornings outside the fort's front gate. "A year ago that wasn't happening," said Captain Phil

Owens, the cheerful and optimistic CIMIC officer who worked in tandem with the Stabad. "Four and a half months ago it was small and took place on one day. Now it's enormous and takes place twice a week . . . that's a real indicator. If people are willing to come and do business here, then they feel secure." In Helmand, though, security was relative. "There might be incidents. There might be suicide bombers or the occasional shooting. But if people are able to get around and do their business, they actually perceive that security is improving." It was as well that, as the soldiers often said, it had never been the intention to turn Helmand into Hampshire.

The bazaar too was booming. The number of stalls had multiplied, as had the variety of the goods on offer. There was plenty of food in the market — flour, wheat, corn maize and spices. Beyond that there were consumer durables — fridges, TVs and radios, and fun items such as clothes and the latest CDs and DVDs. Some of the goods came from far afield, from Kandahar and even across the border from Pakistan. At first sight it looked encouraging. From another perspective it represented only a return to the predeployment situation of plenty as described by Will Pike, though Mark Carleton-Smith would argue that the comparison was false and the impression of calm and plenty illusory.

Improvements were being made to the town. Even so, it would be a long time before the damage caused by bombs, bullets and rockets in 2006 was repaired. The projects varied in size. The lowest level were "consent-winning activities". Patrols went out on the ground to identify small works that could be carried out with a minimum of difficulty and expense, such as clearing a clogged irrigation ditch or simply cleaning up rubbish. Medium-level projects were coordinated with a team from the US Marine Corps, which historically had considerable experience of reconstruction work. The bazaar had recently been equipped with three new transformers, which had the capacity to provide electricity for 300 shops and stalls. Work was also under way to refurbish the mosque. A primary school at the gates of the fort had been redecorated and supplied with new equipment and on a good day thirty or so pupils turned up.

The main projects in view were the construction of a new college and a road improvement programme to surface more than two kilometres of the road that ran through the bazaar, and provide street lighting and irrigation ditches. Altogether $4 million was available to pay for the works.

Getting the inhabitants to accept the largesse had caused problems initially. "A lot of the locals said we don't want to be associated either with ISAF or the government due to intimidation by the Taliban," said Owens. "Some of them said if you pay me a hundred dollars to sweep the streets for three days it isn't worth my while because the risk to my life isn't worth [it]."

When Owens arrived in the spring he had offered help to the local clinic, mending broken windows and replacing tiles to improve hygiene in the wards. He was told by an administrator, "there's no point in doing that because if I take two thousand dollars off you to reskim all the concrete surfaces and do the windows, the amount of intimidation that I will get from the Taliban just isn't worth it". His counterproposal was that they knock the clinic down and build a new one. The benefit would then outweigh the personal risk.

In the minds of the Taliban the receipt of the occupiers' charity amounted to collaboration, and the penalty for collaboration was death. They viewed the arrival of the foreigners as they might the coming of a deadly disease. The illness was contagious, and those who had contact with the outsiders, even if their motivations were mercenary, were carriers. One morning a local worker who had risked working on one of the facilities being built on the base came to the medical officer, Captain James Thompson, asking for treatment for a suppurating hand. Thompson told him to go to a local doctor's surgery next door to the district centre. This apparent lack of charity had a point. The intention was to get Afghans to help themselves and each other. The patient trooped off, looking disappointed. He returned half an hour later. The doctor had refused to treat him on the grounds that if it became known he had aided a man who was working at the base he would be under threat from the insurgents. Thompson patched him up.

Children were as vulnerable to intimidation as adults. When Phil Owens tried to distribute small backpacks with a notebook and pencil to encourage children to go to school, he was told by one little boy that if he was seen with it "the Taliban will tell me not to go to school and I'll get threatened. They'll give me one chance not to go and the second [time] they'll cut my head off."

Even with the improvement in security, contractors were restricted to a tight area. The presence of so many soldiers permitted a reasonable feeling of safety only within an area of one square kilometre centred on the town. Even there, the Taliban were still able to strike. On Monday, 11 August the road-building programme was held up after someone succeeded in blowing up a bulldozer while the workers were off having their midday meal.

The only place where work could go on unimpeded was inside the walls of the base. A house and offices had been built for the governor and a barrack block for the ANA. There was a plan to build a detention centre to hold Taliban suspects before they were flown back to KAF for interrogation. In the meantime the captives who were brought in from time to time were kept in a small concrete shed. One morning there were two prisoners sitting in the shade of the wall, casually guarded by the ANCOP. They had been arrested that morning by a joint patrol in an area known as the Tank Park in the south of the town by the side of the 611, where a number of IEDs had been uncovered recently. One captive was twenty years old, plump and smooth faced. The other was a few years his senior, and thin with a dark ruff of beard. The younger one was indignant. The older, quiet and resigned.

The prisoners maintained they were simple farmers, brothers who had been innocently labouring in their fields when they were picked up. They certainly looked the part in dirty grey and brown dishdashas, plastic sandals and work-chapped hands. "We were cutting grass for our sheep," said the younger one. "Just doing our normal day's work . . . Then the soldiers came by." The two men had been interrogated by the interpreters, who held them until an ANCOP officer arrived. He arrested them and they were being kept at the base pending further investigations. "We don't know why we're here," said the plump one plaintively. "We don't know anything."

They were both volubly anti-Taliban. "They are very bad men," said the older one. "We are here because of them. All they do is harm our homeland. We always ask the soldiers' permission before we go to work in our fields. But now they have arrested us." Despite their protestations they seemed resigned to the prospect that things might go against them. "Only Allah knows [what will happen]," said the bearded one. "We don't have any proof that we're not Taliban. We're innocent but they can say we're Taliban." According to the police he had already been identified as a known insurgent.

They were watched from a distance by Colonel Gilani Brut, the commander of the ANCOP in Sangin. He lay on a charpoy under a tree, smoking and making calls on his mobile sat phone. He had bloodshot eyes that darted about when he spoke. According to him, the younger one was probably innocent. The older one, however, looked like someone who appeared on an American database as a known Taliban operator in the area. After they were lifted a search had turned up an

IED made from four mortar bombs planted by the side of the 611.

For the colonel, the morning's events were proof of how well ANCOP and the Coalition were working together. "We are doing a good job here," he said. "Before we came, policemen were getting killed all the time and they were doing nothing. Now we are working well with the British and Americans and we are happy with them." Gilani had been a security officer all his career. He had served in the NDS before switching to ANCOP. He was an enthusiastic warrior. "I have fought and defeated the Taliban many times," he said. "I shall roll them up like an old blanket."

As it turned out the brothers were telling the truth. Two other men were arrested the following night, hanging around the Tank Park, but this time suspicion seemed well founded. When tested, they had traces of explosives on their hands. To the outsider they looked just like the wrongly accused brothers. They wore the same grubby shifts, the same cheap sandals and the same air of resignation as they squatted on the stony ground, handcuffed and blindfolded with goggles blacked-out with masking tape, waiting for the helicopter to take them off for further interrogation.

If the insurgency was ever to be neutralised it was the likes of Colonel Gilani and his men who would ultimately deliver victory. They had the cultural understanding needed to guess the insurgents' intentions and devise the tactics to counter them. They could draw on a recruiting base that would provide the numbers that were needed to take and hold the ground.

Most importantly, they had the deep motivation that provided the stamina that was the essential resource in a conflict of this kind. The war would be won by the side with the strongest willpower. This was, as ISAF constantly pointed out, Afghanistan's war. All they were doing was to help the legitimate government to win it.

ISAF's name had initially been a diplomatic fiction. In the immediate post-Taliban years the International Security Assistance Force did not merely assist security. It provided virtually all of the government's military capability. By 2008, local reliance on outside help was lessening, though not nearly as fast as all parties would like. By the summer the ANA were taking part in almost every operation of significance. Training the Afghan security forces was a central element in ISAF's mission, and the British Army had been heavily involved from the beginning in Operational Mentoring and Liaison Teams (OMLTs), which instructed ANA units and supported them on missions. In Sangin, a team from the Royal Irish lived alongside an ANA company at the district centre, an arrangement that was repeated in some of the outlying patrol bases.

The company sergeant major of the OMLT in Sangin was Sergeant Major Wallace Mahaffy, a wry thirty-five-year-old Royal Irish veteran with an incisive intelligence and a fund of patience and good nature that made him ideal for the job. The team was working with the Third Kandak of 205 Brigade of the ANA. Mahaffy was anxious to squash any suggestion that the Afghans were playing the role of native levies. "They lead the way themselves," he said. "They conduct the operations themselves. We're merely an outside eye looking over them . . . definitely not leading — just mentoring and looking after them." The ANA were deployed in eleven locations around Sangin with small groups of six or seven British mentors alongside to offer help and advice.

Mahaffy had been impressed on arrival by the quality of the human material he would be working with. "We heard all the horror stories before we came out here but we were pleasantly surprised," he said. "They're courageous, they're gutsy. They'll go for it and they know when not to go for it." Fighting spirit was the essential quality the mentors were looking for and the Afghans seemed to have in abundance. Mahaffy recognised that "what actually fires them up is having a guy killed. It's the same as us . . . you can see it in their eyes. When they see one of their dead soldiers, that's it, they just want to go and kill everything in their path. When you channel them the right way and they go off to do it, they're great."

The Third Kandak was made up of volunteers drawn from all over Afghanistan. Their looks reflected the physical diversity of their country. As well as the dark-haired, dark-skinned Pashtuns there were broad-faced Tajiks and Uzbeks and a few who were as pale as Europeans, a genetic legacy, it was said, of the Soviet invasion. The battalion was commanded by Colonel Rassoul and the brigade by General Muhaydin, who were both in their fifties.

Despite a certain mutual respect for each other's warlike qualities, the British and Afghan approaches to soldiering did not sit together easily. The Afghans were impetuous and fatalistic. Their indifference to risk had been shown by the shooting incident on the road back from the Sangin bazaar. All the ANA troops in all the locations followed the same routine every day. After morning prayers, a detail set off to market to get the day's provisions. In theory, shopping locally rather than relying on trucked-in rations was a good thing. The food was better, which kept the soldiers happy, their business stimulated the local economy and the sight of uniforms in the bazaar was reassuring. The problem was that the soldiers had settled into a fixed routine. The Taliban knew exactly when they would be setting off and set regular ambushes. In the previous three months, three soldiers had been killed on the market run. Yet despite persistent urging by the Brits to consider changing their patterns of movement, the soldiers still jumped into their Ford Rangers every day and headed off to the bazaar.

"We can tell them a hundred times but they are going to have their fresh bread and fresh meat and they're going to the bazaar when they want to," said Mahaffy. "If we say to them, you know, guys, you're going to get killed if you keep doing this the response is *inshallah* [if it's God's will] and that's their way."

The Royal Irish had received a stark lesson in the Afghans' contempt for the basic rules of safety from an incident at the district centre a few weeks after their arrival. An ANA soldier had been having problems mounting an RPG on its launcher and tried to get it to lock by hammering it on the ground. The RPG exploded, killing him and several of his comrades.

One of the main obstacles to harmonising operations was the difficulty of coordinating air power with Afghan ground operations. The Afghans had no air assets of their own. Nor did they have artillery bigger than mortars. They relied on the foreigners' attack helicopters and fast jets and big guns when they got into trouble. The problem was that to provide artillery and air support required disciplines and skills that the Afghans lacked. To call in an air strike or fire mission you needed to give precise grid references to avoid killing your own men. To do that you had to be able to read a map. Most of the ANA could not, though the deficiency was now being addressed in training.

There was a potentially deeper dissonance between the military cultures. The Afghans were hopeless at future planning. It showed in their lack of fire discipline when they clashed with the Taliban. They would shoot every bullet, never bothering to keep a magazine in reserve in case they ran into another ambush on the way back to base. It applied to everything. "The Afghan soldier worries about where he gets his food today, his water today, and he'll think about tomorrow morning when it's tomorrow morning," said Mahaffy.

The mentors took the sensible view that there was no point in trying to do things as they were done at Sandhurst or Brecon, and kept to the forefront the principle that ultimately Afghans would have to do things for themselves. "We have a phrase," said Wally Mahaffy. "We would rather have them do it tolerably than we do it perfectly and that's what we try and stick by."

Progress towards self-sufficiency was, however, dauntingly slow. Looking back after his tour was over, Mahaffy concluded that "there are three stages. One, do it for them. Two, help them to do it. Three, let them do it. We must get to stage three. We are at stage one, moving on to stage two. Stage three is a long way away".

For mentoring to work the instructors had to feel a degree of affection for their pupils. Not all the British soldiers who lived and fought alongside the Afghans did. There was scorn for their indiscipline, particularly when it came to sanitary arrangements. A new ablutions block had been built for the Afghan troops in the base. The toilets packed up within a few weeks. On investigation it turned out they were clogged with the pebbles that the soldiers used to clean themselves with. Many preferred to take a dump in the green spaces of the camp.

Mahaffy had an obvious liking for his charges. He and the other mentors lived with them and shared the food they cooked on the campfires at night and danced with them when they celebrated someone's engagement. "The only way these guys will ever respect us is to get inside their minds and go native," he said. "So it's off with the boots and sit cross-legged on the floor and drink the *chai*. You're here for six months so you might as well get on with it." Somewhat to his surprise he had found the experience enjoyable. "I would do it all again tomorrow, without a doubt," he said. "It's been a pleasure, it really has."

Sometimes the Afghans' rough-and-ready way of doing things had benefits that were not immediately obvious to Western eyes. Early in the tour, Colonel Rassoul had initiated an operation to clear an area south of the base in which one of his men had been killed. Before it began he called a shura of local leaders. The British were long accustomed to holding shuras, as a way of broadcasting their intentions, testing the local atmospherics and, with any luck, picking up information. They approached the task with careful regard for local sensibilities. It soon became clear that the ANA had a different way of doing things.

"As far as we were concerned, a shura was people coming freely to sit down and talk with the local commander, exchange a few thoughts and go away," said Mahaffy. When he arrived at the ANA-convened event, however, he found that the elders had "more or less been brought over by the scruff of the neck . . . and plonked down on the floor. It was non-optional." The round-up took thirty minutes and by the end there were nearly two hundred men squatting on the ground, waiting to hear the colonel. He delivered a harangue, holding them responsible for the death of his soldier and warning suspected insurgents in the crowd that he had his eye on them. Then he strode out. Afterwards Mahaffy asked him "why the grabbing and the plonking them down? He said, 'If I asked them to come freely, how many would come? Maybe twenty. The Taliban would be watching them and by the evening they would have been shot in the head.' " By taking the robust approach, the colonel had got his message across "and probably saved lives in the process". It was the Afghan way of doing things. But it was not an example that the rules the British imposed on themselves allowed them to follow.

For all the cultural differences, the shared dangers of Sangin created real bonds of comradeship between Afghan and Brit. The Taliban did not make any significant distinction between foreign unbelievers and their co-religionists and countrymen who sided with the government. They were both targets. The Allies fought as hard for each other as they did for their own, as had been demonstrated in an incident earlier in the tour when the Taliban launched a series of attacks northwards, up the 611 towards the town. An ANA patrol had lost two dead and had a third seriously wounded and had retreated into Patrol Base Waterloo, which sat on the highway nearly three kilometres south of the Sangin district centre. The casualty would be dead if he was not extracted within sixty minutes. Mahaffy and a Royal Irish team jumped into two WMIKs and with two ANA vehicles fought their way down the road to the base. They arrived at Waterloo in a blizzard of crossfire. The insurgents were plastering the base with RPGs and machine-gun fire and the sangars were shooting back. They loaded the casualty on to the back of an ANA Ford Ranger with a corpse on top of him to provide protection, then steeled themselves for the return journey back to the district centre where a casevac helicopter could pick up the wounded man. "Rounds were going out, rounds were going in, then it was sort of three, two, one, go!" said Mahaffy. Just as the gates were hauled open, Tony Mason, a Royal Irish sergeant who was fighting alongside the ANA, shouted out: "Wally! Have you got any mail with you?" They emerged to see a wave of ANA soldiers advancing at a run across the field opposite the base, charging the insurgent firing points in a row of trees in what Mahaffy regarded as an act of "pure bravery". The diversion allowed the rescue party to race up the road and back to the district centre. The wounded man, who had taken two bullets to the abdomen, survived. The incident had a significance greater than the saving of a life. "The ANA look at us and they know that we put our lives on the line for them." This story and others like it were essential in maintaining morale. Both partners had to know that the other would be sharing equally in a struggle which, even the optimists admitted, had no clear end in sight.

Judged by life in Sangin, progress was halting, the achievements modest, each small success vulnerable and liable to swift reverse. The human material on which success would be built was weak and unreliable. Governor Isatullah ignored official warnings to end his illegal taxation activities. When his men continued to prey on the local economy and were duly arrested, he was forced to resign. There was a heated confrontation at the base, and one afternoon in October he boarded a helicopter and left for good. His replacement got off to a good start but experience counselled against the raising of hopes. "The Afghans simply don't understand what good governance is, what a governor is supposed to do or what a town administration is supposed to deliver for the town," said one sympathetic officer. It was relatively easy to recruit trained individuals in moderately secure places like Lashkar Gah and Kandahar. "But in rural communities it is hard to find locals who are educated, knowledgeable, experienced and respected by the local communities." It was unlikely that the few who were would "head to somewhere like Sangin because of the ongoing risks and perceived lack of security".

That perception only deepened as the summer wore on. The number of IED strikes increased and the devices were now more sophisticated. On 15 August a roadside bomb killed three ANA soldiers on the 611 less than two kilometres from the district centre.

Despite the dangers there was some reconstruction progress. By the end of the year, the new college was almost completed and the first phase of the road resurfacing programme was finished. It was little things, though, which gave the most encouragement. One officer found that "simple daily situations provide a glimmer of hope, such as when a man is willing to walk five miles despite threats and intimidation from the Taliban just to sit in a shura". They were small highlights in a dark picture. There were few who would argue with the same officer's assessment that after more than two years of constant fighting and enormous effort in Sangin "our aims, even the military ones, are a long way off".

CHAPTER
ELEVEN

The White Cliffs of Helmand

Counter-insurgency operations had been memorably described by T. E. Lawrence as "like trying to eat soup with a knife". They were messy, awkward and frustrating. A lot of effort was often expended with very little result. The truth of Lawrence's observation was brought home to 3 Para on another foray into Band-e-Timor, the prime opium-growing belt of western Kandahar where they had started their tour. On the morning of Sunday, 3 August, the Paras took off from KAF to support a mission to grab a "medium-value target" who had his base in the area. The prize was Mullah Multan, another narco baron who had teamed up with the insurgents. The operation had been devised by Regional Command South.

Multan's set-up was a model of efficiency that made full use of his logistics capacity to the equal benefit of the Taliban and himself. He exported raw opium along tracks that ran across the desert, south to the Pakistan border. His vehicles returned laden with arms and fighters. The route also served to evacuate wounded insurgents across the open frontier, where they could be treated in peace. The aim was to swoop without warning in a helicopter assault and to kill or capture Multan and his entourage.

The day started at dawn when they gathered by the runway at KAF for a heads-up from the intelligence cell at RCS headquarters that Multan and his men were at home and the op was definitely on. At 7.45 the green light was given. They piled on to the Chinooks for the short flight along the Arghandab river valley to the objective. The omens seemed good. As they closed on the target, though, they were spotted by Multan and his men in the area. As the Paras descended, they saw three pick-up trucks loaded with men driving away into the fields.

The Chinooks were escorted by attack helicopters. But neither they nor the Predator UAV overhead were able to say for sure that the fugitives were carrying weapons. The rules of engagement were very clear on when they could fire and when they couldn't. The helicopters looked on impotently as the men dismounted from the trucks and disappeared into the vegetation of the Green Zone.

The Paras landed 200 metres from the compound. When they entered, there was no one inside. "It was like the *Mary Celeste*," said Sergeant Peter "Razor" Reynolds of 8 Platoon. "Food was still being cooked, doorways partially open, motorbikes lying down on their sides." They searched a second cluster of buildings. There they had more luck, turning up two PKM machine guns and some ammunition, hidden in waterproofed underground caches. It was getting hot. Razor Reynolds went off to fetch some water. He had spent some time working in the "int" cell and was by his own admission "quite nosy", so when he saw an unusual-looking hatch set into the side of a building he decided to investigate. "I kicked through the hatch, put my head round and it was like another room," he said. "So I walked round the other side and there was a fake mud wall kind of thing. They obviously only used it in an emergency. I smashed the door down, went in there and found a big bundle of money . . . there was drugs and stuff, beds everywhere." Reynolds had stumbled on a Taliban field hospital, complete with stretchers, intravenous drips and stacks of pharmaceuticals.

When the Paras reached the abandoned pick-up trucks in which the gang had fled he made another interesting find. On the back seat of one he found three large bales. "I thought it was just hay first of all," he said. "Then I got my bayonet out and I stabbed into it." The sack oozed a sticky, reddish brown substance and Reynolds was hit by a familiar smell. "I was thinking, what does that remind me of?" He recalled days earlier in the tour, "walking through poppy fields getting the residue all over you and I twigged it must be drugs. I knew that at this time of year there would be a lot of caches of drugs around". He cut open the bales and discovered "bags and bags" of "wet" opium, as the resin is called before it is refined into heroin. In all the haul weighed 70 kilograms and was worth millions of pounds to Multan and the Taliban. The capture of the drugs was, felt Reynolds, "a massive kick in the balls" for the insurgents. They destroyed the drugs with a phosphorus grenade, trying not to breathe in the billowing fumes as the opium went up in smoke.

The compounds clearly were important to Multan's operations. As the day wore on they came across a room with communications equipment, which chirruped constantly. Elsewhere they discovered a cache of mobile phones still in their packaging. But despite the finds, their target had got clean away. The Paras had not even had the satisfaction of a fight.

This was the second major disappointment for 3 Para in a couple of weeks. Eighteen days previously the second-in-command, John Boyd, had enjoyed a taste of command leading an operation deep into southern Helmand to an area known as the "Fish Hook". Again, they had set off buoyed up with the prospect of eliminating a significant commander and blowing a hole in the insurgents' infrastructure. The target was a key figure who was based in an old Soviet fort, which also served as a training camp. According to one officer who took part there was "very, very strong intelligence" that the Taliban leader and his men would be *in situ*. Boyd and a mixed force of 400 British and Afghan soldiers arrived by helicopter on the morning of 15 July to find an empty fort. The suspicion was that the details of the operation had leaked out via the Afghans.

Now they had been thwarted once again and there was frustration in the air as they slumped down wearily at the end of the day in a nearby compound rented from a local farmer. It was to be their home for the next week. As well as the strike operation they were supposed to be reasserting the ISAF presence in Band-e-Timor. The RCS plan had been drawn up by an Australian colonel and was based on the notion that the area was filling up with insurgents who had taken refuge there after being driven north by a big surge from the US Marines in the Garmsir area to the southwest. The Paras' job was to "set the conditions" for the arrival of more American troops, who, it was planned, were going to establish a permanent presence in Band-e-Timor later in the year.

The British were sceptical from the start. Their experience of the early summer had been that it was a relatively benign area and nothing they had heard since had altered that view. According to someone who took part in the planning, however, "it had got quite personal with the Aussie colonel. It was his baby and he was driving it forward at all costs".

As it was, the British misgivings were justified. The daily patrols and searches turned up a few more minor finds but there was no sign of the Taliban. Steve Boardman and his team renewed contacts with some local leaders and plans were made for the newly appointed district leader to come from Hutal for a shura. But the results were disproportionate to the effort involved and soldiers at all levels of 3 Para believed they would have been better employed elsewhere.

Once again the intelligence picture had failed to match reality. The Paras had come to recognise that the only reliable information came from areas where there was an established ISAF presence, such as the Zari and

Panjwaii districts west of Kandahar where the Canadians had been from the beginning, or the British areas around Sangin. There was no centralised ISAF intelligence database and the lack of coherence was intensified by the Allies' tendency to regard each other with varying degrees of trust when it came to sharing what they knew. The Americans were inclined to be fairly generous with their "int" when it came to the British, but were less open with the Canadians. The Canadians, according to one Para officer who dealt with them regularly, "set their intelligence restrictions higher than they need be". In the "Fish Hook" operation, the Paras had been working alongside a Polish team. But before they could pass on any information to them they had to first clear it with the Canadians.

Over the next days, between patrols, there would be plenty of time to discuss what had gone wrong and to think about the bigger questions that the tour was throwing up. The compound where they set up camp was like a thousand others. It was an enclosure about 100 metres square, planted with pomegranate bushes and a few fruit trees. There were two wide-mouthed wells from which the soldiers could haul the water that glinted darkly in the cool depths, 3 metres below. The main dwelling house was a mud-brick cube. Inside was a single living room, completely unfurnished except for a few cheap carpets and cushions stacked against the wall. The only decoration was some painted tinware and an electric clock propped on a long shelf.

246

The soldiers slept on their mats, unrolling them close to the shrubs and trees, as if the foliage would provide a degree of coolness. The stifling warmth of the day lingered on well into the night as the earth exhaled the heat it had absorbed from the pounding sun. It was only in the early hours of the morning that any freshness crept into the air.

Once the last tasks were done and the sentries were posted, they settled down to relax. It was time for a brew, for a fag if you were one of the dwindling number of smokers and for the conversation to begin. Soldiers love talking. It is just as well, given the long hours they spend waiting for a helicopter to land or take off or for their next set of orders to come through. They will talk about anything from football to astrophysics, for in any company there is always someone who is an expert on something unexpected. The talk is usually light-hearted, and often funny, spiced with a wit that is sharp but subtle and only occasionally reliant on obscenity for effect.

Deciding to become a soldier nowadays requires considerable reflection and self-examination. Very few take the step without having thought about what they are doing and making a cool assessment of their own qualities and capabilities. The conversations to be heard in the FOBs and PBs and improvised camps were often stimulating, sometimes surreal and anarchic and always honest. Bullshit cannot survive long in a climate of withering frankness and constant mickey-taking.

When they got away from discussing practicalities, the things the soldiers talked about often had nothing to do with Afghanistan. Talking was an escape and a relaxation, a holiday from the tedium spiked with danger that was Afghan duty. Yet that did not mean they did not think about what they were doing there. It took some probing, though, to unearth what was being left unsaid.

Belief in the cause is by no means a prerequisite for efficient and enthusiastic soldiering. I had seen the British Army on all their main actions of the last quarter-century. It seemed to me that in the Falklands in 1982 the soldiers, outwardly at least, were unconcerned with the principles of sovereignty and self-determination they were risking their lives to uphold, and cared little for the woman who had sent them there. The same was true of the Gulf War of 1991, when the participants were largely unmoved by the plight of little Kuwait, to whose rescue they were charging. In the return match eleven years later, they appeared to regard Saddam as a jovial pantomime villain rather than the monster of Downing Street and White House propaganda.

The truth is that British soldiers welcome wars as an occasion for adventure, an opportunity to add to the glory of their unit and above all a chance to test themselves, their courage, their mettle and their coolness under fire.

But all wars are different. The Falklands and the 1991 Gulf War had been fleeting affairs in terms of the amount of time spent actually fighting. The first lasted weeks and the second days. The initial combat had been equally brief in Iraq in 2003, and the deployment rapidly settled down into a grim and unglamorous policing operation which, politicians had made it clear, would not be allowed to drag on for ever.

Afghanistan was different. The initial thrill of fighting the Taliban might sustain combat virgins through their first tour. It was now obvious, though, that anyone intending an army career would have to return again and again. Afghan duty was becoming as inevitable a part of army life as Northern Ireland had been in the seventies, eighties and nineties. But life was far more uncomfortable than it had been in Ulster and was becoming much more dangerous. The new conditions were already stretching and fraying family bonds, as professional duties took precedence over obligations to spouses and children. Pre-deployment training exercises meant that soldiers were frequently away from home during the run-up to the actual six months of the tour. "It kills the blokes, kills the families," said a company commander. It was the privates and NCOs rather than the officers who would bear the brunt of the repeated tours. Their different career trajectories meant that those with commissions were probably not going to spend more than three or four tours commanding troops in the field. Those without them might have to return to the sharp end again and again throughout their careers.

To maintain the natural enthusiasm that most soldiers feel for front-line operational service, it helped to believe that the hardship and risk were worth it. In the summer of 2008 it was by no means clear where the mission was heading.

The decision to pitch the army into Afghanistan was taken with remarkably little fuss. It was a very bold move, both politically and militarily. Britain was already engaged in an unpopular and unrewarding war in Iraq. The historical precedents were ominous. British armies had fought three wars in Afghanistan since 1838 and suffered disastrous tactical defeats and political frustration. There seems to have been little dissent inside the Cabinet at the decision, however, and the Conservative Party broadly supported the move. They accepted Prime Minister Blair's argument that Britain was fulfilling an undertaking it had given to the United States in the aftermath of the attacks of 11 September 2001 that it would share the burden of building a stable and democratic Afghanistan. The armed services, which were most affected by the decision, seem to have raised only technical questions about the mission. Their instinctive attitude was to respond positively when new tasks and duties were proposed. It was one reason why governments were always so lavish in their public praise for the forces. It was only after proposals hardened into reality that the services' concerns emerged. What opposition there was to the venture came largely from the media, with a number of voices, expert and otherwise, warning of the dire consequences of embracing once again the Afghan tar baby.

The government felt it needed to paint an enticing picture of the benefits that a major military investment in Afghanistan would bring. The mission was presented as a great civilising enterprise. Its aims, as listed by the then Defence Secretary John Reid to the House of

Commons in January 2006, were dauntingly ambitious. The long-term goal was to "help the people to build a democratic state with strong security forces and an economy that will support a civil society". This was to be achieved through a "tailored package of political, developmental and military assistance".

The first task, though, was to establish security. The 3 Para Battlegroup was to "deny terrorists an ungoverned space in which they can foment and export terror". Reid was later to be accused of suggesting that this could be a relatively risk-free business. In an interview with the BBC from KAF in April, shortly after the deployment began, he said that "if we came for three years here to accomplish our mission and had not fired one shot at the end of it we would be very happy indeed". The charge of complacency was unfair. In his Commons statement Reid had emphasised "the difficulties and risks" involved. But these, he declared, were "nothing compared to the dangers to our country and our people of allowing Afghanistan to fall back into the hands of the Taliban".

The notion that Afghanistan, 5600 kilometres distant, was the front line in a war whose effects, if it went wrong, would be felt painfully in the cities of Britain was the one consistent reason given by the government for the decision. Politicians asserted often that more needed to be done to explain honestly and plainly to a sceptical public why Britain was in Afghanistan. But when they spoke about it there was a tendency to use a rhetoric of justification that grew more florid as the months passed, losses mounted and

251

public disillusionment deepened. Foreign Secretary David Miliband claimed in June 2008 that the Afghanistan conflict was as significant to Britain as had been the Second World War.

He told an interviewer from the *Daily Mail*, "why we are there is straightforward. Sixty or seventy years ago the armed forces defended Britain on the White Cliffs of Dover. Now to defend Britain we have got to be in the toughest areas of the world like Afghanistan. So the purpose of the mission is absolutely clear. It is to make sure Afghanistan does not become a safe haven for people who want to plot against the UK."

By the end of the year the Second World War analogy was embedded in the government's language. John Hutton, an intelligent and thoughtful politician who had taken over as Defence Secretary in October 2008, said the forces were engaged in a "vital national security mission". He told *The Times*, "it is a struggle against fanatics that may not challenge our borders but challenges our way of life in the same way the Nazis did". Public opinion was reluctant to accept this interpretation and backing for the war had been showing a long decline. In November 2008 a poll suggested that 68 per cent of Britons would like to see their troops out of Afghanistan by the end of the following year.

Soldiers tended to avoid historical comparisons when assessing the campaign. They did, however, share the politicians' basic view. "We are out there to stop international terrorism proliferating elsewhere," said Mark Carleton-Smith simply. From the ground it was easy to overlook the strategic implications of the struggle. The Taliban were vicious and ignorant, sadists and bullies and haters of women. But they did not seem intent on taking over the world. The insurgents operating in southern Afghanistan were, if anything, narrowly parochial in their outlook. They presented themselves as nationalists, Afghan patriots who were motivated as much by hatred of the outsider as they were by love of Allah. There were some foreign fighters among them who shared al-Qaeda's dream of a global caliphate but they were a definite minority and did not appear to be running the show. The Taliban message was that they wanted everyone to clear out and for them to be left to build Afghanistan to their own grim liking. At first sight it was easy to conclude that the insurgents posed a dire threat to the people they claimed they were fighting to liberate. It was harder to see how they menaced the streets and stations of London, Manchester, Glasgow or Bristol.

To understand the rationale underlying the mission required some effort. It was necessary to think beyond the boundaries of southern Afghanistan. The British expedition to Helmand was part of a pre-emptive strategy. The province, as Mark Carleton-Smith knew well, had been relatively quiet before the Paras' arrival. In 2005 he had been tasked to take an undercover look at the place and report back on conditions. He found there was "a live-and-let-live modus vivendi" between the governor, a corrupt tribal leader closely involved in the opium trade, the other drug barons and a faction who classed themselves as "Taliban". In Carleton-Smith's assessment this was more of a label than a conviction, and they were better regarded as being simply anti-government. Until then they had been left alone by ISAF and the Afghan army and were not seeking to draw attention to themselves. "You could drive around Helmand and drink tea with all sorts of people who today would kill you," Carleton-Smith remembered.

He reported back to London: "There is not to my mind an insurgency in Helmand. But we can create one if we want to." It was a wry joke. His real conclusion was that the stability was superficial and "masked a much more insidious strategic threat which, if left, would have resulted in a resurgent Taliban".

Carleton-Smith did not dispute that disrupting the status quo had changed the place for the worse in the short term. "There's a lot of fighting, it's noisy, it's uncomfortable and it's frightening for a lot of the people. So that smacks of failure and a lack of security." This, however, was "the price of neutering the strategic threat, which would have been [allowing] the Taliban to grow unmolested".

Critics of the war argued that the arrival of the British in Helmand had actually encouraged the Taliban revival. The counter-claim was that it would have happened anyway, as soon as the government and its foreign backers sought to expand central authority into the south. As it was, Carleton-Smith believed that the Taliban had been contained. Helmand was a buffer against expansion. As long as they were preoccupied with fighting the British and Danes there, they were unable to concentrate their forces on Kandahar. Kandahar was Afghanistan's second city and the birthplace of the movement.

There were many who thought that, given the army's great depth of combat and counter-insurgency experience, it would have been better if they had been deployed there, instead of the Canadians, who were relatively new to the business.

But Helmand was where the Brits were and where they were likely to stay. Withdrawal from the province for military or political reasons would bring the Taliban a huge symbolic victory and undermine the foundations of rule in Kabul. The chances of the insurgents driving ISAF out by force of arms were tiny, and despite the persistent alarmist tone of most media reporting, they were a long way from destabilising the Afghan government. Like every commander who had been in Afghanistan, Carleton-Smith urged the need for more troops. But in general, the prognosis was good. "So long as the Taliban are contained . . . then we are doing our job, because over time the Afghan government must surely get better if we invest in the right areas at the right level."

The worst development would be a failure of nerve. He warned that "if the international community were to give up, if we were to give up, I think we would probably consign Afghanistan to another cycle of civil war where frankly all bets would then be off." Breaking off would open up the real and terrifying possibility of "the Talibanisation of Pakistan . . . a lot of those Talibs may recognise that there's a greater strategic prize at home, and that they no longer need to commute to work across the border. And that's the greatest strategic concern to the international community — that a nuclear-armed state collapses."

During 2008 it seemed clear that the Taliban had indeed woken up to that realisation. By the start of 2009 they had gained control of the Swat Valley in Pakistan's North West Frontier province. Through violence and intimidation they imposed their rule on the 1.3 million inhabitants, haranguing them via radio broadcasts against unIslamic activities like selling DVDs, watching cable TV, singing, dancing and allowing girls to go to school. Those who disobeyed their edicts were liable to be murdered. In February their dominance was recognised when the president of Pakistan, Asif Ali Zardari, agreed a "truce" with the Taliban that allowed them to impose sharia law in Swat. The arrangement dismayed the Obama administration's special representative in the region, Richard Holbrooke, who said he found it "hard to understand this deal" and expressed concern that it should "not turn into a surrender". Swat was not part of the traditionally lawless tribal areas on the border but a part of Pakistan proper, only 160 kilometres from the capital, Islamabad.

Most of the soldiers shared the view that their sector of the battlefield was just part of a much broader front and had a direct bearing on safety at home. "I see our job as nothing short of protecting the people of Britain," said a young 3 Para lieutenant. "Making it safe for people like my girlfriend to travel to work with less or no fear of being blown up."

They also felt that the value of what they were doing was little understood, either by civilians at home or the governments of some of the NATO countries that were failing to give more than token support to the mission. "I don't think the British public remain convinced that the war in Afghanistan is about a threat to national security," said an experienced 3 Para major. "They don't see the linkages between the stability of Afghanistan in years to come and domestic terrorism . . . the easy readiness with which you could link [Afghanistan] to 9/11 and the July bombings in London has been eroded." Instead it was the other way round. People were more likely to blame bombs in Britain on our presence in Iraq and Afghanistan and wonder why we were there. They were inclined to think the best way of preventing attacks was to withdraw rather than to tackle the terrorists on their home ground.

Most of the soldiers seemed to believe that the overall strategy was the right one and their struggle and sacrifices were worth while. The main frustration was that there were not enough of them to do their job more effectively.

There was a general belief that public opinion, fed by media coverage that was almost universally seen as carping and unconstructive, would prevent the government from increasing numbers significantly. The extra troops needed were unlikely to come in any quantity from Britain's European allies. Only the

Americans, it was felt, were really "in it to win it". The French, the Italians and the Germans, who did not contribute combat troops to Regional Command South, were making what amounted to a token commitment. Of those who were fighting in the south, the Canadians and the Dutch were only committed to stay until 2011 and 2010, respectively. The Canadians had 2800 troops in theatre, the largest contingent after the US and Britain. They had suffered the heaviest losses of any ISAF nation. By April 2009, 116 soldiers had died and public opinion was deeply sceptical about the value of the mission. One officer wondered how long it would take the Taliban to realise that "the way they are going to fracture the NATO endeavour is to find the weakest members of the coalition and focus all their attack efforts on them".

A 2 Para captain agreed that "NATO, with the UK, USA, Canada, Denmark and Estonia excepted, is not pulling its weight and lacks the moral courage to commit ground forces to the most dangerous areas". France and Germany were "the biggest offenders. The countries that have stepped up to the plate are maxed out — it is these countries that risk losing the support of their own people because of the high casualties and increasing financial cost."

The lack of enthusiasm for the war at home, though, did not seem to affect the spirit with which the soldiers went about their work. Once you were in the field the important thing was to get through the tour, and little time was wasted in reflecting on the bigger issues. With some, though, the public indifference and scepticism rankled. "A" Company contained a number of reservists, who had suspended their careers to come to Afghanistan for the full tour. The life they led, split between the civvy and the uniformed world, gave them a close insight into the attitudes of those in whose name the war was being fought. Among them was a twenty-six-year-old Scotsman who had taken time out from his job as a corporate lawyer in Edinburgh to go to Afghanistan as a platoon commander. Like most, he was grateful for the warm public affection the military was currently enjoying and the general climate of sympathy for the sacrifices they were having to make. But he "felt a bit frustrated when I hear people say we support the troops but we don't support the war . . . I think that just undermines the efforts of the blokes and I think it's contradictory".

He believed fervently that "we've got to be fighting them out here so we are not fighting them back home because [if we don't] that will happen eventually". In the past he had argued the case with sceptics, including his own grandfather, who had asked him what he thought going to Afghanistan would achieve. Now he tended to keep his opinions quiet. He agreed with his bosses that the best way to explain his absence was by saying he had gone off on an attachment to a bank for six months. Like John Hutton, he saw the struggle as having the same moral dimensions as the Second World War. "Sixty years ago people stayed the course," he said. "They saw what was bad and they said we are not going to have this change our way of life."

Another reservist was a civil servant in a London ministry. He was equally sure that the effort was worth it, and had also encountered indifference or unreflecting opposition among friends and colleagues. "Clearly there is . . . a direct cause and effect between what is going on here and al-Qaeda, the Taliban and terrorism throughout the world," he said. "That wasn't the case for Iraq. I think there is more reason to be in here than certainly there was in Iraq and it's just maintaining that level of commitment . . . it's difficult, especially when casualties start mounting." In some ways the effectiveness of the strategy in tying up terrorists so they were not able to reproduce the success of 9/11 had caused it to fade from memory and made it harder to justify.

It was supposed to be a conflict with global significance. But everywhere, homecoming soldiers encountered profound and dispiriting ignorance, not just of the situation in Afghanistan but of the very nature of soldiering. A 3 Para corporal returned to his native New Zealand after his tour to find "the average Kiwi has no real idea about our situation. I've also found a lot very naive. You wouldn't believe the amount of times virtual strangers have asked me that horrible question 'so how many people have you killed?' and then gawked at me expecting me to launch into some Rambo-like tale of blood and guts with a grin on my face."

He was clear about his reasons for being in Afghanistan and the order in which he listed his priorities was telling. They were "to bring stability and peace to the people of Afghanistan, to combat militant Islam and at some stage to curb the traffic of narcotics out of that country and into the wider world, which is for me very important as I'm very much a hater of drugs".

Some encountered a slight atmosphere of embarrassment among civilians at home, which would have been familiar to Tommies returning to Blighty from the trenches. "Often I feel like they're walking on broken glass and tend not to ask me much about the tour," said a young lieutenant. "Questions are generally confined to benign topics such as what the weather was like or how was the food? I get very few questions about serious topics. The people at home are a world away and don't really have a clue what's going on there. They mostly appear to be too busy with their own lives and don't seem to perceive the threat that there is."

Public opinion was, for many of the soldiers, of strictly limited interest. Soldiers, especially members of a volunteer army, operate in a semi-enclosed world with its own values and codes of conduct. Their outlook often differed from that of the society from which they had been drawn. That was something that they recognised and took satisfaction from. By joining the army they had passed through a portal to a place where honesty and duty counted more than they did in civvy street and people cared as much about each other as they did about themselves. "Civilians are a lot more selfish and everything's about getting from A to B," said a veteran colour sergeant. He found civilian life was "not very friendly. We're not afraid of talking to people even if we don't really know them. If you bump into someone out on the ground . . . you become friends. You don't see civilians do that because there's a lack of trust." Civilians inhabited a domain the soldiers had chosen, at least temporarily, to leave behind. The words and thoughts of the outside world barely carried over the barrack wall, and when they did they often went unheeded. Behind it lay a world that was satisfying, sometimes exciting and most of all felt like home.

Corporal Mike French and Corporal Marc Stott were two of the battalion's outstanding younger NCOs. French was twenty-seven. He had the regiment in his blood. His father and his uncle were ex-3 Para. He had signed on aged sixteen and started training three months later as soon as he was legally able. The waiting time had been spent working in a garage. "I hated it," he said. "I joined the army and never looked back." Stott's father had been in the navy and at first it had been thought that he would go for the Royal Marines. During his researches he decided the Paras looked more interesting. He was twenty-four and, like French, a veteran of the fighting in 2006.

French had specialised in combat medicine and combined skill as a healer with a continuing enthusiasm for fighting. He had been in Inkerman with "B" Company, where his body armour saved him when he was hit in the side by red-hot shrapnel from an RPG while patrolling with Stu McDonald. Despite weeks spent in Musa Qaleh, one of the hottest spots in 2006, the buzz of being in a contact never faded. "My heart still pumps every time that first round wings past you," he said. It was the same for Sergeant Major Stu Bell. At thirty-eight years old, Bell was one of the older men in the battalion. He had served in Helmand in 2006, where he entered 3 Para legend. He was unloading mortar rounds off the back of a Chinook in the middle of a firefight when it took off prematurely. Seeing the ground receding, he jumped off the ramp rather than abandon his mates, hurting his leg badly in the process. Bell had volunteered to go to Inkerman as a mortar fire controller, where he had enjoyed himself during the 27 July patrol. He was a good-natured man, looked up to by the younger Paras, who started life as a baker and was as expert with a piping bag as he was with a mortar barrel. But he was honest about the hot-blooded rush of elation mixed with fear that combat gave. "I don't think anybody could say that getting shot at isn't exciting," he said. "It can also be nerve-racking and it can be scary, depending on how serious the contact or the incident gets. Whichever side of the fence you sit [on] . . . it makes your heart race."

Whatever their higher motivations, almost every soldier wanted to experience combat at least once in their career. "The blokes obviously enjoy the time out here," Stott said. What bothered them was when they were "sat around doing nothing . . . they are just thinking I can't wait to get home". But "when you're out doing your job, that's when the lads are happy because they are doing what they want to do . . . this is what they joined the army for. They are out here fighting, they are toe to toe with the enemy."

The only praise that really counted was that given by other soldiers. French, like many, was not interested in homecoming parades or civilians buying him drinks. "To be honest I don't really care," he said. "People don't really appreciate the army the way I think they should but I know your family do and your friends do . . . But your random civilian, I don't really care what he thinks . . . it's me that's out here."

The civilian world seemed to find difficulty in accepting that the soldiers had made a free choice. "All these people [are] whingeing, 'Oh, bring our troops home'," said French. "They don't think of asking what do our troops want to do? The majority of our lads, if they were told you're going to Afghanistan or you can stay home if you want to, they would be, like, 'oh, Afghan, six months, lose some weight, get a good tan, save a decent amount of money . . . I'll go to Afghan.' "

There was more to it than that. The experience, in Marc Stott's view, literally made a man of you. In his section was a private who had turned nineteen the previous month. "When he first came into the platoon he was a normal eighteen-year-old who wanted to do his own thing and thought he knew best, [as] eighteen-year-olds do," he said. "[But] he's changed so much out here . . . he's turned into an adult . . . and he's turned into more of a man and he's gone home and he's seen his mum and he came back and he said to me that his mum's said she's proud of him. She said how much he has changed."

And it was not just the men who relished the test. It was now commonplace to see women on any front line in southern Afghanistan. They were medics and translators or, like Corporal Marianne Hay, dog handlers. Hay was twenty-four years old from Banff in Aberdeenshire, one of the Royal Veterinary Corps experts who conducted the explosives and ammunition searches. She had experienced as much danger as any of the Paras. "When they're going to exploit compounds [or] tunnels they'll take me as well," she said. "I'll just go in and search it." She felt bad about putting her springer spaniel, Deanna, in first, but "if there's something in there it's going to be quite dangerous and the guys are more important at the end of the day".

Marianne Hay did not have to be in Afghanistan. She had volunteered and sometimes she wondered why. She had days "when I can't believe I'm here and I think I'm bloody stupid for coming out". But then there were the others when "I absolutely love it and I've even thought about asking to extend and do a winter tour because I think it would be nice and cool . . . I like watching all the guys and the bond they've got with each other and the laugh they have and all that."

The truth that civilians overlooked on the occasions when they thought about what the army was doing in Afghanistan was that the soldiers were pursuing their own personal goals as hard as they were any task set for them by politicians. In August, however, a huge operation was in the making which offered great scope for both public and private satisfaction.

CHAPTER
TWELVE

Convoy

The Kajaki turbine project had an epic quality that set it apart from the rest of the army's Afghan duties. During the preparations it sometimes felt as if the psychological boost it gave the soldiers was as great as the practical benefits it was intended to bring to the inhabitants of southern Afghanistan.

In peacetime the task would have been difficult but manageable. It involved delivering more than 200 tonnes of components across 100 kilometres of rocky track to the powerhouse of the Kajaki Dam, which held back the Helmand river in the hills of the upper Sangin Valley. The insurgency turned it into a major test of logistical and military skills. Negotiating the route would be hard enough. The bigger problem lay with the Taliban, who could be expected to menace the convoy with IEDs, indirect fire and, when it entered close country, direct attack, at every opportunity.

It was a challenge, but one that everyone was up for. Getting the turbine to Kajaki would prove something, to the soldiers themselves, to an outside world that was doubtful of the value of the Afghanistan enterprise, and above all to the people they were there to save. The extra electricity it generated would light the lives of 1.8 million Afghans and power economic growth. Success would count as a real achievement, the high point not only of Herrick 8 but of the two years that British troops had been in the area. The operation would give the British Army the chance to put on a glittering demonstration of its abilities, from the logistical muscle and know-how that the physical move required to the war-fighting that would be needed to protect it. The second task would fall, in the main, to the Paras. They were delighted to be given it.

The project was one of the early improvements planned by the Americans after the 2001 invasion but it had been sitting on the shelf for several years. When running at full capacity the plant at the dam had the potential to supply energy to the whole of Helmand and boost supplies to Kandahar city, 90 kilometres away. At present it was operating at only a fraction of its potential. It had been built to house three turbines but only two had ever been installed. Now it was down to one. The people of the Sangin Valley had electricity for only a few hours a day and relied on generators to light their homes and pump their water. The electricity they did receive was subject to a "tax" by the Taliban. Farmers had to pay the insurgents not to blow up the power lines or murder the technicians who worked at the plant.

Kajaki was a battered symbol of past foreign endeavours to better lives in southern Afghanistan. The dam was built in 1953 with money from the United States Agency for International Development (USAID).

Shimmering behind it, blue in the sunlight, was a vast reservoir of 1.2 cubic kilometres of water which was piped down the valley to trickle through more than two hundred thousand hectares of previously barren land.

The Americans later helped the Afghan government build the hydroelectric plant below the barrage. It was opened in November 1975. The event was marked by a marble plaque in English and Dari on the wall by the main entrance. The following year USAID commissioned two 15.5 megawatt generating units with room left for a third. One turbine was taken away for repairs in May 2006 and had not come back. The British Army would be delivering the third turbine, thirty-three years late.

The spirit of Afghan — American cooperation was still alive at the powerhouse, a square-built concrete vault planted below the dam alongside a mesmerising mill race that jetted out of a hole in the rocks at a rate of 3850 cubic metres per second with a force that would pulverise any creature that fell into it.

The plant was supervised by a short, solid Texan called George Wilder, who worked for the Louis Berger Group, the American contractors in charge of the project. He was sixty-two years old and had long experience of engineering projects in remote and wild parts. He looked and spoke like a Texan is supposed to. He wore jeans and a hard hat, rings and chains of heavy gold, and smoked with old-fashioned zeal. But he had spent his working life outside America and had no desire to go home. He had lived alone at the dam since the end of 2004. "It's a strange life," he said. "It takes a special person to stay here. You have nothing to do here, totally nothing." He was nonetheless determined to stay there until the end. "I have never left a job unfinished in forty-four years," he said. "I will leave when all [three] turbines are in and producing energy. [Only] then will I call it quits."

The chief engineer was Sayed Rassoul, who was "like a brother". He had worked at the plant for twenty-eight years. He led a team of forty-three workers, white-bearded, dignified men, most of whom had been there since the beginning. They had kept the place going through thirty years of war and insecurity. Nowadays the threat was from the Taliban, who controlled the surrounding countryside. After many attempts to capture the dam complex which had been repelled with high losses to the insurgents, they had apparently decided to allow it to function, provided the locals kept up the protection payments. The arrival of the turbine presented them with a clash of interests. The success of the operation would dent their claim to control events in the area. But if they sabotaged the delivery they would be demonstrating in the clearest way the falseness of their claim to be on the side of the people. The staff officers planning the operation had left open the possibility that the Taliban could be persuaded to allow the convoy through unmolested, either by force of argument or the payment of bribes. Even so, experience taught that maximum protection would still be essential.

Despite the inspiring nature of the project, there were some who saw it as a waste of effort. If George

Wilder was going to stay at the dam until electricity was coursing down the valley from three turbines spinning at full revs, he might be there for a long time. Delivering the turbine was not the same as throwing a switch that would light up southern Afghanistan. It had to be installed. The distribution system was ravaged by warfare and neglect. Hundreds of kilometres of power cables and dozens of substations were needed to carry the electricity to where it was needed. This task, given the fragile or non-existent security, might take years. At the highest levels of the Helmand PRT there were officials who regarded the operation as a sideshow, promoted by the Americans to demonstrate that reconstruction was working. The British role, in the words of one senior diplomat, was to "ride shotgun". The military, on the whole, took a more positive approach. They regarded the institutional caution of the civilian bureaucrats as an excuse for inaction. The longest journey started with a single step. Too much scrutiny was a recipe for paralysis. In the discouraging environment of Helmand anything was better than nothing, and it was not as if there was much to show for all the British energy and money that had been poured into the mission.

There were seventy men and women labouring in the heavily fortified PRT headquarters in Lashkar Gah. They supported the four mixed civilian and military Stabilisation Teams based at the main nodes of reconstruction, Gereshk, Garmsir, Sangin and Musa Qaleh. The headquarters was a pleasant spot by Afghan standards, with a garden, an open-air dining area and gym and rows of neat prefabricated offices and accommodation blocks. It was still a dreary place in which to spend any time. There was nothing to do and nowhere to go. An armoured car and armed escort were necessary for the trip into town. The inmates plunged into their work, slaving over computers and producing endless reports from early morning until ten and eleven at night.

But for all their industry, achievement on the ground was slow. The development doctrine now dominant in Whitehall might have altered to give primacy to governance rather than big building projects. But some physical reconstruction needed to be done to give substance to the mission's *raison d'être*, and in all categories progress was measured in centimetres. British ministries were spending about £57 million on non-military schemes in Helmand in 2008/09. They were working to a plan that had been agreed with the Afghan government. It was structured around seven themes. They were politics and reconciliation; governance; security; rule of law (justice, police and prisons); economic development; counter-narcotics; and strategic communications. In short, all the basic functions of a state.

They found it difficult to spend the money allocated. A report issued in late 2008 revealed that DfID had been able to disburse only half the designated funds and had "not been able to deliver all its planned development projects". The environment simply did not allow it. "The high level of insecurity in Helmand makes delivery of all types of aid, including the most basic humanitarian assistance, difficult," the report explained.[1]

There were some improvements to report. The British embassy website listed "achievements since 2006". There were fifty-nine schools open in Helmand, which was an increase of twenty-five, eleven of which were built by the PRT. Pupil enrolment had risen by 10 per cent. That still meant that only 55,000 children were going to school out of an overall population of 745,000. According to the website, the government-contracted health supplier Ibn Sina was now able to operate clinics in all of the district centres in which Britain was working. But the level of treatment they offered was basic and the rural population had to make arduous and dangerous journeys to reach them. Anyone suffering from other than a minor ailment was force to travel to Kandahar. There were some genuine achievements in sight, however. More than $300,000 was being spent on a district health clinic in Musa Qaleh and a similar amount on another in the area which, by the end of 2008, was operational.

There were a few good news stories to tell about economic development and officials were eager to recount them. A commercial bank had opened in Lashkar Gah and a restaurant in Musa Qaleh. A marble factory had been privatised and a local businessman was investing $6 million in an oilseed press that would form part of an agribusiness park. Small businessmen

---

[1] National Audit Office/Department for International Development, *Working in Insecure Environments*, p. 18.

had benefited from loans worth £100,000. Some seemed to signify real progress, such as $1.3 million spent on improvements to a canal, which increased the supply of water to the fields of 10,000 farmers. British funding had resulted in nearly 2500 new wells being dug, which benefited more than 400,000 people. About sixty kilometres of main highway had been resurfaced and repairs done to roads in Lashkar Gah, Sangin, Musa Qaleh and Gereshk.

The same towns had received some benefit from quick-impact projects. These had been built by local Afghan reconstruction companies but managed by the Royal Engineers on behalf of the PRT. The latest figures available showed that 114 had been completed, forty-two were ongoing and sixty more were planned.[1] Much of the work was related to security, building permanent vehicle checkpoints and improving base facilities, or piecemeal schemes that would have only a limited effect. By far the biggest construction project being planned for Helmand province was a huge expansion of the Bastion base, tripling its size to accommodate the surge of American troops into the area planned for 2009.

For all the effort and expenditure there was nothing that could be said to have brought about a major transformation in the quality of life in Helmand. It was nobody's fault except the Taliban's. Every project came with a caveat that it would be carried out "security

---

[1] Parliamentary answer to Tobias Ellwood, MP, from Bob Ainsworth, Ministry of Defence, 9 June 2008.

273

conditions allowing". Security conditions rarely did, or at least not the uninterrupted freedom from risk that would allow major work to be done. Every scheme was liable to suspension or to lying dormant on the drawing board, waiting for a period of stability that never arrived.

The Kajaki turbine project offered the chance to snap the bonds of frustration and deliver something big and meaningful. It was to be called Oqab Tsuka, Eagle's Summit, a name that reflected 16 Air Assault Brigade's insignia. There was a purposeful buzz in the air in the Camp Bastion headquarters of 13 Air Assault Support Regiment, the brigade's logistics arm, which had been given the job of carrying the components to the dam. They were part of the Royal Logistic Corps (RLC). The Loggies were the biggest outfit in the army, the "Really Large Corps", as they liked to say, but they were unknown to the general public. Their comrades in combat units sometimes treated them with good-humoured mockery for the unglamorous nature of their duties. Everyone knew their true value. Nobody could fight for five minutes without the support of the RLC. But it was not often that they got the chance to run their own show, and they were revelling in the opportunity. The regiment's CO, Lieutenant Colonel Rufus McNeil, would be in charge of the operation for most of the journey, handing over to the Paras only for the last 8 kilometres of the way. "There's a lot of risk in it and it's a very unusual role for the regiment," he said. "I'm running my own battle space which is normally something a battlegroup would do . . . it's great. It's a real challenge . . . it doesn't happen very often and so it's nice to prove that we can do it." McNeil was all too aware that they had to make the most of their chance, "otherwise I'm sure we'll get locked away in our log box again". Every one of his unsung heroes and heroines was looking forward to proving they were up to the task.

The Paras were equally excited at the prospect. 3 Para were to have responsibility for protecting the convoy when it entered the last and most dangerous phase of the journey, the belt of Green Zone known as Kajaki Sofia that lay to the south of the dam. As well as his own men, Huw Williams would have command of two companies from 2 Para and the support of an ANA *kandak* together with their Royal Irish mentors. He could also call on lavish artillery and air resources. The operation was a new departure for the Paras as much as it was for the Loggies, and one that they found inspiring. Williams had taken to heart Mark Carleton-Smith's rule that "we shouldn't be counting our success on how many rounds we fired . . . sooner or later you've got to start reconstructing and developing". Williams liked the thought that when people asked "what did you do in your six months?", instead of replying "we had this many contacts and fired this many rounds, we'll be able to say, 'Well, we got the turbine in which produces fifty-three megawatts of power and [provides] electricity for so many thousand people . . .'" Nonetheless, as they made their preparations there was every expectation that many rounds would fly before the turbine was home. "It's going to be a hell of a fight to get in," was his deputy John Boyd's prediction a few weeks before D-Day.

The inherent risks of the operation as it was first conceived were considerable. The proposal had been around for some time. Huw Williams remembered it from his previous tour in 2006. "They talked about how are we ever going to get the other turbine up here and I remember saying then that it's nigh on impossible." What had changed was the increased number of troops on the ground and the fact that there was now a string of forts running up the 611, which was the obvious route for a land convoy to take.

Even so, the journey would be full of hazards. The components would arrive in-theatre by air at Kandahar. The only way to Kajaki from KAF was westwards along Highway One before turning north on to the 611 at a point between Lashkar Gah and Gereshk. Highway One was paved. The 611 was a broad track, rutted, potholed and strewn with rocks. It followed the course of the Helmand river, passing through Sangin on its way to its final destination of Kajaki. The first problem was not so much its condition as its predictability. Once the convoy was trundling along it, the Taliban would have all the time they needed to prepare their IEDs. A trial run in the early days of planning had turned up twenty-one roadside bombs along the 45 kilometres between Sangin and the junction with Highway One. Securing its length was impossible. The vehicles would inch forward while each step of the route was cleared for bombs. They would be crawling through country bristling with additional danger. For much of the way, the 611 was flanked by stretches of Green Zone. Its ditches, dense crop fields and myriad compounds were the Taliban's natural habitat. From within its depths they could launch a constant succession of ambushes which ISAF's massed guns and aircraft would be unable to prevent.

For all its drawbacks, when 16 Air Assault Brigade began drawing up their plans, the 611 was the only practical route. Delivery by air had been considered and ruled out. There was no helicopter big enough or strong enough to lift the components, the lightest of which weighed 15 tonnes. The task would have been simple for a fixed-wing transport, such as the C-130, the faithful battlefield moke which was a familiar sight lumbering across the skies of Helmand and Kandahar. There was even an airstrip across the Helmand river from the hydroelectric station, which had been built by the Russians during the occupation. After their departure it was taken over by local traders, who built small shops the length of the runway. It would be easy to patch it up. The problem would be getting the kit across the river. It was spanned by a narrow wood-and-scaffolding bridge that would collapse under the weight of a heavily laden lorry. Building a new one was dismissed as too time-consuming and expensive. So a road convoy it was.

There was always the possibility that there was another way to get to Kajaki. The bare desert outside the thin bands of Green Zone was criss-crossed with tracks and, in summer, dried-up river beds, which local people used to make their way in jalopy, in pickup or on motorbike between the sparse communities dotted about it. Aerial surveillance failed to detect anything that looked like a recognisable route, however. If there was one, it would have to be found on the ground. If anyone was capable of discovering it, it was the Pathfinders.

The Pathfinders were an elite within an elite. They were 16 Air Assault's reconnaissance unit, roaming the area of operations in their WMIKs, seeking the ground truth that would underpin operations. They were highly trained and radiated *esprit de corps*. Their commander was Major Matt Taylor, who had been Ops Officer for 3 Para in 2006, a job that often kept him a frustratingly long way from the front lines. Now he was at the tip of the spearhead and enjoying himself enormously. In the third week of July they were sent on a ten-day patrol into the country north of Highway One on the Helmand-Kandahar border. They were to roam the districts of Malmand, Wushtan and Ghorak which lay due east of Sangin and the 611. The area lay along the Malmand river, a wadi in summer, which opened the way to the Sangin Valley and the proposed turbine convoy route. Any information they could gather would be useful in the preparations for the Kajaki operation. The Pathfinders were tasked with finding out what they could about the strength and methods of the local Taliban. They were to test the attitudes of the local people towards ISAF and to gather information on narcotics production and trading. They were also told to keep alert to any alternative routes that might cut out total reliance on the 611.

278

They started patrolling on 19 July and carried on for a week, moving from village to village, holding shuras with the inhabitants and building up an impressive picture of the realities of local life. At the same time they were monitoring traffic and questioning travellers. On the morning of 25 July, the Pathfinders' second-in-command, Sergeant Chris Tilley, was tasked to set up a checkpoint on what appeared to be a well-used track just north-west of the Ghorak district centre. The road ran through a gap, the Ghorak Pass, which split a 1500-metre-high massif stretching almost all the way to Kajaki. "We crested the hill and saw what was quite a major carriageway and there was quite a lot of traffic on it," Tilley said. "The first guy we stopped we questioned quite thoroughly and [asked him] where are you going and why are you using this route?" The man at the wheel was a young taxi driver. He had six passengers crammed into his beaten-up family saloon and he was on his way to Kandahar. He was "chatty and helpful". He told Tilley that he chose the route over the 611 because "I don't get jerked about by the [Taliban], I don't pay road tax to the ANP, I'm not robbed by the Afghan security forces and it's safe from IEDs". In a sentence the taxi driver had just summed up the perils of travel in southern Afghanistan for the poor, suffering peasantry.

When Tilley learned where the man was coming from, his interest quickened sharply. The taxi driver had set off from Kajaki. He made the journey frequently, as did other taxi drivers, who charged their fares 800

Pakistani rupees (approximately £7) for the four-to-five-hour trip to Kandahar.

It sounded too good to be true. Matt Taylor's initial thought was that ISAF had been in the area for two years. He reasoned that "surely if [the route] was as good as it [seemed] then it would have been found by now". They moved to another stretch of the track and questioned more drivers. "Pretty much the same answer came back," said Tilley. "We don't get messed about, it's a direct route and it doesn't go through any Green Zone. That's when Matt started ringing the bells in headquarters."

Security considerations were not everything, however. The road had to be able to take enormously heavy loads. To the Pathfinders' experienced eyes the surface of sun-blasted earth and rock looked solid enough. That judgement seemed to be reinforced by the appearance of occasional lorries grinding along the track. Their report back to Brigade was cautious but highly encouraging. "Despite being marked on the map as little more than a track, the patrol noted that [it] was capable of taking HGVs in one direction at a time," Taylor wrote. "The route between Kajaki and Kandahar appears to be fairly direct and the lack of [Taliban] presence was the stated reason why most people preferred to use it." He concluded that "a reconnaissance of this route should be conducted to assess its suitability as an alternative route to Highway 611". An expert from 13 Air Assault Regiment was taken along on a subsequent patrol to examine the route. He confirmed that it was a goer. The desert track was given the code name Route Harriet and the planning for the turbine operation swung on to a new course.

The Pathfinders had good reason for feeling pleased with themselves. Their discovery had saved a huge amount of time and reduced danger levels. The route-proving exercise showed that the surface of Harriet was actually better than that of the 611. The security benefits were even more significant. According to Chris Tilley, "the real advantage [was] the fact that it goes through open ground". There was no Green Zone flanking the path from which the Taliban could safely emerge to plant IEDs or which they use as cover for ambushes. Harriet ran through broad expanses of bare desert in which the slightest movement was instantly detectable. They could still lay IEDs but the convoy's countermeasures were well up to dealing with that. "It's a lot better than fighting through close country with people being able to engage at short distances from concealed positions," said Matt Taylor. There was still a sector of the route where the risks were high, however. On the final leg of the journey, the hills on the approach to Kajaki would channel the vehicles on to the 611 for the last 8 kilometres to the dam, through the high crops and half-hidden compounds of Kajaki Sofia. Its safety would then be in the hands of Huw Williams and his men.

Even with this discovery, the move still presented enormous practical difficulties. The first concerned transport. The main vehicles at the Loggies' disposal were HETs, Heavy Equipment Transporters. The rig comprised a Canadian-manufactured eight-by-eight Oshkosh tractor unit which towed a British-made seven-axle King trailer. A HET could carry a 70-tonne Challenger tank. But it was designed to do so on the smooth autobahns of northern Europe, not the rocky tracks of southern Afghanistan. The road clearance was a mere 28 centimetres.

The heaviest component was the stator, the electromagnet which wrapped around the turbine and which came in two halves. Each weighed 29 tonnes, but armour plating to give protection from Taliban bullets added another 9 tonnes. On a smooth road this would present no problems. On Route Harriet it meant constant stopping and starting while burst tyres were changed, snapped axles were replaced and severed power and hydraulic lines were reconnected.

By 16 August three of the seven components had arrived at KAF, flown in on an Antonov AN-224 transporter, one of the largest aircraft in the world. They were shifted to the workshops of 7 Air Assault Battalion of the Royal Electrical and Mechanical Engineers (REME) in the outskirts of the base, where the work of armouring got under way, assisted by 3 Para's Light Aid detachment under WO Steve Wooller. In the excitement surrounding the project, the turbine had taken on a mythical quality. Seeing it for the first time was a slight disappointment. To the ignorant eye it looked like a collection of anonymous lumps of grey-painted metal. It was old technology, and none the worse for that, manufactured in a place where they still made sturdy, utilitarian machines. Examination revealed a small metal plate screwed to the side of each part bearing the name of the Shanghai Huaming Power Equipment Company of China.

On a blistering Saturday afternoon the REME team was hard at work, welding together sheets of 24mm mild steel boxes to fit around the components. Despite the apparent solidity, the kit was surprisingly delicate. A lucky round from an AK47 or a piece of RPG shrapnel hitting one of the parts could be enough to wreck it and send the whole project sliding back to square one. Each armoured component would then be packed in an ISO container and loaded on to a HET. This was where a second problem arose. To load the containers required a heavy-duty crane which would then have to be transported to Kajaki to complete the unloading. There were two at KAF, which were supposed to be able to lift 50 tonnes. When the first one was tried it broke under the strain of a test weight of only 11 tonnes and the chain and hook on the second snapped. If the cranes could not be made to work there was an alternative. Lieutenant Colonel Simon Warner, who was in charge of the Equipment Capabilities team, had the use of several Foden military recovery vehicles, each of which could lift 12.5 tonnes. He was confident that, between them, the Fodens could manoeuvre the kit on and off the HETs, albeit with some difficulty. According to Sergeant Gareth McKenna, who would be in charge of the loading and unloading, the Fodens had "the turning circle of the QE2".

D-Day for Oqab Tsuka was initially set for 27 August, though the date seemed likely to slip. The plan was that, under cover of darkness, the convoy would rumble out of the gates of KAF and head west along Highway One. In the middle would be eight HETs bearing the seven components and, it was hoped, a functioning crane. The column would be topped and tailed by a phalanx of armoured vehicles supplied by the Canadians. They would roll slowly through the night along 30 kilometres of metalled road before turning off north into the desert, where they would stop at a rendezvous point. There they were due to meet up with a second convoy, which would set off slightly later from Bastion for the shorter journey eastwards through Gereshk. It was made up of twenty Leyland Daf "drops" logistics vehicles, each loaded with a container filled with 18 tonnes of stores and three fuel tankers carrying 20,000 litres of diesel. There were Vector Explosive Ordnance Disposal [EOD] vehicles for locating mines and roadside bombs, armoured diggers to clear the route and tipper trucks loaded with gravel and fascines, giant plastic pipes strong enough to fill a collapsed bridge or culvert. Scattered along the length of the column were a variety of WMIKs, Viking and Mastiff armoured vehicles armed with .50-cal machine guns and GMPGs. Together there would be well over a hundred vehicles making a convoy 5 kilometres long. Twenty-four hours before the column set off, a detachment from the Queen's Royal Lancers mounted in Vikings would go ahead to provide overwatch at the Ghorak Pass, the main choke point on the route. UAVs would be hovering overhead at all times, scouring the ground for any threatening movement.

To the men and women who would be operating the vehicles, Oqab Tsuka was a chance for once to feel the glow of the limelight. Their work was in many cases just as hazardous as that of the "teeth arms" fighting units patrolling the Green Zone. The enablers spent their days slogging along desert routes keeping the FOBs and patrol bases supplied, braving IEDs and ambushes every day. No one ever wrote about them or filmed them. They had to be content with their own pride in their professionalism.

They were used to long hours without sleep and the thumping heat of the desert. This operation looked set to be the most gruelling of all. Once they had started, the intention was not to stop unless forced to by breakdown or enemy action. No one had any idea how long the journey might actually take, but by the most sober projections the column was unlikely to proceed at anything more than one kilometre an hour, and the distance from Highway One to Kajaki was more than seventy kilometres as the crow flies.

Yet for all the inevitable sweat and tears and the prospect of spilled blood, they were ready for it. "Everyone is looking forward to it," said Corporal Warwick "Stretch" Bromgrove, as he made final preparations. "Everyone is a bit nervous because this is uncharted territory for us. But this is what we've worked for, this is the brigade's main mission. We all want to do a good job and make sure this [turbine] gets up there." There would be a huge weight of responsibility on some very young shoulders. Corporal

Dani Hanwell, a twenty-four-year-old from Stoke-on-Trent, would be in charge of communications throughout the operation. "I can't say I'm not nervous but I think it will be fine," she said. "I've got a good feeling about this next op, a good feeling."

The convoy would get through come what may. With the massed logistic and military might at ISAF's disposal anything other than complete success would be a humiliation. The unknown factor was how hard the fighting would be on the way. And that was something the Taliban would decide.

CHAPTER
THIRTEEN

The Enemy

Who were the Taliban? Even after two years the soldiers seemed to have only a blurred picture of the people they were fighting. What was sure was that they defied simple definition. Their identity was localised, shifting character from area to area. Inside any band of insurgents there could be several different elements, each with its own attitude and agenda. For all the intense surveillance and the mass of information collected in the field, it was not clear how they organised themselves or how decisions were taken and orders transmitted.

The Taliban bundled together a coalition of the ideological, the criminal and the disaffected who, for the time being at least, had a shared interest in fighting the foreigners and the Afghan government. At its core was the rump of the old regime that had been ousted in 2001 and was now seeking to return to power by the same means by which it had first won it. It was still led by Mullah Mohammed Omar, the movement's founding father, who had remained at the top throughout its fluctuating history. Its outlook remained rooted in Deobandi Islam, a deeply conservative strand of the faith which sprang up in India in the nineteenth century, at least in part as a reaction to British rule. It was at heart a religious rather than a political movement. Over the years, its alliance with Osama bin Laden and al-Qaeda had introduced a global jihadi element to its ranks. It included foreign volunteers from Islamic or Arab countries but the majority of fighters were Pashtuns, either from Afghanistan or refugees from decades of fighting who lived in the border areas of Pakistan where the madrasas provided a steady flow of recruits. In the opening stages of their post-2006 resurgence, it was Afghanistan they were most concerned with. Their mission was to expel foreign unbelievers and return the country to theocratic rule inspired by their version of sharia law.

Those were the simple outlines. Inevitably the detail was more complicated. If religion was the most significant element in the Taliban identity, it was also formed by historical, economic and tribal forces. It was a multilayered organisation, and each layer felt a different degree of commitment to, and relationship with, the cause, so much so that it was better, as Mark Carleton-Smith suggested, to regard the word "Taliban" as a label rather than a definition. Sandwiched in the middle was a stratum whose interest was neither religious nor political. The opium producers were concerned only with business. Yet their support for the movement, as everyone came to realise, was central to its operations, and the narco-barons, their underlings and the fighters led an intertwined existence. They were mutually parasitic growths.

The success of the Taliban in inflicting a low but steady level of casualties, punctuated by occasional attention-grabbing operations, had produced some exaggerated assessments of their military capabilities. No soldier believed that the insurgents were capable of inflicting a conventional defeat on ISAF. That, though, was not where their abilities or their intentions lay. "The view of the Taliban often portrayed in the media is of a slick, committed and dynamic organisation that fuses the latest technological methods with the tactics of the traditional guerrilla," said Captain Jon Cox, 3 Para's Intelligence Officer. "[But] although the Taliban may have leaders and individuals who fit this mould, I believe that the organisation is better described as robust, stubborn, deep rooted and slow to respond." It was only belatedly that they had shifted towards asymmetric tactics and away from the costly confrontational approach that they had used in the early days of the British deployment. In a way their learning difficulties were irrelevant. In this war it was durability which counted. "The Taliban . . . know that they only have to outlast the NATO mission in Afghanistan to win," said Cox. The insurgents were supposed to have a saying: "You have the watches but we have the time". It was true enough. The foreigners were running against a ticking clock, set to a Western tempo. They were striving to get the Afghan security forces and governmental institutions into good enough shape to take over the burden of countering the insurgency on their own before the politicians and electorates of America and Britain decided the effort was not worth the losses. The transformation was slow and arduous. If the mood swing occurred before it was substantially effected and the outsiders withdrew, there would be little doubt about the result. It would mean bloodshed and chaos, from which the Taliban would probably emerge triumphant.

That was the big picture. It was the smaller canvas which concerned the soldiers on the ground, and that altered from district to district. Commanders were constantly trying to improve their understanding not only of how the Taliban operated but also of their relationship with local communities. The prize, as everyone said, was the people. The assumption underpinning the entire operation was that the support of the inhabitants was actually available to be won. There were times when the soldiers wondered about that. The peasant fatalism was confusing. It could be interpreted in different ways. Did the lack of overt enthusiasm for the prospectus they were offering equal sympathy for the Taliban? When they did meet a positive response, was it anything more than mere courtesy, telling the questioner what he or she wanted to hear, the quicker to send them on their way?

Sometimes, though, the information-gathering produced valuable results, lifting a corner on the obscure world in which the soldiers moved and allowing them a glimpse into the minds of those they were there to help. The Pathfinders' ten-day patrol in July had not only found a new route to Kajaki. They had also gained an insight into the interaction between insurgents and farmers in the area through which the turbine convoy would be passing. They had been charged to gauge the "atmospherics", the term used for the prevailing local attitudes towards ISAF forces, and to investigate narcotics activity in the districts of Malmand, Wushtan and Ghorak, which lay between 12 and 25 kilometres to the east of Sangin. The country was poor and drought-stricken. The lack of water had driven many families to take refuge in Kandahar. The exodus had to some extent been balanced by the arrival of refugees fleeing the fighting in Sangin. Everywhere they went the Pathfinders found people willing to talk to them. The message they received was encouraging. The inhabitants seemed mostly to hate the Taliban. Until now, they had had very few contacts with ISAF and were willing to take at face value the prospect the mission offered of greater security and a better life.

The Pathfinders set off after midnight on 21 July from FOB Price, the ISAF base in Gereshk, and arrived in Malmand district just inside the Kandahar border with Helmand at mid-morning. They were travelling with a detachment from Afghan Task Force 444 (ATF), a small Afghan army unit that was to prove invaluable in winning the confidence of the farmers and encouraging them to speak honestly and freely. As soon as they arrived they were dicked by small groups of males who watched them from a hillside. For the moment, though, the Taliban kept their distance.

The following day they moved into Malmand village and the translators issued an invitation by loudhailer to a shura which, in keeping with the doctrine of presenting an "Afghan face" whenever possible, was

291

conducted by the ATF. They soon learned that Malmand had considerable significance to the insurgents. The Malmand bazaar was the main opium-trading centre in the district. It was where the farmers brought their crop to sell to local drugs merchants, who took it off to laboratories for initial refining. There were, they learned later, fifteen opium-processing plants in the neighbourhood of the village. The product was then moved under armed escort to the Iranian border for onward export, to end up eventually on the streets of London, Paris, Amsterdam, anywhere where people took any form of heroin. The locals called those involved in the trade "smugglers". The smugglers worked with the Taliban, who protected their interests in return for payment, and who nurtured the climate of lawlessness in which they could carry on their business. On market days the traders arrived with Taliban escorts, mounted in Toyota Land Cruisers and Corollas and bristling with weapons. The smugglers were the most prosperous people in the area, but they did not go in for ostentatious displays of wealth. Outwardly they seemed to live in the same mud-wall compounds as everyone else. It was only if you were invited inside one that you saw any evidence of the comparative luxury in which they lived.

The importance of Malmand to the opium trade had grown since ISAF closed down the Sangin drugs bazaar. The insurgents were determined that the Malmand market was not going the same way. They kept watch over it from three compounds near by. Ten days before the visit, a local ANP commander had turned up at the bazaar with his men. In the three-hour firefight that followed several policemen were killed. The police were forced to withdraw and the Taliban dumped the bodies of their victims on the road outside the village.

The elders seemed happy to see the Pathfinders and particularly the ATF, and hoped that their appearance was the start of a regular presence. Their main concern was the lack of water. The cultivable land beyond the reach of the river valley irrigation systems relied on wells to water the crops and was acutely vulnerable to drought. The lack of water meant many were excluded from the opium trade, which was the best way for a poor farmer to make any money. Poppy was a thirsty crop. Instead the Malmand farmers had to grow wheat. Life seemed to be on a level with the Europe of the Dark Ages. There was no school in the village or the surrounding area, and the one primitive clinic near the bazaar was poorly attended because of fear of the Taliban, who had burned down another one in the area. The elders expressed the timid hope that the arrival of the outsiders might be a sign that life was about to change for the better.

The Taliban that the villagers lived in such fear of appeared to be their own kin, members of the Ishakzai and Noorzai tribes, which predominated in the region. Some were from Malmand itself. Others were "outsiders", a designation that covered anyone from more than a few kilometres away. They included the chief commander, who came from Sangin.

Intelligence reports indicated the insurgents had been watching the recent comings and goings closely. Following a second shura in a hamlet near by, the Pathfinders set up camp for the night on a hillside that gave them a clear view of their surroundings. As dusk was gathering there was a loud explosion and a missile impacted close to their position. It appeared to be a 107mm rocket fired from the south-west, and the man who fired it was spotted running away. The Pathfinders opened up on him with their .50-cals and grenade machine guns. When that failed to stop him they launched a Javelin missile, which scored a direct hit. An hour later another rocket landed near their position but this time the shooter escaped.

The following day they moved north to Wushtan, a village on the banks of the Ghorak Mandal wadi, which ran east to west through the Ghorak Pass. It was the main conduit to Sangin, and trucks, cars and motorbikes were moving briskly in both directions. They set up a vehicle checkpoint and with the help of the ATF questioned some of the drivers. The fourth car they stopped aroused the Afghans' suspicions. The driver refused at first to answer their questions. When eventually he began to talk he claimed he had never seen any Taliban around. The ATF searched his car and soon turned up some suspicious items. They found a length of twin flex and a small piece of wood like half a clothes peg which had a metal sheath on one end. They were both identifiable as components of a pressure-pad-operated IED. Faced with the discovery, the driver became more forthcoming. He admitted that there were Taliban in the area who moved around in convoys of six vehicles and attacked ISAF forces whenever they could with mines and rockets. He was assessed as being too lowly a player to be worth arresting and was released. Later an intelligence intercept heard the Taliban expressing relief that he had not been caught carrying "pumpkins", one of their code words for explosives. The ATF and Pathfinders would stop more suspicious young men in the following days but in the absence of clear-cut evidence there was no point in detaining them.

Everywhere they went people were willing to talk, particularly to the Afghan soldiers. They were friendly but understandably cautious, given the insurgents' ruthless punishment of "collaborators", real or suspected. The Taliban were hated and feared. The inhabitants had a particular loathing for the foreign fighters from Pakistan and the Arab world, who "thought they were superior" and were "telling the Afghans what to do and destroying the country of Afghanistan". The Pathfinders reported that one group of village elders said that "if the foreign Taliban could be destroyed this would help them to speak to the local Taliban and change their views on the government and ISAF". This seemed to reinforce the often expressed hope that there were "reconcilable" elements inside the insurgent ranks who could be persuaded that their interest lay in coming over to the government side.

Other villagers said they would like to see them all dead and derided the local insurgents in the most insulting language in their vocabulary as "the wives of

Pakistanis and Arabs". The attitudes of the local Taliban did not suggest they were susceptible to influence. Their behaviour was a head-on contradiction of their claims to be the champions of the people against an oppressive government and their foreign mercenary backers. There was no sign of the "alternative administrations" their spokesmen claimed were being set up all over the country. Their interest appeared to be in anarchy rather than order. Everything they did seemed at odds with their projected image as the upholders of stern and conservative traditional values. It began with their deep-rooted involvement in a drugs industry that they had done their best when in power to eradicate as sinful and unIslamic. They stole from the poor and protected the rich. They taxed travellers and turned up at people's homes demanding yoghurt and bread which they never paid for. There were many stories of beatings and threats. One elder told how he had stopped one of the prowling Land Cruisers when it appeared in his village and asked the men inside their business. He was immediately assaulted by the gang's leader.

The men they spoke to were reluctant to give detailed information about insurgent personalities or operations. They were showing remarkable courage by even meeting the members of the patrol. Intelligence revealed that the Taliban were tracking its movements closely. Everyone knew what the Taliban did to those they accused of being ISAF "spies", a term that could cover anyone who had the most glancing contact with outsiders. A few days before, two insurgent vehicles had arrived in one of the villages, having travelled all the way from Musa Qaleh, looking for a man who was "working for the government", but had to go away disappointed, having failed to find him. If they caught him he would be as good as dead. One of the local commanders was notorious for his treatment of prisoners and was said to have a "knife that would cut the truth out of them".

The peasants lived an existence that was fragile and filled with fear. There was no one and nothing to rely on. Their dusty fields taught them that nature itself was treacherous. They knew from bitter experience that it was foolish to expect much from their fellow men.

Yet they continued despite everything to hope. In every village the Pathfinders and ATF visited they were told that they were desperate for any help the government could give them, willing to risk the punitive reaction from the Taliban that development would inevitably bring. They were all aware that the insurgents were murdering poor labourers who had seized the chance of earning a few dollars repairing Highway One in the south of the province. Their plight was stark evidence of the enormity of the reconstruction task. There appeared to be not a single properly functioning medical facility in the area. There were no schools. Some of the boys received instruction in the Koran from local mullahs, and the Pathfinders were told of one teacher who taught not only Dari but a rudimentary science class. But the vast majority of the people were condemned to illiteracy and ignorance, with only their hands to help them in the relentless struggle of daily existence. The governance that was spoken of had no meaning for them. Kabul might as well be on Mars. The only flag that the Pathfinders saw flying was over the single Afghan National Police station in the area.

This, as it turned out, was the one small rock of decency sticking out of the sea of violence, insecurity and intimidation. As they went about their travels, the Pathfinders and the ATF had picked up good reports of the local police and their leader, Commander Fiateh Mohammed Khan. Hearing praise for the ANP was a highly unusual experience for ISAF soldiers in Afghanistan. The men who made up much of the force were generally regarded as degenerates and thieves, drug addicts and sexual predators, who were at least as bad as the criminals they were supposed to combat. In their defence it could be said that they were paid virtually nothing and, by putting on uniform, they were exposing themselves to great danger. In 2008, insurgents killed 868 policemen, more than three times the number of Afghan soldiers who died. The international effort to build efficient Afghan security forces had concentrated on the army and it was only belatedly that the importance of the police was recognised and greater effort devoted to their training and conditions.

Commander Fiateh Khan and his men showed what an effect a clean, dedicated force could make. Their behaviour appeared to be a model of decency and efficiency, surpassing the most optimistic imaginings of the ISAF propagandists.

In one village the Pathfinders were told by the inhabitants that they had regularly received unwelcome visits from the Taliban, who had set up base in a neighbouring settlement. They demanded food and money and tried to take over the running of the local mosque. They also set up a checkpoint on a local route and levied a "tax" on the drivers. When the elders reported their problems to Fiateh Khan he turned up with his men. The Taliban prudently withdrew. The police chief gave money to those who had been robbed and instructed the elders to "tell him quickly when the Taliban next came to the area". The Pathfinders heard similarly encouraging stories in almost every village they visited. Here was a real example of local forces providing local security. The last time the population had seen ISAF troops was three years previously, when some Americans had come through. One local man remarked that the police were "specifically liked because they were a constant Afghan force in the area".

The Pathfinders met Fiateh Khan on 26 July when they visited Ghorak village. He was short and slim with a neat moustache and had a friendly, confident manner. He belonged to the Popalzai tribe and came from Ghorak, where his headquarters stood on rising ground overlooking the village. There were fifty men inside the base, who moved around in six jeeps, four of them seized from the smugglers and their Taliban allies. The fort was scarred with mortar splashes and craters gouged by RPG strikes. The last attack had been ten days previously by six jeep-loads of Taliban. A month before they had come under mortar attack for several

299

nights in succession. The raiders were based in Malmand, and the commander had responded by launching the raid on the Malmand bazaar which the Pathfinders had heard about when they first arrived. He and his men might have suffered some losses but they had "killed lots of Taliban". The police were clearly doing their job.

They produced ten IEDs they had seized from a smuggler's jeep, improvised out of an assortment of munitions, including a round from a British grenade machine gun which had failed to explode.

The commander and his men were, as the Pathfinders reported back, a "good news story for the ANP". They were carrying out a difficult task, providing a degree of security in the strategically important area of the Ghorak Pass. But they were surrounded by their enemies and felt their isolation. Fiateh Khan made it clear that he hoped the patrol was the first sign of an increased ISAF and Afghan security force presence in the area. More immediately he was desperate for ammunition, which was in short supply. Matt Taylor backed his request for more support. Whether it came or not depended on what was available, and in southern Afghanistan there was never anything like the resources needed to meet the area's colossal security requirements. It was men which were required far more than material.

The absence of any serious obstacle to their growth meant the Taliban clustered parasitically on daily life like ivy on an oak tree. Throughout the ten days that the Pathfinders were patrolling they had stood by and

300

watched and waited. The intelligence intercepts showed they frequently had "eyes on" the column. But despite much talk of impending ambushes there were no more attacks after 22 July. There was no doubting they had the means to launch one if they wished. This was country the turbine convoy would be passing through in a few weeks' time. The territory beyond was planted even more thickly with insurgents. One way or another, the Taliban in the area would have to be neutralised.

CHAPTER
FOURTEEN

Close Quarters

On 12 August 3 Para began deploying for a series of operations to force the Taliban on to the defensive in their strongholds close to Kajaki. "B" Company were sent to Musa Qaleh, which, despite all the energy and resources that had been poured into the place, was still anarchic and volatile. "A" Company went to Inkerman. The deployment had two aims. They were to disrupt and damage the Taliban and reduce their capacity to send fighters into the country along the turbine route. At the same time they were to mislead the insurgents as to where the route would run. By attacking the Taliban in the Musa Qaleh area and in the Green Zone north of Sangin they would encourage them to believe that the convoy would be travelling up the 611.

There was reason to believe that the insurgents already knew about Operation Oqab Tsuka. The Taliban had often seemed remarkably well informed about ISAF's intentions. If they didn't know they would soon find out. It had been decided to extract the maximum psychological advantage from the event in the struggle for hearts and minds. It was going to be an "influence" spectacular that would demonstrate the

302

scale of the foreigners' largesse and the benefits of their presence. When the time came there would be leaflet drops and radio broadcasts to tell the local population what was happening. For the time being, though, the news was to be kept secret from the outside world, and the Ministry of Defence had issued a Defence Advisory Notice, which asked the media to keep silent on the grounds that premature publicity could damage national security.

"B" Company flew into Musa Qaleh as it was reeling from another blow to its precarious security. The week before, twelve tribal elders had been kidnapped by the Taliban and intelligence reports spoke of an influx of foreign fighters and heavy weapons from Pakistan. The indications were that the insurgents were preparing to go on the offensive.

At 7 a.m. on 14 August, Stu McDonald led his men out of the gates of the Musa Qaleh district centre and into the streets of the town. Much had changed since the last time the Paras were there. They had departed in October 2006 following a summer-long battle with the Taliban. They handed over security to the local elders, but after only a few months the insurgents seized the town. British and Afghan troops had driven the Taliban out again in December 2007 and the place had recovered some of its old vigour. It was full of life as the patrol set off, and crowded with vehicles carrying goods and customers to the bazaar. The suicide-bomber threat was high and as usual some of the drivers were impatient. One tried to drive through the line of troops as it made its way down the wadi opposite the base, ignoring the shouts and mini-flares and stopping only when a couple of warning shots clanged into the bonnet. Among the soldiers was Sergeant Craig Allen, a veteran of 1 and 3 Para, who had left the full-time regiment but served as its official photographer. He noticed that such incidents appeared to be almost routine. The driver and his passenger reacted "with amazing calmness", he said. "The Afghans are so used to firearms, so used to war that there was [just] a shrug of the shoulders. The ANP came and had a look at it and again there was a shrug of the shoulders and the two young men walked off . . . and that was it."

The patrol was big, more than a hundred men. The plan was to push into the Green Zone north of the town up the river valley and make their way to an ANA patrol base only a few kilometres distant. They would flush out any Taliban who were in there and "smash" them if they chose to fight. The operation was supposed to last five hours. It ended up taking nearer twelve.

They tabbed along in the rising heat through the ramshackle outskirts of town and into the maze of fields and compounds. It seemed to Allen that the pattern of life was "pretty normal, lots of locals sitting around watching us go by, people working in the fields, plenty of kids about". Progress was slow and deliberate. "It was the usual stop-start you get on these company snakes," he said. "When you reach an obstacle the guys have to get across and the whole thing slows down. Everyone gets down on one knee and then sits down and then you get up again and so it goes."

And so it went for forty minutes until the calm was split by two rounds cracking over their heads. No one had seen where they had come from but now they knew the enemy had "eyes on". At the same time, intelligence picked up a surge in communications chatter. Up and down the long line of soldiers, minds cleared and muscles tensed.

It was a quarter of an hour before the first real contact. An RPG fizzed through the air, exploding behind them, and heavy machinegun rounds chopped through the greenery and smacked into mud walls. This time someone identified the firing point on the roof of a compound. The Mortar Fire Controllers called a grid reference and bombs flew towards the insurgent positions. The firing stopped. The Paras moved out of cover and on to the next compound. After that a sort of rhythm developed. The two platoons moved forward systematically, hooking left and right, heading northwards with the river on their left. They were "pushing the enemy", said Allen. "Trying to keep them moving so that they couldn't get a fix on us, and trying to get a fix on them — very much a cat-and-mouse game."

A standard methodology had evolved for operations in the Green Zone. One group would advance, take a compound and climb on to the roof, using it as a fire base to provide overwatch for those following behind. It was slow work, hot and heavy, and on a long day like this day was turning out to be exhausting. Soldiers by and large were happy with the quality and quantity of the weapons and kit available. But if there was one universal complaint it concerned the weight of the loads they had to carry. The combined burden of body armour and helmet, weapons, ammunition, water and food could add up to 54 kilograms that routinely would have to be carried for eight hours at a time.[1]

The compound-clearing continued methodically for a quarter of an hour. Then 5 Platoon, which was leading on the right, ducked for cover as a wave of heavy machine-gun bullets thumped into the walls around them. The firefight went on for fifteen minutes. Once again the mortars were brought up to pound the firing points. That, said Allen, "set the scene for the day. We'd have a meeting engagement with them, there'd be

---

[1] Technical innovations never seemed to lighten the overall load. The new Osprey body armour and Mark 6 Alpha helmet were widely unpopular. One veteran of 2006 recalled that the protection they wore then "was like a smoking jacket but now it's been binned and we've got something that weighs about four times as much". There were constant complaints that it was difficult to tuck your rifle into the bulky shoulder piece and that the helmet slid down over your eyes when you sighted along the barrel. "If you can't see the enemy because of the kit that is issued to you then what good are you going to be?" asked one corporal. The soldiers would happily trade mobility for extra protection. "All we ask for as troops on the ground is to be as light as we can," said a senior NCO. "We don't mind carrying extra ammunition and night vision kit because that helps us to do our job, but not something that's restricting our movement." They believed that the emphasis on protection was an official response to uninformed domestic public concerns about casualties. The suspicion amongst the Toms', said a sergeant, "is that the kit is designed not so much to save our lives but as a bit of arse-covering for the politicians."

a firefight. We'd try to win it by putting down more fire than they did but they wouldn't generally hang around, and then we'd try and get the mortars on them as quickly as possible to catch them before they bugged out." The intelligence intercepts picked up traffic indicating the mortars were causing casualties. But there was plenty of fight in the Taliban and the Paras were in for a long day.

For many of the soldiers the events of the morning fitted into something that was now close to a routine. They knew from the outset whether or not a "contact" was likely by the presence of the dickers, the young men watching on rooftops in the middle distance talking into mobile phones. Then came the increase in radio chatter, adding to the sense of inevitability. "You don't know where or when it's going to erupt so there is that build-up of tension and you're walking along looking for the next piece of cover," said Allen. When the shooting began he found it "almost like a release . . . because at least it's started and you know where you stand".

Once they got through the first gust of fire things got steadily better. "The noise, the psychological weight of it drives you down into cover . . . you can feel how close it is and you can check. Is it right at us? Is it to our front or left or right? You get more of a feel for how safe it is . . . once that wave has gone over, then you can move around and start to do things."

Each contact was dragging them farther away from their line of march and the ANA base. By the end of the afternoon there had been five clashes. Night was falling when they finally struggled into their destination, weary and thirsty, for most men had either finished or were on the last dregs of the 5 litres of water they had calculated would be enough for a five-hour outing. The patrol base was in three fortified compounds. The Paras' arrival had put a strain on space. They sank down where they could and tried to make themselves comfortable. British soldiers took to heart the old military maxim that "any damn fool can be uncomfortable" and went to great trouble to create a tiny patch of calm and domesticity whatever the circumstances. Afghanistan tested their skills to the limit. They were each issued with a "pod", a bendy metal frame, big enough to take a sleeping mat, over which they stretched a zip-up mosquito net. It created a small, private enclosure inside which you could escape from the relentless communality of army life. "It gives you a little space of your own that's relatively dust free and you can administrate yourself in there, you can get changed . . . sit and read or whatever," said Craig Allen.

They had the luxury of a quiet morning while their vital comms batteries were recharging, then set off in the early afternoon. This time, they took enough water and rations to sustain them for a whole day. There were few complaints about the food these days. It was wholesome and tasty and there was a lot of it. A one-man, one-day ration pack came with a main meal, a stew or curry or pasta dish, pudding, biscuits, processed cheese, high-energy cereal bars, powdered fruit drinks and chocolate bars that turned to liquid as soon as they hit Afghan airspace and never regained solid form.

The programme was to investigate the area around the telecoms tower near Musa Qaleh. It was a regular target of the Taliban, who treated mobile phone masts as an extension of ISAF's electronic surveillance network. During the afternoon the Paras searched six compounds and turned up a few bits and pieces of kit. There was only one contact, when they were attacked with small arms, mortars and RPGs. It was counted a relatively quiet outing compared with the day before.

The following morning they were out again, with no more specific purpose than to push north into the Green Zone for eight hours and see what happened, before returning to Musa Qaleh district centre to get ready to pull out. Stu McDonald was determined, said one of the patrol, "to have one last crack at the enemy". He got his wish just before 9 a.m. when two RPGs flashed towards the lead platoon, followed by a wave of heavy machine-gun fire. Unlike the previous engagements, this one was launched from very close quarters. The first grenade struck a few yards from the lead section, showering them with debris. McDonald and his HQ team were caught out in the open and had to scramble for cover behind a mound of bricks. This, to his undoubted satisfaction, gave the OC the opportunity to bang a few rounds back at his attackers with his SA80 before retiring to more substantial cover to direct the firefight.

The battle was developing very well from the Paras' point of view. For once they were right up against the enemy, "feeling their breath", as one sergeant put it, and could use their firepower to dictate events. One soldier darting into an alleyway by a compound found himself face to face with a Taliban fighter standing a few yards away. They were both so startled that neither got a shot off and the insurgent bolted.

The fact was that the Taliban usually held the initiative. They knew the ground far better than the soldiers and the Green Zone was an ideal environment in which to practise their chosen tactics of harassing attacks which inflicted few casualties but placed a constant strain on their opponents' nerves and resources. They could move around unencumbered by the huge burden of kit with which the Brits were lumbered. It was their choice when they encountered their enemy whether to fight or flee. If they decided to engage it was on their terms, and they usually broke off when they felt the odds moving against them. It was rare for the sweating British soldiers, making their way through the high, concealing crops, to feel that they were really at grips with the enemy. But that was how it seemed that morning.

The enemy were stuck in a compound, pinned down with mortar fire and, according to intelligence, taking casualties. "The adrenaline was going and the whole company was up and pushing forward," said Allen. "We had them on the back foot and . . . for a change they were having to think on their feet and get out of the situation so that was quite a good feeling."

They pressed on to the limit set for the day's operation then broke off the engagement. They were in good spirits as they trekked back to the district centre to be airlifted back to KAF in preparation for the move to Kajaki. It seemed a promising start to the big operation.

"A" Company had completed their deployment to Inkerman on 13 August for the second op in preparation for Oqab Tsuka. This, according to the company sergeant major, Steve Tidmarsh, was "very much a deception plan". The idea was to give the impression that a major push was under way to swamp an area that until then had been a safe haven for the Taliban, an important transit route and the site of several opium-processing labs. The insurgents would have to defend it. The action would draw them into the area and, it was hoped, fix them there. The Paras' arrival caused some initial confusion among the Taliban. The intelligence intercepts revealed that they could not decide whether the arriving helicopters were merely delivering supplies or rotating troops or were a sign of something bigger.

They were soon to find out. The company group with its attachments numbered 180 soldiers, a lot of men and a lot of firepower to bring to bear on a relatively confined space. They were to set up a base a little to the north of Inkerman which would give them a good jumping-off point to the area of Green Zone where the insurgents were most active. The first thing was to locate a likely spot. That evening a patrol set off to recce the possibilities. They found a compound that seemed perfectly sited, on high ground in the desert to the east of the 611, which divided the cultivated and barren areas. It had good all-round arcs of fire and a view of the road. The sentries could keep a constant watch for anyone planting IEDs, which would significantly improve 2 Para's peace of mind when they set off on their patrols. It also faced the Green Zone and the "Putay track", which was a favourite insurgent trail. The compound was small and the soldiers would be living on top of each other. But the advantages outweighed the downside, and Steve Boardman and the NKET team were soon discussing terms with the owner. They settled on a rent of $600 for a few days' occupation and their new landlord seemed very pleased with the arrangement. He moved his family, sheep and poultry to another compound on the far side of the 611. Neighbours later revealed that one of his sons was a prominent figure in the local Taliban.

Before the main force moved in, the area had to be checked for IEDs. That was the job of the engineers and the dog handlers. The Paras had their usual expert, Corporal Marianne Hay, who had been with them for most of the tour. She was efficient, good-natured and courageous, going in first, taking big risks to ensure her comrades' safety. They were grateful and full of praise and respect. "She's very proactive," said Tidmarsh. "She goes forward with the lead sections and asks for work to do." She had an excellent rapport with the soldiers, who somehow managed to treat her as a woman as well as a fellow soldier without awkwardness or condescension. The debate back home about whether women should be allowed on the front lines had long ago become irrelevant. They already were, and none of the predicted dramas had come to pass.

The company started to move into the compound an hour before first light on 15 August. As dawn came up they could see the first dickers, young men on small motorbikes, watching intently from a distance on the desert tracks to the east. Soon the insurgents' radio nets were buzzing. The Taliban were talking in the transparent code they employed for security. Tidmarsh was briefing his men about where the sangars should be sited when the first mortar landed. It was followed by bursts of small-arms fire, which appeared to be coming from five or six different directions. Tidmarsh, Sergeant Peter "Razor" Reynolds and Corporal Mark Skinner clambered on to a compound roof and began pouring fire back with the GPMG and a .50-cal. Over the next hour they fired about sixteen hundred rounds at the enemy positions.

At the same time, the company's 2 Platoon was coming under fire from RPGs, heavy machine guns and small arms. They had been pushed out to the west of the base facing the Green Zone to deter any direct attack on the compound. The shooting was coming from a treeline behind a wide irrigation ditch about 150 metres distant. They were also being hit from a compound 20 to 30 metres away. The stand-off went on for about an hour before the 3 Para mortar barrels were in place and the platoon commander, Lieutenant Matt Clamp, could call in a strike. The short distance between the Paras and the enemy meant that the rounds would be landing "danger close". "There was no room for messing about," said Clamp. "Everyone was covered with dust from the rounds exploding." The barrage drove the attackers back and the firing died away.

The attacks soon began again and went on all morning from several firing points around the base while the soldiers humped sandbags to the sangars and built up their positions and supply convoys shuttled to and fro from Inkerman. It was a lively introduction to the operation. "It was good," said Tidmarsh. "The lads enjoyed it." It was a concept that was hard for a civilian to comprehend but very easy for a Para or any member of any combat unit. "If you're a front-line soldier you want to fight," he said. "We can do anything that people ask of us, but predominantly Parachute Regiment soldiers enjoy fighting."

For some of the young Toms who had just joined the company it was the first time they had been in real action. It was the most important moment in their formation as soldiers, an experience that no amount of training could replicate or completely prepare them for. "It gives the reassurance that people can shoot at you and you're not necessarily going to be killed," said Tidmarsh. "That not every bullet has got your name on it." They also proved to themselves that they could function properly in extreme conditions and that the drills they had learned were effective.

During the course of the day they were able to put most of them to use. The Taliban seemed determined not to allow the Paras to set themselves up in a location that obviously posed a serious threat to their operations. An air strike and a creeping barrage from the 105mm guns failed to deter them. It was the actions of 2 Platoon and 1 Platoon, who were sent out to support them, which eventually drove them away. Throughout the morning they pushed deeper into the Green Zone, clearing compounds, until at about noon the Taliban appeared to have had enough and fell back into the enveloping maize fields. By nightfall the Paras were settled into the new stronghold, which was named Patrol Base Emerald.

Having established the foothold, Matt Cansdale jumped forward. The stretch of Green Zone opposite the base was beyond the patrolling range of the Inkerman garrison, which conducted operations inside an area covered by the .50-cals and GMPGs mounted on the FOB's walls. The new strongpoint threatened the insurgents in a sector where they had previously felt safe.

His tactics were designed to erode their comfort zone and maximise their insecurities. At 3 o'clock the following morning, three hours before first light, a patrol crept out of Emerald, crossed the road and slunk into the deep shadow of the maize fields. They searched for an empty compound they could use as a launch pad for the day's operations, then laid up there until dawn. The result, said Tidmarsh, was that by the time the enemy woke up, the Paras "had already set up our defences so when they started to identify where we were, we could then decisively engage them and kill them in an area of our choosing".

The day was spent in a series of fleeting engagements in which the Taliban showed caution, breaking off as soon as the mortars began thumping in. The Paras felt confident and in control. Private Matt Tonroe, a sniper, was climbing up and down compound roofs, providing overwatch as the platoons moved systematically through each other. He was twenty-four and a veteran of Herrick 4. He found the current tour less nerve-racking than the desperate days of 2006. This time the Paras could be pretty sure that they would always "overmatch" the Taliban in any encounter. "In 2006 we'd go out there and every time we'd get smashed," he said. At the end of the tour he had considered leaving but decided eventually to stay on and was glad he had. "This time it's more fun," he said.

He was ranging his weapon on a rooftop in the middle distance in the direction of the Taliban positions during an intermittent firefight when "this bloke just sort of minced out with his AK slung over his shoulder". He disappeared from sight for a few minutes but when he came out again Tonroe was ready. He shot him twice. "He mustn't have known what hit him," Tonroe said. When they reached the position later they found signs of prolonged occupation. Tonroe assumed his kill had persuaded them to pull back. "His friends will have seen their mucker fall," he said. "They just bugged out after that." They left in a hurry for they forgot their usual practice of extracting all battlefield casualties, dead or alive, and left the body behind. They searched his clothes and discovered a passport but the picture in it did not correspond with the dead man's face. He was clearly identifiable, however, in a small photograph album they found. It showed him surrounded by his comrades, all smiling and waving their weapons, the sort of snap carried by soldiers everywhere.

After this encounter Cansdale decided to call it a day. On the way back the Taliban made it clear the Paras could expect a return engagement the following day. They were ambushed and it took them twenty minutes to win the firefight.

The next morning they set off early again, finding a compound and laying up until light crept over the fields. By 6a.m. women and children could be seen trekking out of the area, a sure sign that trouble was looming. The only inhabitants now were men intent on killing each other. The patrol searched through several compounds, finding nothing, and at about 9a.m. Cansdale gave the order to "go firm". They took up positions in three compounds and settled down for a brew. Intelligence had been reporting all morning that the Taliban had been tracking the patrol and were preparing an ambush. The attack was likely to come without warning.

The maize in the fields was dense enough and high enough for a man to get within a few metres of you and still be invisible. The company's tea break came to a sudden end when fire erupted on three sides. "They hit us hard," said Steve Tidmarsh. "It was accurate, sustained fire with airburst RPG, small arms, PKM." Tidmarsh was on the roof of one compound. "I was shouting to the lads, 'Identify the enemy position, win

317

the fucking firefight!' " Razor Reynolds, the 8 Platoon sergeant, was crouched behind a wall that appeared to be disintegrating under a blizzard of bullets, alongside some engineers and a medic. He counted down "three, two, one and we all knelt up as high as we could and we all fired at the same time". They were shooting into the maize field on the other side of the wall, aiming as best they could at the smoke and muzzle flash from the attackers' rifles and machine guns. "It was crack, crack, crack all around us," said Reynolds. "They were smashing us and they just kept smashing us. We just kept firing and firing." The shooting from the maize field would slacken and die away and for a few minutes they thought they had indeed "won the firefight", but then it would start up again.

The 8 Platoon commander, Lieutenant Ivan Rowlett, stood up to try to get a better look at the enemy positions. As he did so a burst of fire stitched a line of bullets cartoon-style around his head. Tidmarsh was amazed to see him "smiling and laughing. I said, do it again, sir, and I'll hit you!"

They were pinned down and they would need outside help to extract themselves from the most difficult situation they had yet encountered. Cansdale called in the guns from Inkerman and 105mm rounds began to land around them, covering them with dirt. He also called for air support, but it was some time before the request was granted, which led to an exchange between Cansdale and 2 Para headquarters, which were monitoring events from Sangin. About an hour after the fight began the men were relieved to hear the rumble of approaching jets. A few minutes later the ground shook as a Harrier began a series of strafing runs. The appearance of aircraft was usually the signal for the insurgents to retreat. As the engine noise faded away, silence returned to the Green Zone. The Taliban had lost at least five men in the action. The Paras' good fortune had held once again. The insurgents, though, had manouevred with skill and cunning, making full use of the advantages that the Green Zone gave them. Even with the discovery of Route Harriet, the convoy would still have to pass through 8 kilometres of the Green Zone that lay south of Kajaki. And that was where the Paras were going next.

CHAPTER
FIFTEEN

Fields Of Fire

As he put the last touches to his security plan, Huw Williams was hoping for the best while preparing for the worst. It was possible that the Taliban would decide it was in their interests to let the convoy through unmolested. Or they might regard the operation as a challenge to their authority that would have to be resisted. Given their inherent nihilism, which seemed to overwhelm any calculation of long-term gain, the worst-case scenario seemed the likeliest. Williams still wanted to hold the door open. Most of the men the soldiers were fighting were rooted in the local soil. They belonged to the tribes and families whose support they were trying to win. Peace would come only when they were crushed by force of arms or persuaded to cooperate and accept the government's authority. Here was a chance to engage with them by other than military means and to test the possibilities for compromise. The British had already negotiated a settlement with the Taliban, albeit at one remove through the medium of local elders, when agreeing the pull-out from Musa Qaleh in October 2006. The turbine operation might provide them with an opportunity to cut the sort of deal that would have come naturally to their Victorian forerunners in the region.

It seemed to Williams that the different elements inside the insurgents' ranks would have conflicting attitudes to what was a significant development in the play of power in their area. It was possible that local commanders might recognise the political and practical benefits of standing back. By allowing the convoy through they would be demonstrating the sincerity of their claims to have the interests of the people at heart. Once the turbine was in place they would be able to tax the electricity humming down the power lines. The Taliban, though, were driven by instinct and emotion as much as by logic. Williams suspected their warrior pride would not allow them to step aside and there would, at the very least, be some token attacks. They were unlikely to pass up the opportunity "to pick at us at the edges . . . kill a few soldiers en route". These attacks were more likely to take place on the journey out than the journey in. Once the turbine was delivered, there was no further advantage, and all bets would be off. "Then it's just a free-for-all," Williams said, and this time they would know which route the convoy was going to take.

There was also the attitude of the "Tier One Taliban", Mullah Omar and the exiles who sat in Quetta directing the campaign, to consider. They would want the last word in decisions affecting so important an event. It seemed unlikely that they would cede to the government the propaganda equivalent of an open goal.

The situation seemed to contain an interesting possibility. The tension between local and external interests might be exploited to create a rift between the Taliban commanders on the ground and the Quetta Shura. The planners had soft and hard power at their disposal and they used both in tandem as they went along. The most effective non-military weapon in Afghanistan was money, and ISAF had plenty of it. An attempt had been made previously to buy the acquiescence of the insurgents by paying both them and tribal leaders who could exert some control over their actions. In the end it had come to nothing. "They negotiated with the wrong people," said a senior Helmand Task Force officer. "They paid off the wrong people and it just didn't work. You have got a real potpourri of tribes all the way up the upper Sangin Valley so there are an awful lot of people you need to square away." They included the Taliban foreign fighters who were unlikely to accept a ceasefire no matter how tactical and temporary. The chances of success were too slim to be worth serious pursuit.

There was another, more subtle way of softening up the insurgents. The most dangerous leg of the journey was the stretch through Kajaki Sofia, the belt of cultivated land south of the dam complex. It ran along the eastern bank of the Helmand river and to the west of the 611, and was prime poppy country. It was beyond the patrolling range of Inkerman to the south and Kajaki to the north. The insurgents were strongly established inside it and seemed determined to hold the ground, routinely shooting at helicopters when they overflew the area.

But their occupation depended to some degree on the passivity of the population. Williams hoped local leaders would use what influence they had with the insurgents to persuade them not to disrupt a development that would undoubtedly bring major benefits to the miserable lives of the inhabitants. He planned to use ANA officers and the mullahs who were attached to every Afghan unit to hold "key leader engagements" in all the villages along the 8-kilometre stretch of the 611 that led to the gates of the dam complex. They would explain exactly what was going on. The message was that the soldiers were not interested in grubbing up their poppy fields. They were there to help the people, as agents of the central government, who would be given the credit for the impending improvement to their lives. They were also to pass on practical instructions. Everyone was to keep well back from the road and the convoy to minimise the risk of being mistaken for insurgents and shot. These messages were to be reinforced later with leaflet drops and broadcasts. The latter were beamed to the radio sets that had been distributed throughout Helmand, tuned to a wavelength that pumped out news and upbeat messages from Lashkar Gah.

The leaflets were printed in colour and showed four frames of a strip cartoon. The first pictured a large lorry, with the turbine on the back, passing through a bazaar on its way to a distant reservoir while local people went peaceably about their business. The next

323

showed the same scene but with the addition of power lines, buzzing with electricity, while the amplified call to prayer blared out from a loudspeaker on the mosque. Below, the remaining frames spelled out the alternative. Scowling turbaned gunmen are shooting up the convoy before being flattened by ISAF missiles.

The ANA arguments would be sweetened by cash. The passage of the convoy would disrupt local life. Farmers and their families who lived in the compounds nearest the route might be forced to move out of their homes for a few days. The ramshackle bazaar at the southern end of Kajaki Sofia would have to shut down temporarily. In return for these inconveniences ISAF was willing to hand over sizeable compensation payments. The assumption was that some of the money at least would find its way into the hands of the Taliban. It seemed a small price to pay for the life or limb of a soldier.

Behind the soft words lurked the big stick. The elders would also be used to communicate with the Taliban. They were to let them know that the visitation was only temporary. For the time being at least, ISAF's interest was in the turbine only and there was no intention to build a FOB in Kajaki Sofia or disrupt their drug operations there. The message, said Williams, was that "we're just going . . . to take the convoy through, then we're going to get out . . . leave us alone. If you try and stop us then we will destroy you."

Williams certainly had the means to carry out the threat. Come D-Day there would be a thousand ISAF and Afghan troops swamping the area. From his own battalion he had "A" and "B" Companies along with the FSG, the Mortar Platoon and the Patrols Platoon. He was also given command of "X" Company of 2 Para, who were based at Kajaki Dam, and the battalion's "D" Company were due in from Sangin a few days before the operation began. That added up to five hundred fighting soldiers. They would be supported by an ANA *Kandak*, which brought in another four hundred, together with their Royal Irish mentors. The men on the ground could call on indirect fire support from the mortars and the 105mm artillery pieces perched up on the hills overlooking the dam. This would be supplemented by devastating air power from Apache attack helicopters and a variety of "fast air" jets.

D-Day had been set for 27 August. The Paras began to arrive at Kajaki five days before. The base meandered along a plateau that sat above the Helmand river. It had been named "Zeebrugge" by the Royal Marines who wintered there in 2006/07 after the navy's famous attempt to blockade the Belgian port in April 1918. It was a picturesque and healthy spot. The garrison lived and worked in low, stone-clad cabins, and the spaces in between were shaded by pine trees. There was water everywhere — in the river, in the fountain that played outside the gates of the camp, and in the reservoir that glittered in the bowl of mountains that lay behind the dam. In the morning and the evening the soldiers went there to swim and jump off the rocks into the cool, clean depths. Kajaki seemed more like a hunting lodge than a military base, and that, according to local legend, was what it had once been, a royal retreat used by the last king of Afghanistan.

Like many places in Afghanistan, Kajaki had seen a succession of foreigners come and go over the years. The Russians set up a base there during the occupation to protect the dam. It also served as an R&R centre for weary Soviet soldiers. Their tenancy had come to an end in gruesome fashion. Everyone who passed through Kajaki was familiar with the story of the Soviet garrison's last stand. By the end there were only a handful of soldiers left, holed up in a two-storey barrack block at the camp's southern gate. When the mujahedin finally broke in they flayed them alive, playing their screams over their own military radios so that the commanders in HQ could hear the death agonies of their men. No one knew whether the story was true. You did not need to be particularly imaginative, though, to sense a slight chill in the air and a pang of desolation as you stepped out of the bright sunshine and into the concrete hallways, still blackened by the smoke of the battle. This was relieved, though, by the graffiti left behind by the Afghan troops who were the last to occupy it. The walls were covered with delicate drawings of flowers, and large female eyes, ringed with kohl, weeping pear-shaped tears. It was a marked contrast to the pneumatic, pouting pin-ups torn from *Nuts* and *FHM* plastered over the walls of the quarters of their Brit counterparts.

The accommodation blocks were crowded out but it was a pleasure to sleep in the open air. The Paras set up their pods along the concrete walkways. At night you could lie peacefully on your cot looking up at Orion glittering through the branches of the pine trees, lulled by the rumble of the jumbo jets ploughing the stratosphere, plying back and forth between destinations the peasants in the mud villages below could barely imagine, let alone conceive of visiting. Every now and then the calm was shattered by a chilling sound. One of the stray dogs that the soldiers had adopted would start to howl. The cry would be taken up by another, then another, until the whole valley was echoing with the eerie and supernatural-sounding chorus. The explanation was that one of them had spotted a lurking jackal and was warning the others. The phenomenon brought a touch of Transylvania to the deserted landscape.

On the opposite bank from Zeebrugge lay the village of Tangye. The original cluster of houses, with mosque and bakery, had grown into a commercial centre after the Russians were driven out. They left behind a strip of runway, which was soon transformed into a bazaar when rows of single-roomed shops sprang up on either side of the concrete. There was no life in the bazaar now. The constant fighting between the Brits and the insurgents had driven away many of the inhabitants. The area south of the camp, Kajaki Olya, was empty after dark. The fields and the compounds that lined the road for the first three or four kilometres were abandoned, though their owners came back during the day to work the fields. The Taliban had been pushed back by the successive waves of British soldiers who had washed through Kajaki so that the front line was several kilometres away and Zeebrugge was rarely troubled by indirect fire. The soldiers still faced a threat from IEDs when they went out on patrol, however. New arrivals were met by the sight of a shattered Jackal armoured vehicle sitting outside the compound which had been caught in an IED blast while carrying out a recce along the 611.

The insurgents were getting increasingly skilful in the way they planted their bombs. Not long before 3 Para arrived, a 2 Para soldier had been caught in a blast that no amount of drills and training could have prevented. He was taking part in a patrol to what was effectively the Taliban front line north of the base. The column set off on Tuesday, 22 July, crossing the bridge to Tangye then heading into the dusty hills. Their destination was a compound that they had fortified on a previous visit. It was on rising ground and commanded a good view of the enemy territory beyond. When they arrived they began improving the defences, shifting around the sandbags. Private Louis Smit of 2 Para, who was driving a quad bike carrying water and ammunition for the patrol, was 50 metres away when he heard the explosion. "We realised somebody must have set off an IED so we went on the net . . . for two or three minutes there was dead silence. Then they were screaming for a medic." Lance Corporal Jan Fourie, a South African like Smit, raced forward to the compound, now billowing with smoke and dust. Smit gunned his quad, forcing it up the steep slope. When he arrived Fourie had already applied tourniquets to Lance Corporal

Tom Neathway, who was loaded on a stretcher. He was the victim of a clever booby trap triggered by the movement of one of the sandbags. The bomb had blown off both his legs and it looked as if he would lose his arm. To Smit's amazement Neathway was "talking and making jokes . . . he was calming us down, saying stuff like 'I don't think I'll ever drive my Subaru again' ".

As they loaded him on to the quad the insurgents launched an attack on the compound with RPGs and small arms and they extracted in the midst of a firefight. Smit was heading to a rendezvous point with a Vector armoured ambulance which was following the patrol. On the way they reached a difficult stretch where Smit and his quad bike had got stuck before. "I thought to myself I'll just put a bit of welly on," he said, but the vehicle jammed against a tree trunk and he and his two companions had to unhook the trailer carrying the stretcher and lift it around the obstacle. They reached the ambulance, loaded the casualty in the back and drove to the designated landing site. As they waited, Smit and the ambulance driver, Corporal Jason "Jay" Barnes, did what they could for the wounded man. The casevac helicopter arrived quickly to fly him to the field hospital at Bastion. It looked as if Neathway would survive. Smit had been impressed by Barnes's performance. "I congratulated Jay Barnes," he remembered. "I said, 'You did well, mate.' "

They set off on the short journey along the track that led along the river back to Kajaki with a WMIK leading the way. Smit followed on his quad and the Vector ambulance brought up the rear. They had gone only a few yards when there was another huge explosion. The ambulance disappeared in a cloud of dust and smoke. Smit grabbed his med pack and the stretcher and ran back to see the Vector lying on its side with its tracks blown off. Jay Barnes was dead. There were two other men in the back, including one who had been hurt in the initial blast. The ambulance had been hit by another IED planted by the insurgents, who had clearly been observing the soldiers in the area closely enough to predict their likely movements.

Barnes was twenty-five years old and came from Exeter. He was a member of the REME on attachment to 2 Para and had been in Kajaki for three months. He was an armourer by trade and much admired for his skill, and also his willingness to do whatever was asked of him, such as driving the ambulance on the day of his death. "He was not one to be left behind when there was an operation to be conducted," said his company commander, Major Grant Haywood. "He was first class, never one to call time when there was a job to be done . . . he died as he lived, placing others first and doing what he wanted to do so well without fear or complaint. Nothing exemplifies this more than the last moments before his passing."

The spot where he died was just across the river from the base. The incident demonstrated the near-impunity with which the insurgents were able to operate outside the hours when the soldiers were on the ground. In these conditions there was no possibility of exercising governance beyond the limits of British control, and the office and residence of Kajaki's district leader were sited inside the base. Mullah Abdul Razzak was an impressive figure, as bulky and as slow-moving as a grizzly bear. Like a grizzly, his apparent cuddliness was deceptive. As with many men of authority on both sides of the conflict he had once belonged to the mujahedin, joining them when he was a nineteen-year-old student and fighting the Russians for eleven years. The soldiers liked to believe that he had played a part in the grisly fate of the Russian garrison, though when pressed on the subject he merely smiled and looked enigmatic.

Abdul Razzak lived in style in a pleasant villa, surrounded by orchards and gardens and protected by his own bodyguards, who treated him with careful deference. He was shown similar courtesy by the British. It was more than mere politeness. The governor was said to be an influential figure in the area. He had three brothers living in Kajaki Sofia and, despite the fact that he was literally in the enemy camp, managed to maintain links with the insurgents. "I know all the local Taliban commanders," he boasted. "I know their fathers and their grandfathers."

He had good reason to hate them. They had killed one of his brothers, dragging him out of a taxi when he was on his way from Kajaki Sofia to Lashkar Gah to check on Abdul Razzak's wife and six children, who lived there. In Afghanistan, though, life had to be lived as it was. The circumstances did not allow the governor the moral luxury of shunning his sibling's murderers. Accommodations had to be made and deals struck. He spoke regularly to the insurgents by walkie-talkie radio.

This made Abdul Razzak a potentially vital player in attempts to persuade the Taliban to leave the convoy alone.

At noon on Monday, 25 August, Huw Williams held a shura with Abdul Razzak in his compound. The meeting took place in a low-ceilinged room around a long table with the governor sitting at the top. Overhead a harsh strip light beamed down and a large fan churned the air. The meeting was a formality, an official display of the governor's engagement in the big event. He was to present the public face of the operation to the 5000 inhabitants of Kajaki Sofia. They would not need to be persuaded that it was a good thing. "Everyone is really happy about the convoy and with the upgrading of the dam," the district leader said. "This is a real improvement in the performance of the government." The feeling was that Governor Mangal in Helmand was "really doing his job". The success of the operation would mean "a real defeat for the Taliban and a real boost for the support for our side".

Abdul Razzak was expected to front shuras with local figures in the run-up to the convoy's arrival. He would broadcast warnings that if anyone approached the convoy they would be regarded as insurgents and shot. Intelligence reports were warning of the possibility of suicide bombers attacking the vehicles as they passed through Kajaki Sofia. He also undertook to put out his own feelers to the Taliban and oversee the elders' contacts with the insurgents.

Having finished the diplomatic part of his day's work, sharing a lunch of lamb and rice with Abdul

332

Razzak, Williams returned to his planning. The base was filling up. Over the previous two days, 2 Para's "X" Company had pushed south, clearing and securing compounds on either side of the 611 in Kajaki Olya, making room for the new arrivals. By Monday, 3 Para's "B" Company had moved into a complex of houses and storerooms a few kilometres south of Zeebrugge. "A" Company set up in an empty compound nearer the base. That afternoon, the Afghan *kandak* and their Royal Irish mentors arrived and deployed the following day at their own temporary base near the Paras. "X" Company and their bomb clearance detachment were scouring the ground for IEDs as they worked their way down the 611. They soon found them. One had been improvised out of a 10-kilo oil drum, packed with home-made fertiliser explosive. It was a "victim-operated" device which exploded when someone stepped on a pressure plate. The plate was made out of two pieces of plastic foam. One surface was studded with ball bearings, the other with tinfoil. The weight of a footfall would complete a circuit and blow the charge. The bomb had been discovered by a metal detector, but as Captain Liam Fitzgerald-Finch, the RLC explosives expert in charge of clearing the route, was only too aware, the insurgents were increasingly using non-metal components. He and his men would be extremely busy over the coming days. As soon as darkness fell the Taliban bomb layers emerged to plant their surprises in the culverts and potholes of the 611. One had been shot dead the night before in the act of setting up an IED.

333

"X" Company's progress down the road brought them closer and closer to two known Taliban strongpoints. One, called "Flagstaff", was next to a distinctive stand of trees on a slight bend to the north. It was about 5 kilometres from the southern gate of the base. The other, "Vantage", was just to the north-west of it, in the Green Zone, where it bordered one of the channels of the Helmand river.

The positions were thought to be solid and well placed to give good fields of fire over the road, the cultivated areas and the bare hillsides on the southern side of the road from where the convoy would approach. So far the insurgents were showing every sign of wanting a fight. On the evening of 25 August, from the village of Paysang on the west bank of the river, they had opened fire with small arms and airburst RPGs at two American Cobra helicopters whose pilots had decided to take an unauthorised excursion to view the Kajaki Dam. Intelligence reports said there were about three hundred fighters in the area, of whom about a hundred were in the southern zone. They had been watching the regular arrivals of Chinooks and had drawn their conclusions. They had confirmation of the imminent arrival of the convoy through the leaflet drops, which had now started. But they seemed to doubt that the soldiers were there solely to protect the turbine and anticipated a move to occupy their haven and break up their narco-labs. Messages were intercepted ordering fighters in the north to move south to bolster the defence.

On the morning of 26 August, "X" Company set off to take another step closer to Flagstaff and Vantage. Intelligence reported that the insurgents were interpreting this as the start of the big operation. This suited Williams's plan well. In fact only two platoons would be involved in the day's activities. "It will be interesting to see what they say when they see a whole Afghan *kandak* coming their way," he said. The purpose of the exercise was to sting the Taliban into action. "Today is just probing," he said after the morning gathering in the windowless briefing room at the base. "All we're doing is poking them with a stick, getting them to fight back and starting a process of attrition." Once they opened fire they could expect a swift battering from the 105mm guns on the hill and a pounding from the two Para battalions' mortars. They would also have to endure the deadly accuracy of the GMLRS rockets sited near Sangin and aerial bombardment by fast jets and Apache helicopters. To use a phrase that was often heard as the soldiers discussed the forthcoming operation, if they popped their heads up, "they are going to get smashed".

The Sparrowhawk West OP, which lay at the southern end of the ridge that loomed over the base, would provide a grandstand view of the day's events. That morning, a group from 3 Para set off on the ninety-minute climb to reach it. Among them was Stuart Hale, who had spent several months in Kajaki in the summer of 2006 fighting off fierce attacks from the Taliban, who were intent on scoring a symbolic victory by capturing the most significant piece of infrastructure in Helmand. At the time he was a sniper with Support Company and passed his days in the OPs scanning the valley below. He had returned to Afghanistan with the battalion as a corporal serving in the intelligence cell. Hale was a changed man, mentally and physically. He had lost his leg when he stepped on a mine after scrambling down from his position on the Normandy OP to engage a group of insurgents who had set up a checkpoint on the 611 below. One of his 3 Para comrades, Corporal Mark Wright, had been killed that day going to the rescue of Hale. Four others had been wounded, two of them also losing limbs.

Hale had seized the chance to go back to Kajaki when it was offered. It was the last mile of a painful personal journey, and he hoped that completing it would bring a measure of release. Media reports focused naturally on the fatal casualties in Afghanistan. The wounded were anonymous. The advances in battlefield medicine meant that men who a generation ago would have died of their wounds now survived. Some, like Hale, had been able to go back to their units, though not necessarily in a role that they would have chosen before. Stu Hale had once had the ambition of joining the SAS. That would not happen now. But he was determined to gain as much of his old fitness and mobility as possible, certainly enough to carry him back up the mountain under his own power to the scene of the disaster.

He had survived, but when he looked back it seemed that his wounding had been a less shocking experience than the process of recovery. "The actual incident itself

. . . until Mark got hit wasn't traumatic," he said. "It was almost surreal. We were laughing and joking thinking, Christ, if we're finding this funny there's not much anyone else can throw at us that would dampen our spirits."

But his resilience was pushed to the limit when he reached the UK. He had been taken to Selly Oak hospital in Birmingham, where he found himself in the same ward as Corporal Stuart Pearson, who had also lost a leg in the mine strike and who also returned to the battalion. Hale was unconscious for five days, and when he woke up found it difficult to distinguish between dreams, or rather nightmares, and wakefulness. He suffered from paranoid delusions. "It was horrific," he said. "You get the impression that everyone is out to get you. You hallucinate. I had two doctors come in to speak to me. One of them was trying to coax me and calm me down and explain what was happening." The doctor was dressed in blue. When he went, "a green doctor would come in. He would tell me how as soon as my family was gone he was going to slit my throat and cut off the machines and bleed me to death."

Hale was completely powerless. "I had all these pipes going into my mouth to feed me nutrients so I couldn't scream for help." His mother would stroke his hair and soothe him as he struggled to tell her his imaginings, but the words would not emerge. "It was like an old Punch and Judy show," he said. "You know — 'He's behind you!' It was horrible."

For a time he suffered the delusion that his injury dated from a tour of Iraq in late 2004 and he had been lying in hospital for two years. He had a "crystal-clear hallucination" that his girlfriend Shannon was waiting outside the ward, unable to face coming through the door because his injuries were so horrific. After a few days the nightmares tapered off and were replaced by surreal fantasies. He thought the then French President Jacques Chirac had come to visit him and that all the orderlies were members of the SAS. Part of the madness was caused by the drugs, part by the trauma. It passed, to be replaced by the physical ordeal of learning to walk again.

He had been lucky. The blast had taken off a portion of his leg just above the ankle. It meant that the point of amputation was through the knee, giving him a better chance of walking evenly on a prosthetic leg. He went from Selly Oak to Headley Court, the Defence Medical Rehabilitation Centre near Epsom in Surrey. Initially he spent three months there, on and off. He and Shannon had a child on the way, a little girl they had named Sophia. She was due in late December. He was determined to be standing up when he saw her come into the world. He kept his promise to himself. "Sure enough, on the day she was born I was in the hospital on a walking stick," he said delightedly. "It was amazing." From then on his injury "paled into insignificance. It wasn't about me any more. This was nothing."

That morning at 9 o'clock Hale and his companions were dropped off from a Pinzgauer carrier at the foot of the first peak. A stony path snaked up the barren hillside to the Athens OP. On either side of the narrow track were rocks splashed with white paint which had turned a dirty grey over the years. It was a warning that the area was still strewn with the mines that the Russians scattered everywhere. Stu Hale led the way up the steep slope, swinging his arms and bounding forward, pivoting on the metal and plastic of his right leg. It was hot work toiling up the hillside but the air on the first peak was fresh as it rose from the slate-blue water of the reservoir, stretching below to the east. We paused for a breather, then plunged down the next steep dip before climbing up again towards the Normandy OP position, which was no longer occupied.

The "X" Company patrol was well under way and the sound of gunfire was drifting in from the Green Zone. There was a steady bob-bob-bob from a .50-cal followed by the lazy, seashore swish of heavy bullets flowing through the air. Regimental Sergeant Major "Moggy" Bridge reported progress from the information coming over the net. The Taliban had attacked "X" Company with RPGs from Vantage. 2 Para's Patrols Platoon, which was providing overwatch on the hills to the east of the highway, had fired back with the heavy machine guns. There was a flat banging behind as the mortars from Zeebrugge opened up, then a rushing noise as they flew over, on their way to Vantage, followed a little later by hollow, drumbeat thuds as they landed.

We stopped below Normandy and stood back to give Stu a few minutes of solitude to look down on the tawny folds of hillside where he and his mates had suffered. There was nothing to distinguish it from any other hump of desert in Afghanistan. He stood silhouetted against the flawless blue of the sky, shading his eyes from the glare bouncing off the bleached earth and rocks, looking down the winding valley and the lush green band of crops and trees now smudged with smoke from the fighting.

There was a little farther to go to reach Sparrowhawk. The sun was high now but Hale seemed to have barely broken sweat. He set off again, bounding confidently along the rising and falling track that ran along the ridge. The Sparrowhawk OP was busy as the men manning it scanned the battlefield with outsized binoculars from behind sandbagged sangars, reporting back the slightest motion on the ground. They could see everything from up there. In the fields on the far side of the river figures were stooped over the crops, the men in grey and black, the women in startling blue chadors that echoed the shade of the sky. Children were playing and donkeys stood placidly awaiting their next burden. It looked like an idealised picture of peasant life. On the other side of the river, a kilometre or so away, the fields were empty. The only figures in the landscape were men in uniform, moving slowly and methodically between the compounds that lined the 611.

The observers in the OP were concentrating on the shoals, gravel banks and fields directly across the river. Intelligence reports suggested that a Taliban mortar team was lurking there. Then, out of the anonymous dun and green patchwork there was a flash and a puff of smoke. A few moments later grey smoke blossomed at the foot of the hill below the OP right next to the compound where "B" Company had set up its temporary base, followed by the thump of the explosion. A Light Counter Mortar Radar (LCMR) kit was set up in front of the position and was swivelling to and fro. Its function was to track the trajectory of mortar bombs and the next one, it seemed, was heading in our direction. We ducked into the shelter under the observation platform and the missile landed harmlessly 200 metres away. Two more mortars followed, one from the south and one from across the river. The observers radioed back the grid reference of the firing point given by the LCMR for the mortar lines to respond. Then there was a bang like a giant door slamming, followed by a slithering noise as artillery shells from the 105mm battery next to the dam spun through the air towards Flagstaff and Vantage, sending up pillars of smoke and dust. The noise they made would drift back then the land would sink back into silence, invaded occasionally by the drone of an airliner overhead.

Around noon it was time to head back. Stu Hale once again led the way with the same confident, bouncing step. When we reached the camp he returned to his bed space, neatly set up on the concrete walkway next to the main accommodation block. A large drawing in felt tip of the Parachute Regiment winged insignia was propped next to his cot. He seemed subdued and reflective. Revisiting the scene had brought back to him memories he had forgotten, "a feeling of despair which I couldn't remember before, to be honest . . . it was a bit eerie". He was also struck by the change that had taken place in the countryside in the preceding two years. When he last looked down on the 611 from the OPs "it was really thriving. There were kids running around, old people". Now, apart from the fighters, it was deserted. "It's a shame," he said. "All those houses, all that effort that people put into [things] and now it's just all dead."

It was a bleak image. But at least the prospect of the arrival of the turbine convoy was there to lighten the picture. "It has got to be a step in the right direction," Hale said. "If this gets pulled off at least some of it will have been worth it."

CHAPTER
SIXTEEN

"Something our Parents will Understand"

Early on the morning of Thursday, 28 August, the convoy carrying the turbine and its key components rolled out of KAF and set off west along Highway One on the first leg of its epic journey. About half an hour later, another column laden with the logistical necessities to support the operation left Bastion and headed eastwards. At first light they joined up at a rendezvous point a few kilometres to the north of the highway. D-Day had slipped by only twenty-four hours, a considerable achievement given the number of logistical cogs that had to click into place if the enterprise was to succeed.

Dawn came up on a remarkable sight. Nearly 150 vehicles sat throbbing and revving in the desert, wreathed in a fog of dust and grit. They ranged in size from the giant HETs carrying the heaviest kit to the Mastiffs and WMIKs that would protect the force as it crawled northwards to Kajaki. No one knew how long the journey would take. It depended on how many physical obstacles and IEDs were encountered and how many ambushes were launched.

So far, though, reality had matched the plan. The two elements of the convoy meshed easily, scarcely pausing before they set off. Then, after barely a kilometre, the dramas began. The engineers at the front of the column found a bomb planted at the side of the route. It was a new and unusual type and it took a while to deal with. At the same time, tyres on the HET carrying the crane blew out. To Lieutenant Colonel Rufus McNeil, the commander of 13 Air Assault Support Regiment and the master of the convoy, the ruptured tyres were more worrying than the IED. "This spelt real trouble," he said. "We had to take the crane off, put it on another vehicle and repair all the tyres." The gloomy thought struck him that "if that was an indication of what the journey was going to be like it was going to take us potentially weeks to get there". As the day wore on, though, progress improved. The crane weighed 85 tonnes and was the heaviest bit of kit being carried. There were more breakdowns and blowouts but thanks to the skill of the drivers and the repair teams, the convoy kept moving. The initial plan had been to roll on through the night. By the early hours of 29 August it was clear that exhaustion and the difficulty of clearing the route of bombs and obstacles in the dark made that aim impossible. The convoy stopped at 3a.m. and everyone curled up where they could to grab two hours of blissful sleep.

While the convoy ground northwards on the initial
day of its journey, the Paras and the ANA were
launching the first stage of the operation to secure the
route down through Kajaki Sofia. They had spent
the preceding days probing along the 611, testing
the Taliban's reactions. While they edged south, the
artillery and mortars bombarded the insurgents'
positions, killing at least a dozen fighters. It now
seemed likely that when the big push came they would
stand and fight. Senior commanders had been away in
Musa Qaleh when the build-up began and had only just
returned. There were intelligence reports of another
200 fighters and "prestige weapons", thought to be
recoilless rifles and additional heavy machines, being
moved into the area. Huw Williams still wanted to leave
the insurgents a way out from their strategy of
confrontation, and on the evening of the 27th a
loudspeaker was set up at the nearest point to the
insurgents' positions to repeat the message that the
British and government troops had no intention of
moving in to Kajaki Sofia.

By the morning of the 28th the Paras' lead sections
and the ANA *kandak* fighting alongside them were only
500 metres from Flagstaff and Vantage, the insurgent
strongpoints that lay to the west of the 611. The main
stage of the operation was about to begin. Before it
started Huw Williams had requested a relaxation of the
Rules of Engagement to allow troops to fire on
positions where the enemy were presumed to be
without having to positively identify them first. "I
suppose . . . most people would interpret it as all gloves

345

are off," said Williams. "We're now war-fighting as opposed to any pretence of counter-insurgency." It was a precautionary measure that in the end was not needed. But it sent a signal to his officers and men that their commanding officer was giving them all the means, physical and legal, to do their job.

The ANA had been tasked with taking Vantage, the first objective, which lay to the right of the 611, where the Green Zone sloped away to the shingle banks of the Helmand river. It was an important moment in the development of the ANA. This was the first time they had played such a prominent part in a major operation. Their performance would provide hard evidence upon which their progress towards the distant goal of taking charge of Afghanistan's security could be judged. Even so, it had taken a political fight to get them in the line-up. They had been included in the original planning but diverted away from the operation on the orders of President Karzai, who wanted them to go to the Nadi Ali area to the south, where a Taliban build-up had been reported which threatened Lashkar Gah. The intelligence was confused and another false alarm was suspected. Mark Carleton-Smith, Regional Command South and the Americans insisted that the practical and symbolic importance of the *kandak*'s presence was paramount and the president was forced to back down.

Now, in the rising heat of the morning of 28 August, they were poised to launch. The attack was preceded by a heavy mortar and artillery bombardment on Flagstaff and Vantage. It was intended as much as anything as a demonstration of the futility of resistance. The message, according to Major Ben Howell, the battery commander, was "your best course of action is not to fight us and quite honestly we don't want to fight you".

It was certainly delivered with force. At 6 a.m., from the heights of Sparrowhawk, you could see the compounds flickering with fire as the first mortar rounds hit. The .50-cal in the OP joined in, spitting bright tracer rounds in dipping arcs that sparked as they struck the walls. Soon a banner of grey smoke trailed over the healthy green of the fields. In the space of a few seconds, six 105 shells landed on Flagstaff. The grouping was immaculate. Thick sepia plumes leapt skywards, held their form for thirty seconds, than bled into the innocent blue, like ink dissolving in water. "Spot on," said Private Scott Bunwell, one of the Sparrowhawk observers, approvingly.

Within a few minutes both enemy positions were smothered in smoke. There was a burst of fire from the direction of Vantage but it lasted only a few seconds. An intelligence report came over the net. One of the Taliban commanders, watching the bombardment from a distance, was urging his men to hold their positions until reinforcements reached the area to support them with heavy machine guns and mortars. Soon afterwards the first Afghan soldiers were moving across a paddock in front of the compound, ready to storm it. "There's fuck-all to assault," exclaimed another observer. "They've all bugged out."

The fall of fire was being observed and adjusted by Sergeant Paul "Buck" Rogers, of the Second Battalion of the Royal Regiment of Scotland, who was attached to the RHA. His skin was red and raw and his lips dry and flaking, baked by the long hours in the sun clamped to his binoculars, peering with merciless eyes at the ground below. The radar had shown the ghostly outlines of eight or nine men leaving the compound after the initial bombardment, scrambling down the rat runs that led out the back. As they fled they were caught in a shower of mortar fire. Now only one figure was showing. It was, someone said, hard not to feel sympathy for the poor bastard. "Not me," growled Buck. "I've lost too many good mates to feel sorry." He had managed to get only five hours' sleep in the last forty-eight hours and kept going on constant brews and fags. When he tried to kip his brain wouldn't let him. "There's a little guy sitting on your back," he said. "As long as there are people on the ground, I can't sleep. It's a fraternal thing."

By 6.54a.m. the Afghans had cleared Vantage. On the hill, there was a moment or two of quiet. The only sound was the wind rustling in the camouflage netting. Down in the valley, smoke and dust lay lightly on the fields like a morning mist. The lone insurgent had disappeared from the radar screen. It had been decided to spare him and he was now presumably burrowing frantically into the Green Zone. He was a lucky man. Intelligence had heard an area commander asking his sub-commanders how many men were left. The answer came back that they were unable to say. No one was answering their radios.

Now "D" Company of 2 Para, led by Major Mike Shervington, were closing on Flagstaff, which lay beside a distinctive stand of six or seven tall trees on a bend in the 611. They hung back while it was hit with an air strike. There was no sign of the aircraft delivering the bomb. It was too small to see, an unmanned Reaper drone, lost in the immensity of the sky. The 500-pound bomb burst right on the target. The blast was followed by a ripple of further explosions as the strongpoint's ammunition dump went up.

Intelligence reports said the Taliban were preparing to send a suicide bomber on a motorbike towards the advancing soldiers. It seemed possible. The bombardment had attracted an audience. Not far from where the bomb had landed a gaggle of young men on the 125cc machines that you saw all over the region had gathered, whether out of curiosity or hostile intent was impossible to say. "If I see someone moving down on a motorbike, can I job him?" asked one of the men on the .50-cal. But as the Paras' lead section neared Flagstaff the young men dispersed.

Everyone on the hill was eager to fight. They were still talking about the way they had dealt with one of the mortar teams that had been harassing the area two days before. They had managed to get "eyes on" two insurgents and opened up with the .50-cal. The team escaped unhurt but left behind the tripod that supported the mortar barrel. When dusk fell the men returned to retrieve it. Up in the OP they were waiting with a Javelin. The missile scored a direct hit. Everyone on the hill knew someone who had been killed or maimed and had no sympathy to spare for the perpetrators. "After what's happened to friends of mine I'd kill them all," said one. The man who fired the Javelin had been close to Tom Neathway, the IED victim from Kajaki, as well as two of the three Paras killed by a suicide bomber at Inkerman in June. He had felt no qualms as he sighted on the men creeping through the darkness and pressed the trigger. "It was good to have a bit of revenge," he said.

As the Paras approached Flagstaff, the only sign of resistance was an occasional burst of small-arms fire coming from a bunker a hundred metres or so to the south of the position on the far side of the 611, next to a compound with a bright green door. Whoever was inside was showing suicidal determination. The mortars and the 105mms had each taken a turn at hitting the bunker but had failed to silence it, and every now and then there was another spurt of ineffectual fire. A pair of American Apaches was on station overhead, black gnats in the blue, tirelessly buzzing back and forth. Just before 9.30a.m. one of them turned away and moved towards the bunker, talked into position by a Joint Tactical Air Controller on the ground. No flash was visible as the missile was fired, just the ball of fire as it hit the bunker, leaving a smoking pit.

It was the end of the morning's action. Fifteen minutes later the Paras entered Flagstaff without meeting any resistance. The position had been reduced to churned earth and a few shattered walls. The surrounding compounds were almost untouched. There was little sign of the occupants. The casualties had been removed, leaving only splashes of blood, and the stores had gone up in smoke when the first bomb was dropped.

Once the fighting had begun, the area had started to empty. To the south of the battle zone, straggling lines of civilians, about thirty or forty of them, made their way across the gravel bars and around the oxbow pools towards the west. Most were women, carrying bundles and trailing little gaggles of children. They were heading for a flatbed chain ferry, carrying a few cars and motorbikes, waiting to carry them across the main waterway to the safety of the western bank.

Williams called a pause so as to pursue the diplomatic side of his plan. That afternoon Steve Boardman organised a broadcast, inviting the leaders of Kajaki Sofia to come to a shura the following day. The intention was to try and persuade the Taliban, via the elders, to give up and fall back. Even after the exodus of the morning there were still many civilians in Kajaki Sofia. Their presence would put tight restraints on the Paras if they had to fight to secure the rest of the road. The first stretch of the route was all but empty. The next sector was thickly populated. President Karzai was already angry at the numbers of civilians being killed by ISAF actions. He let it be known that he would be watching the forthcoming operation closely. The British did not need to be told to be careful.

There were good reasons why the Taliban might decide to hold off. According to intelligence reports they had suffered heavy losses. At the outset there had been about two hundred fighters in the Kajaki Sofia area, including the reinforcements drafted in when 3 Para appeared. Of those, it was reckoned that fifty had been killed, fifty wounded and fifty had deserted.

On Friday, 29 August, Steve Boardman and the district leader Abdul Razzak drove with their escorts to a canopy of intertwined trees at a spot a few kilometres south of the base to the side of the 611 to conduct the shura announced the previous day. Fifty-five men gathered to hear what the district leader and his friends had to say. Abdul Razzak and Boardman were to give the elders a message to pass on to the insurgents. At the same time they wanted to strike an agreement on a tactical approach that would reduce the risks to both the soldiers and the local population. Abdul Razzak repeated the message spread through leaflets, radio broadcasts and by loudspeaker about the limited aims of the operation. He offered cash in compensation for the disruption the passage of the convoy would create, and asked the leaders to cooperate in allowing the soldiers to move freely in a 300-metrewide band either side of the 611. The elders left to hold their own discussions and another shura was called for 10.30 a.m. the following day.

Overnight, the question of civilian casualties took on an extra urgency. An American team had been inserted onto Black Mountain, a feature to the south of Kajaki Sofia, with the task of preventing any move by the Taliban to reinforce the area from Musa Qaleh. From there they had launched a series of offensive operations. On 30 August, wounded civilians, some of them badly injured, turned up at Sangin and FOB Inkerman saying they had been attacked by foreign troops. Such incidents gave a hollow ring to ISAF claims that their presence would bring security to the local population.

News of the blunder did not appear to have affected the Brits' negotiations with the Kajaki Sofia leaders, though. When Boardman, Abdul Razzak and Colonel Rahim, commander of the ANA *kandak*, returned at 10.30 on the morning of Saturday, 30 August, for the next meeting with the elders, they found that the crowd was twice as big as the day before. Ninety-two men had turned up. The British brought with them apples and oranges and bottles of water. The idea, said Boardman, was to "set the scene and make it as genial as we could". Among the crowd, it was safe to assume, were a number of Taliban. Once again the district chief opened the meeting. He emphasised the benefits the turbine would bring and encouraged the hope that it was the start of a process that would lead to the building of schools and hospitals. He was followed by Colonel Rahim, who spelt out the damage the insurgency was doing. The fighters were either outsiders who had no right to bring their violence to the area or local men whose campaign was only destroying the lives and property of their families and friends. Then it was Steve Boardman's turn. Like the rest of the British team he had taken off his helmet to try "to get a bit closer and a bit more personal. So I just took my helmet off, put my weapon down and went down in and amongst them". He began by saying that "the turbine itself was nothing to do with ISAF or the British or Americans. It was actually a gift from the Afghan government to the Afghan people and it should be seen that way."

His next remarks were made to everyone but intended for the Taliban in the crowd. He insisted that the British had no intention of building an FOB in Kajaki Sofia. Their sole interest was in protecting the convoy as it came through. Ideally, that would happen without a shot being fired. But if a single bullet was aimed at them they would respond with all the force they possessed. He warned the inhabitants that British and Afghan forces would be roaming around their homes on either side of the road. Families could leave if they wanted to, but if they chose to stay their compounds would not be searched. He also promised ISAF would pay the elders $25,000 for their help in securing the 611 and as compensation for closing the bazaar. The money would only be paid, though, once the convoy had unloaded and the troops had extracted.

The meeting went on for two hours. When it broke up it seemed to Boardman that "the elders were happy. They said that they wanted to talk to the Taliban to get their agreement and they wanted to come back later in the afternoon at four o'clock". The British and the Afghans believed that the agreement was now in the bag. The Taliban at the shura had allowed the elders to signal their agreement, so the consultation appeared to be a matter of form rather than substance. Boardman and the team climbed into their vehicles and drove back to Kajaki to draft a formal agreement.

When they returned to resume the shura the atmosphere was genial and positive. Boardman had in his pocket a paper signed by Huw Williams and Abdul Razzak committing them to the undertakings given earlier. It was now time for the elders to sign. Before they did so there were some points that they said the insurgents were anxious to clear up. The Taliban seemed remarkably cooperative. They were offering a ceasefire that would start from the time of the meeting. They also proposed going out that night to clear away the bombs they had planted along the 611, asking that no troops move on the road that night to avoid deadly misunderstandings. They were worried that they might still be liable to arrest. Boardman replied that if they weren't carrying weapons they would be indistinguishable from any other local male and would be left alone. The main sticking point was the duration of the ceasefire. He was told that the Taliban were prepared to offer only four days.

Boardman generated an aura of calm and good humour. His steel-rimmed specs and bald head made him look more like a schoolteacher than a soldier. But his strong belief in the goodness of human nature, essential if he was to do his job, was shot through with an iron streak of Northern common sense. The convoy was still some distance away. If, as seemed likely, there was a mechanical breakdown or a physical hold-up, then it would take more than four days to get the vehicles and escorts in and out. He insisted the ceasefire must last a week. The elder shook his head. "The initial response to that was . . . 'no, we can't do that' ". It dawned on Boardman that the man he was talking to was actually a Taliban commander, a

355

realisation that was subsequently confirmed by the district leader. The "elder" said that if a problem developed they could sit down and negotiate an extension to the ceasefire. Boardman held his ground. The man asked for a recess and retired for a huddled conversation with the others. When he returned he announced that they "needed to go and talk to the Taliban leaders".

They disappeared for an hour and returned with another demand. The Taliban wanted to be given forty-eight hours' notice of the convoy's final move. Boardman refused. "I said, no, that's not open for negotiation," he recalled a few hours after the meeting. The only issue for discussion was the length of the ceasefire and "everything else [was] set in stone". The elders retreated, promising to call Abdul Razzak on his satellite phone that evening with the Taliban's final decision. Boardman returned to camp. Williams was there to greet him as he climbed down from the Pinzgauer, a smile on his earnest face and a film of dust on his glasses.

At the evening briefing Williams insisted on the strictest discipline to ensure nothing was done to jeopardise the ceasefire. The soldiers were to react forcefully if their lives were threatened. But "if one shot is fired at you, use your own initiative", he said. "One shot overhead from one lone scared Taliban who is immediately grabbed by the man next to him" should not spark a firefight. "We're not going to throw it away over one shot flying harmlessly over our heads." Williams had been surprised that the Taliban had agreed to any ceasefire at all. At 8.10p.m. the district leader received a call on his mobile satphone telling him they were prepared to extend it to a full week.

There was a feeling of satisfaction in the air in Kajaki that night. The Paras sensed they were on the brink of achieving a great success that had been brought about by calculation and negotiation. The "smashing" could stop and no one was sad about that. The Taliban had been forced to compromise. When the elders first reported signs of their willingness to cut a deal they were demanding the right to search the convoy to verify that it was not carrying a new "secret weapon" designed to menace Iran. Now they were offering to clear IEDs from the 611.

Williams was delighted at the turn things had taken. There was no question of his ability to force the convoy through, but there would inevitably be collateral damage and innocent people might be killed. "I would hate to cause so much disruption that you then start to question whether the plan was worth it," he said after the meeting.

But the optimism was tempered with caution. Williams had no doubt that the Taliban's new attitude reflected the weakness of their position. "We've given them a face-saving measure. They can say, 'We let the turbine through because that's what the elders wished for.' But really the turbine would have got through either way and they'd have lost even more people. So I think we have given them something they can't really say no to." Still, the ceasefire decision had delivered "the perfect scenario". His last words as he went off to work on the following day's plan were "I just hope that it holds".

About thirty kilometres to the south the convoy was preparing to stop for the night, looking for a safe place where they could defend themselves and grab a few hours' sleep before resuming their journey. The next stage would take them through the Ghorak Pass, a choke point that made a good spot for an ambush. The journey had been slow, fraught with breakdowns and burst tyres as the HETs dragged themselves up and down the wadis that criss-crossed the terrain. The column stretched and shrank, from 15 kilometres in length when things were going well to 4 kilometres when they closed up while the specialist teams went to work, repairing a broken vehicle or clearing an IED. So far they had encountered only a handful of explosive devices. They had come under several small-arms and mortar attacks but no one had been hurt and the convoy had rolled on without stopping to engage, reassured by the helicopters and jets watching overhead. As they settled down by the side of the vehicles, it seemed that the worst of the journey might already be over.

Before Steve Boardman went to bed he sat down with a brew in the cookhouse to write up his report for Brigade. He was careful to tell those who came up to congratulate him that he was "not Neville Chamberlain. I won't be saying 'it's peace in our time'." But he went on, "I do think it's got the potential to be a bit of a coup."

A few shots were heard that night from the area south of the base, fired by nervous Afghan sentries and provoking no response. The only activity reported was a few figures moving on the 611 during the evening. It seemed the Taliban were making good on their promise to clear the road. The main disturbance came from the ISAF side. Bangs and thumps drifted down from the north of the camp where an Australian operation was taking place, causing Williams to worry that the commotion might threaten the ceasefire.

But in the morning the calm still held. Families were moving back from the compounds nearest the road. The way seemed clear for the Paras to echelon through each other down to the rendezvous point with the convoy while the Afghans secured the ground on either side of the 611. Even with the ceasefire, the soldiers would remain extra vigilant. Williams was concerned that rogue commanders might ignore the agreement, and there were intelligence reports of a threat from a suicide bomber. He was determined to keep his side of the bargain. To avoid spooking the insurgents, check-firing weapons and demolishing bunkers were forbidden, and any IEDs that were found were to be marked and driven round rather than destroyed.

At 8.30a.m. Williams and his team boarded their vehicles and drove out of the southern gates of the camp and down the rutted, rocky highway to the bend in the road where the signing ceremony was to take place. Abdul Razzak followed behind in his white pick-up flanked by his bodyguards. The grove of trees by the roadside was all set up for the meeting. There

359

were rows of plastic chairs underneath the boughs and cheap carpets covered the dirt. All that was missing was the elders. For a few minutes, the soldiers and interpreters milled around uncertainly. The district leader held a muttered conference with some of his team. He pulled his Thuraya mobile satphone out of his brown waistcoat and punched in a number. There was a brief, low conversation. Then Abdul Razzak pressed the "off" switch and turned to Williams and Boardman, shaking his head. The elders would not be coming. The deal was off.

Later the story emerged that after the shura of the previous day the details of the agreement had been relayed to Quetta for the leadership's approval. Overnight they had sent back word forbidding the ceasefire to continue. The truth was impossible to verify. For the moment, though, all that mattered was that the local commanders were reneging. Boardman reported that the commanders had told the elders "they are not just not honouring the agreement, they want to fight".

The news was met with resignation rather than disappointment. Soldiers were wary of drama. In their vocabulary the word was synonymous with "trouble", as in "no dramas", meaning everything's fine. Everyone switched into their professional roles, barely missing a beat.

It would be a busy day. Williams and his headquarters group moved along the road to a compound just behind the forward edge of his troops. It seemed hard to believe that the insurgents really wanted a fight. Anyone who raised his hand against the soldiers now was almost certain to die. Williams still hoped he could scare at least some of them off by argument, and if not, with a show of force. The interpreters began broadcasting warnings to whoever was lurking ahead. Through the megaphones their voices sounded tinny and menacing. "Any act of violence against ISAF or the ANA will be met with overwhelming force. If you threaten ISAF or the ANA you will be destroyed."

The message was reinforced by the rumble of an approaching jet, which made a deafening, earth-shaking pass at 250 feet. It had arrived at the CO's request. It was to let the insurgents know "this is what we have and we're prepared to use it", he said. It was not what he had wanted. "I just feel sorry for the local people," he murmured as it flashed over the treetops.

The Taliban were taking no notice of the warnings. As 2 Para's "D" Company advanced down the road at the head of the column, they saw men moving into compounds overlooking the 611, 1.5 kilometres south of Flagstaff. When they got closer, they came under fire from small arms and RPGs. The Paras paused and called in artillery and mortar fire. It arrived a few minutes later, landing with a flash and crash, snuffing out the resistance and setting the pattern for the rest of the day. Each time the column moved forward it was shot at from compounds. Each time it would trigger a devastating response, not only from the gun line at Kajaki and the mortar teams that were following the advance, but from the GMLRS battery near Sangin and the aircraft that were constantly overhead.

There was a web of electronic linkages between the rifle companies at the front, the Joint Tactical Air Controllers on the ground behind them, the pilots in the air and the unseen controllers at the airbases. The soldiers identified where the shooting was coming from and passed the grids back to the JTACs, who forwarded them to the pilots. This afternoon there was an American B1 bomber in the sky which had flown thousands of kilometres to Helmand from the Indian Ocean base of Diego Garcia. The pilot's voice was cheerful and detached as he chatted to the JTAC, Flight Lieutenant Adam Freedman of the RAF. He was given the grid reference for the troublesome compound. Then there was a pause for comment from the CO or anyone else with authority to object or intervene back at the relevant bases.

At 2p.m. the target erupted in flame. It had taken a direct hit from a GBU-38 satellite-guided 500-pound bomb, followed quickly by another. The sound rolled over the Paras' compound two kilometres away and a fountain of dove-grey smoke, 30 metres high, soared into the flawless sky. Three men were seen heading southwards from the area of the blast. They were "squirters" in military-speak, who were bugging out of an area that had got too hot for them. They were cut down with a sheaf of 105mm shells as they ran.

It seemed colossally, insanely wasteful. The villagers had been offered $25,000 to buy their goodwill. But one of the bombs being dropped with such abandon cost more than ten times that.

The advance was going steadily. There was plenty of time to chat as the Paras sat around in the compound in the shade of the fruit trees amid the churned-up earth of the previous days' bombardments. The decision to renege on the ceasefire seemed to bring no gain to the Taliban, not even the satisfaction of a glorious death taking a few of their enemies with them. "They could have been wealthy and alive," said one of the Royal Irish mentors. "Now they're fucked." For the British, the insurgents' decision to carry on was no more than a nuisance in military terms. In the longer run it could bring benefits, driving a wedge between the local population and the insurgents. The Taliban knew that the people wanted the turbine. Yet, apparently on the orders of their faraway leaders, they had tried to block it, and their futile resistance had swamped the fields and compounds with fire and death.

"I don't think it's damaged us at all," said Huw Williams. "It's damaged them. We've done everything properly. We agreed everything by shura, which is the Pashtun way . . . we've done everything we said we were going to do. They haven't. I just can't see the logic in it." It could be, he thought, that there was little point in trying to do so. "Perhaps that's the problem," he added. "Sometimes we try to see logic in a Western way and that's where we go wrong."

Having made their choice, the insurgents stuck to it. Their dwindling manpower meant that on Monday, 1 September, they were unable to do more than loose off a few token shots to which the British barely bothered to reply. By mid-morning the convoy was approaching the FRV, the Final Rendezvous in the desert a few kilometres east of the 611, where they would shake down and regroup ready for the last leg of the journey. The column had passed through the Ghorak Pass without trouble. There had been a few more minor shooting incidents and more IEDs but the main trouble had been the terrain. The track got worse the closer it got to the 611. The engineers were kept in constant action, working through the night widening, grading and filling in to prepare a path that the HETs could negotiate.

By midday, from the roofs of the compounds lining the 611, the column was just visible in the distance. It lay in the plain between two mountain ridges, glittering in the heat haze, waiting for the last stretch of track to be cleared of IEDs. Rufus McNeil drove forward with Major Joe Fossey, OC of the engineers. When they reached the 611 they got out and walked. The only noise was the occasional thud as some IEDs were detonated by controlled explosions. Otherwise, McNeil felt, "it was quite evidently safe. We thought, this is not going to be the scary proposition we imagined it might be. There was not a soul in sight. The Paras had cracked it".

The landscape was not completely empty. Setting off in a Pinzgauer to meet up with the arriving force, we came across a group of men and boys squatting under a tree in a dusty field on the right-hand side of the road. Around them, green, tattered flags flapped on tall poles.

It was a graveyard and the men were there to bury someone. They looked towards us with blank faces as the vehicle clattered past.

When we returned the group was still there. The ceremony was almost over and men were shovelling dirt into the grave. One of the interpreters had been talking to the mourners and recounted the story. They told him the dead man had been killed the day before by a rocket fired from a helicopter while he was sitting on a motorbike. "They say he's just a farmer but I think he's not a farmer, he's a fucking Talib," he said. In the background another interpreter was repeating a message over and over again through a loudspeaker on the walls of the compound. "Please leave this area because our soldiers are patrolling . . . stay in your compounds . . . keep yourselves and everyone else inside your houses . . . God be with you . . ."

It was dusk before the convoy reached the road. It took another seven hours to grind its way along the last eight kilometres of its journey between the high walls of the compounds, watched over by an unbroken line of sentries. It was here, about two kilometres from Zeebrugge, that the convoy suffered the sole serious casualty of the epic journey up. One of the trucks carrying a turbine component developed a fault and the driver, Lance Corporal Lee Bentley, got out to investigate. As he stretched out under the trailer the suspension failed and he was crushed under the load. His pelvis was broken in three places. The agonising process of extracting him to be stretchered back to the camp on a quad bike before being flown back to

Bastion took time. The delay meant it was just after 2a.m. before the convoy arrived at Kajaki. It loomed out of the darkness, in a cacophony of squealing and hissing brakes, wreathed in clouds of dust. The soldiers came out to greet it and the knackered, sleep-starved crews flopped out of the cabs in a flicker of camera flashes. There were smiles and cigarettes and brews. Every successful mission brought its glow of achievement. Often in Afghanistan the accomplishment was merely to have survived. But for everyone, the soldiers and the storemen, this felt like something different, a human victory that outshone anything that they had done by force of arms.

The saga was over and the participants could feel proud. "We all talk about the mission being focused on reconstruction," said McNeil. "This was the clearest evidence for us that we had done something towards that. Most of what we do is sustaining the force . . . keeping them alive in the field. It's a valuable job but it doesn't make you feel like you're taking Afghanistan forward. This made you feel like you were contributing to the bigger picture."

When talking to his men, Huw Williams had often described the convoy mission as the ideal operation to finish on. Now, as the tail of the column passed safely through the gates of the camp, the Paras' part was almost over and their accomplishment complete. "Some of our operations might be regarded as spurious," Williams said. "Everyone can see the value of this . . . All our friends will read about it. It's something our parents will understand. We will be able to say to ourselves, 'You helped to see it through.' "

It was a feeling that united everyone as they stood, thankfully, under the canopy of stars in the early morning freshness of Kajaki on 2 September 2008.

CHAPTER
SEVENTEEN

Homecoming

A few hours after the turbine components had been winched off the HETs the convoy was on its way again. There was just enough time for a swim in the blissfully cool water of the reservoir before the vehicles were grinding back down the 611 and on to the desert track. By now everyone was exhausted and adrenaline reserves were running dry.

It had always been feared that the journey back would be more dangerous than the journey out, and so it proved. The Taliban knew the likely exit route and their IEDs were waiting for the column as it slogged slowly home. Three soldiers were wounded in one bomb strike. Then, as the convoy neared the end of Route Harriet, the insurgents launched an ambush, just as the vehicles were about to rendezvous with a patrol that had gone out to meet them from a Canadian FOB. An American soldier was killed in the clash. "We hit it, we handled it and got through it," said Rufus McNeil. But it was a relief to be back in Bastion and counting the days until departure.

The turbine operation attracted some sceptical comment. The machinery would not be installed until the spring of 2009. Given the elastic quality of Afghan time, no one was counting on that deadline being met. Civilians in the PRT pointed out that even when the turbine was working there were no power lines in place to carry the electricity out. The soldiers, though, believed that all great enterprises had to start somewhere. McNeil's instinct was to "just get on with something. Show a bit of progress, and progress breeds progress". If the project was not fully completed until 2012, then the operation would still be a success.

The Paras felt the same way. Their part in the epic had been the high point of their tour. The satisfaction was great. It was comforting to have a concrete achievement to point to as they headed home. They arrived back at their Colchester barracks on 27 September to a joyful reception from their wives and families. In Britain, though, there was a mood of disquiet and scepticism towards the mission that got deeper every week. The soldiers knew better than anyone the ground truth of the situation. Their experiences had given them insights that made it hard for them to share the monochrome views of opponents and supporters of Britain's Afghan policy who had little or no contact with the realities of the place. It seemed unwise to be dogmatic about anything amid the swirling military, political and cultural uncertainties of Afghanistan. There were, though, several things of which the soldiers felt sure.

The tour had reinforced their confidence in their ability to carry out the basic task they had been set. There was general agreement that the quality and quantity of weapons and equipment were steadily improving. Every soldier wanted more heavy-lift helicopters, which would give them swifter and safer travel around the battlefield. The most frequently heard complaint concerned the weight of kit they had to carry, and particularly the Osprey body armour and Mark 6A helmet, which were, in the words of one corporal, "roundly hated" by all the soldiers. Osprey provided superb protection against small-arms fire and shrapnel. The downside, according to another corporal, was that it "wrapped around your body like a thermal layer . . . it may seem like a small point to some but when you spend six to seven months wearing this sort of stuff in thirty-five-plus-degree heat, it's not". Dissatisfaction was intensified by the fact that body armour specially designed for extreme heat was commercially available and was issued to British special forces.

To an outsider there seemed to be another major target for legitimate criticism. Living conditions in the FOBs from where most of the fighting was done were appalling by any standards, and a stark contrast with the quality of life back at Bastion, KAF or Sangin. The latrines and ablutions were primitive and everyone was guaranteed a dose of diarrhoea and vomiting. Daily existence seemed unnecessarily harsh. Why was it so difficult to provide proper fridges so soldiers could look forward to chilled water when they staggered back from patrol? Things seemed to have gone backwards since 1897 when Winston Churchill wrote that "arrangements for the comfort and convenience of the troops of the Frontier Force are unequalled. They live more pleasantly and with less discomfort on active service than does a British regiment at the Aldershot manoeuvres."

Most of the soldiers seemed stoically unconcerned about the privations. They were more interested in the technicalities of their tasks. There appeared to be a consensus that tactics and drills as they had evolved since 2006 were the right ones for the circumstances. They accepted the need for constant patrolling, taking the fight to the enemy and maintaining pressure to keep the insurgents off balance, despite the near-constant exposure to danger that this approach involved.

They were prepared to endure the risk because most of them had faith in the value of the mission. They believed that fighting a war thousands of miles distant brought a greater measure of security to their families and friends at home. They were also committed to the notion that, despite the destruction and the loss of civilian life, which were felt with real sorrow by the soldiers, they were helping to build a better future for Afghanistan and creating the conditions in which peace and prosperity could germinate. Many also saw themselves as engaged in a battle against an evil of which, as young people, they had some personal experience. "If what I'm doing reduces the number of heroin overdoses in the world then it has been worth it without a doubt," said one sergeant. The main regret was that, for the time being at least, they were doing nothing to wipe out the poppies that grew all around them.

They also believed that, no matter how slow, painful and limited it might be, some progress was being made. It was measured in centimetres rather than kilometres. When asked about it, they invariably replied that it was "two steps forward and one back", but nonetheless they were moving, if not always in a straight line, at least in the right direction. There were dissenting voices. One officer had come to the conclusion that the declared aims of the mission were bogus and the real objective had been to maintain Britain's long-term strategic relationship with the United States on which UK defence policy was fundamentally based. "I don't think that when we signed up to the mission we ever expected it to turn out so bad," he said. "Now that we're in it, we're trapped against our will." He did not "subscribe to the view that by fighting the terrorists in their country we are preventing them attacking ours . . . every day we radicalise more people". Nor did he believe that their presence was benefiting the Afghans. "If that is the case then we've screwed it up in spectacular fashion," he said. If he was an Afghan he would "rather live under the Taliban than try to survive in the middle of a bloody war for the foreseeable or indefinite future".

Soldiers were more likely, though, to try to search for a glimmer of hope among the smoke, fire and bloodshed. The uplifting moments they experienced usually involved contact with local people. A Royal Irish officer spoke of patrolling one morning at dawn into a village outside Sangin. "We arrived at the mosque to find all the elders together at morning prayer. We waited off to one side until they were done then started chatting to them. They told us we were the first ISAF patrol ever to visit the village and they were absolutely delighted to see us. We spoke for an hour about how we could help each other out." There were further visits and some aid projects were carried out.

The soldiers had long ago come to the conclusion that talk of large-scale construction was fantasy and that no serious work could be done until the land had been pacified. Progress was crippled by the lack of resources, and particularly of fighting soldiers. The main difficulty, according to one Para officer, was "primarily insufficient forces to achieve the mission. We have the ability to hold ground but lack the capacity to project force and dominate our area of operations. Consequently any success is localised as we lack the ability to influence the population at large". The British were pulling their weight but the same could not be said of other major European nations. The British soldiers had mixed feelings towards the Americans, who, according to a Para captain, were "friendly and respectful but they really do see us as the poor cousin". The United States were at least taking the mission seriously, however, and were "in it to win it", as demonstrated by President Barack Obama's decision to send 17,000 further troops to Afghanistan.

Morale is difficult to quantify in readily measurable terms. From direct observation it seemed that most soldiers were glad to be in Afghanistan, if only for their own personal fulfilment. Any NCO or private soldier in the army now can expect to do multiple combat tours of Afghanistan. The officers' career path is different. There are more choices open to them and they are less likely to have to return to the front line again and again. Most, whether commissioned or not, claimed they would be willing to serve there again. "I'm not sure if 'happy' is the right word," said a sergeant. "But I feel it is my duty to go back. Quite simply I believe what we are trying to do there and I believe it makes a difference to the safety of everyone, my family included, in the UK."

Sustaining the current levels of willingness and commitment depends to some extent on the belief that effort is being shared and commitment reciprocated. Contact with Afghan society could be dispiriting. "The primary obstacle to complete an immediate success is simply the Afghan," said one Para captain. It was a thought that struck everyone sooner or later. It was not the Afghan soldiers who attracted disapproval. They were a bright spot in the picture, and those who came into contact with them regarded them on the whole with respect. It was the venality of many politicians and administrators which aroused contempt.

The soldiers spoke of themselves as "holding the ring" until the national security forces and government could take charge of their own affairs. The Afghan army might be struggling towards that end, though it was still a long way off. But the government representatives the Paras encountered often seemed to regard the ISAF deployment not as a historical opportunity to build progress but as a chance to enrich themselves. The rulers displayed a dismaying contempt for the ruled.

"Everyone in a position of importance seems to be out for personal gain," said a major. "Until the Afghans buy into their own country and take responsibility then we will continue to fight uphill." The rot went almost to the top. Yet despite countless warnings, Karzai was unwilling to move against the worst offenders, claiming he needed the tribal power they wielded for the bigger project to succeed.

His government, it seemed, was unreformable, and progress would have to await a change of leadership. There was a bigger problem, though, looming behind the feebleness and venality of the Karzai administration. The insurgency the British were fighting was in Afghanistan. But they were merely grappling with the tentacles of the beast. The brain and the vital organs lay in Pakistan. Events there were beyond British control. Even the Americans had only limited powers of intervention. Throughout 2008 and the beginning of 2009 the soldiers in Afghanistan watched as the government of Pakistan acquiesced in the Talibanisation of the northern and frontier areas, a process exemplified by the "ceasefire" that ceded the Swat Valley to the fanatics.

Without action to destroy the Taliban in their safe havens in Pakistan there could be no serious progress against the insurgency in Afghanistan. Without the arrival in power in Kabul of a government genuinely committed to good governance there could be no hope of persuading the population to commit themselves fully to the state. In the spring of 2009 there was little

375

to suggest that these preconditions were likely to be met in the near future.

Soon after they arrived home from Afghanistan, the Paras started preparations for their return. They will go back in 2010. Looking forward, there was little expectation that things would have changed dramatically for the better. No one had ever expected to be able to defeat the Taliban militarily. The one circumstance that might have raised such a hope was unattainable. Even with the forthcoming American "surge" it seemed unlikely that ISAF and the Afghans would have the resources to seal the border. Pakistan had neither the means nor, it seemed, the will. For the time being, though, it was the military effort that was paramount. There was little to encourage hope that political initiatives would produce better results in bringing peace and progress to Afghanistan. Overtures by the Afghan government to the insurgents and interventions from the Arab world appeared to get nowhere. The Taliban was too incoherent an organisation to be a serious partner in negotiations and the aims of those who directed it were too extreme and absolute to be accommodated without a betrayal of every value the mission was meant to be upholding. The best the soldiers could hope for was to contain the insurgency, buying time for the Afghan security forces to build their competence. In the meantime, the reconstruction effort would remain hesitant and dislocated, dependent entirely on a mercurial security situation.

Viewed through civilian eyes, the Afghanistan mission seems daunting, uninspiring, thankless. Soldiers see it differently. The daunting, the uninspiring and the thankless were "what they did", and they did them for financial rewards that seemed pitifully inadequate to civilian eyes. The exploits of the Paras in 2006 and the troops who succeeded them had generated a surge in recruitment, and there would be no shortage of newcomers anxious to test themselves against the men who went before them. Huw Williams found watching them in action "humbling". "I never once witnessed them being afraid," he said.

Unlike soldiers of their fathers' generation, these young men and women are facing a future of repeated, high-risk deployments. There are many older soldiers who are now in line for a third tour of active service in Afghanistan, a prospect that arouses mixed feelings. "After two tours I would rather deploy elsewhere," said a captain. "But I can imagine that one day, perhaps three to five years away, I would happily do another tour. It is my job, after all."

It is duty, finally, that will drive the soldiers back. They get professional satisfaction from their service in Afghanistan and will continue to do so, but without a sense of progress and a feeling that the discomfort, dislocation and sacrifice are worth it, the rewards are bound to diminish. At the same time the physical and psychological stresses on the soldiers will mount and the strains on marriages and families intensify. They are risking their lives in a conflict that attracts little public enthusiasm and considerable doubt. They have been warned that it could last a generation. The Paras and their comrades will see it through as they always have.

377

Their courage and resolve and good humour will endure as long as the political will persists to keep them in Afghanistan. But the years ahead will test their qualities to the limit.

Abbreviations, Acronyms and Military Terms

AFC	Army Foundation College
AH	Attack helicopter (i.e. Apache)
ANA	Afghan National Army
ANCOP	Afghan National Civil Order Police
ANP	Afghan National Police
ATF	Afghan Task Force
CIMIC	Civil-Military Cooperation
CO	Commanding Officer
DfID	Department for International Development
Dickers	Taliban spies who pass on information about troop movements
EOD	Explosive Ordnance Disposal
FOB	Forward Operating Base
FRV	Final Rendezvous
FSG	Fire Support Group
GMG	Grenade Machine Gun
GMLRS	Guided Multiple Launch Rocket System
GPMG	General Purpose Machine Gun
Hesco Bastion	Steel mesh containers lined with polypropylene fabric, filled with stones, sand and gravel, used as protective barriers
HET	Heavy Equipment Transporter

HGV	Heavy Goods Vehicle
HLS	Helicopter landing site
HPRT	Helmand Provincial Reconstruction Team
HQ	Headquarters
HRW	Human Rights Watch
IED	Improvised explosive device
ISAF	International Security Assistance Force
ISO	Containers conforming to International Organisation for Standardisation specifications
TAC	Joint Tactical Air Controller
KAF	Kandahar airfield
kandak	Afghan National Army battalion
KIA	Killed in action
LAV	Light Armoured Vehicle
LCMR	Light Counter Mortar Radar
Leaguer	Temporary camp in desert
Loggies	Members of the Royal Logistic Corps
NATO	North Atlantic Treaty Organisation
NCO	Non-Commissioned Officer
NDS	National Directorate of Security (Afghan)
NKET	Non-kinetic effects team ("Team Pink")
OEF	Operation Enduring Freedom (US)
OMLT	Operational Mentoring and Liaison Team
OP	Observation post
PB	Patrol Base
PID	Positively identified
PKM	Soviet design type of general purpose machine gun

PRT	Provincial Reconstruction Team
RAF	Royal Air Force
RCS	Regional Command South
REME	Royal Electrical and Mechanical Engineers
RHA	Royal Horse Artillery
RLC	Royal Logistic Corps
ROE	Rules of Engagement
RPG	Rocket-propelled grenade
SAS	Special Air Service
Shura	Meeting with representatives of local communities
Stabad	Stabilisation Adviser
Terps	Interpreters
UAV	Unmanned Aerial Vehicle
UN	United Nations
USAID	United States Agency for International Development
Wadi	Dried-up riverbed
WMIK	Weapons Mount Installation Kit

Acknowledgments

As with *3 Para*, this book is founded on the words of the participants. I am profoundly grateful to everyone, soldier and civilian, who so generously shared with me their thoughts, their experiences and their insights. I would particularly like to thank Lieutenant Colonel Huw Williams of 3 Para and his deputy, Major John Boyd, for their help and hospitality. Captain Ian McLeish was a model of patience and thoroughness in his responses to all my queries and requests. I would also like to pay tribute to the warmth and good nature of the soldiers of the Royal Irish Regiment who looked after me in Sangin. It is about time someone wrote a book about them. Researching in the field I was reliant on the goodwill of the media ops officers in Kandahar, Bastion and Lashkar Gah. A big thank you in particular to Squadron Leader Al McGuinness at KAF for his unfailing helpfulness and good cheer.

I owe a huge debt to Annabel Wright and the team at HarperCollins for their skill and professionalism, which they manage to combine with great good humour despite the burdens imposed by the deadline. Truly, grace under pressure. I would also like to thank

Arabella Pike and my agent David Godwin for their crucial role in the genesis of *Ground Truth*.

Mary Jo Bishop and Patsy Dryden did a wonderful job of transcribing the interviews. In Rome, *grazie mille* to Tertia Bailey, who diligently quarried out valuable background data as she awaited the birth of young Arthur.

Finally, as always my greatest thanks are due to my wife Henrietta. As I sometimes point out, usually rather late in the evening, *I am a very lucky man* . . .

Also available in ISIS Large Print:

Special Forces Heroes

Michael Ashcroft

Over the last century, Britain's Special Forces have performed a whole host of operations with unequalled skill, secrecy and bravery. From the Cockleshell Heroes' daring 1942 raid deep into Nazi-occupied Europe, to the rescue of hostages from the clutches of terrorists at the Iranian Embassy in 1980, to the dangerous sorties into enemy territory during the Gulf wars.

It takes a truly special sort of courage to go undercover behind enemy lines, or to be part of a small, elite unit in a hit-and-run raid against a far larger power. Fascinated since he was a boy, Michael Ashcroft set about assembling what is believed to be the largest private collection of British Special Forces medals in the world. Here he traces the origins of those teams as well as detailing the action-packed accounts behind over 40 medals, recognising the astonishing valour and ingenuity displayed by servicemen.

ISBN 978-0-7531-8422-6 (hb)
ISBN 978-0-7531-8423-3 (pb)

Their Darkest Hour

Laurence Rees

Award-winning writer and filmmaker Laurence Rees has spent nearly 20 years meeting people who were tested to the extreme during World War II. He has come face-to-face with rapists, mass murderers, even cannibals, but he has also met courageous individuals who are an inspiration to us all.

Here he presents 35 of his most electrifying encounters, from Estera Frenkiel, a young Jewish woman given the chance to save ten fellow Jews from deportation and death to Hiroo Onoda, a Japanese soldier, so fanatical that he refused to surrender for 29 years after the end of the war.

The devastating first-hand testimony in *Their Darkest Hour* is both a lasting contribution to our understanding of the war and a powerful insight into the behaviour of a human being in crisis.

ISBN 978-0-7531-8310-6 (hb)
ISBN 978-0-7531-8311-3 (pb)

Operation Millennium

Eric Taylor

"Operation Millennium" was the terrible culmination of months of pressure from "Bomber" Harris to get this new and deadly strategy accepted. It was an extraordinary feat of organisation involving 1,048 bombers, over 6,000 aircrew and 53 British airfields. To ensure success, "maximum effect" was the order. The Royal Air Force waged a campaign against any airmen who showed faltering commitment, ruthlessly trying them by court martial.

The atmosphere of night bomber stations is vividly recalled — the comradeship, the pity and the fear. The raid on Cologne is remembered by the crews of Bomber Command and the unlucky citizens of Cologne who endured the night raids. Eric Taylor has interviewed Britons and Germans, whose eye-witness accounts testify to the horror and heroism on both sides.

ISBN 978-0-7531-5665-0 (hb)
ISBN 978-0-7531-5666-7 (pb)

Bomber Boys

Patrick Bishop

The 125,000 men from all over the world who passed through Bomber Command were engaged in a form of warfare that had never been implemented before. Between 1940 and 1945 they flew continuously, stopping only when weather made operations impossible. There was nothing romantic about their struggle. Often barely out of boyhood, they lived on bleak bases, flying at night on long, nerve-wracking missions that often ended in death. In all, 55,000 were killed, counting for nearly one in ten of all the British and Commonwealth war dead.

In this powerful and moving work of history, Patrick Bishop brilliantly captures the character, feelings and motivations of the bomber crews and pays tribute to their heroism and determination. They were among the best of their generation, who were called on to carry out one of the grimmest duties of the Second World War. *Bomber Boys* brilliantly restores these men to their rightful place in our consciousness.

ISBN 978-0-7531-5675-9 (hb)
ISBN 978-0-7531-5676-6 (pb)